BOTTLING
SHIPS & HOUSES

RONALD C. ROUSH

TAB BOOKS Inc.
Blue Ridge Summit, PA 17214

Notices

Dremel is a registered trademark of Emerson Electric Co. (Dremel Manufacturing Division).
Weldwood is a registered trademark of Roberts Consolidated Industries.

To my wife, Suzanne, and all her animals for their terrific patience.

FIRST EDITION
FIRST PRINTING

Copyright © 1985 by TAB BOOKS Inc.
Printed in the United States of America

Reproduction or publication of the content in any manner, without express permission of the publisher, is prohibited. No liability is assumed with respect to the use of the information herein.

Library of Congress Cataloging in Publication Data

Roush, Ronald C.
 Bottling ships and houses.

 Bibliography: p.
 Includes index.
 1. Ship models in bottles. 2. Architectural models in bottles. I. Title.
 VM298.3.R68 1985   745.592′8   85-19683
  ISBN 0-8306-0975-X
  ISBN 0-8306-1975-5 (pbk.)

Contents

	Acknowledgments	vi
	Introduction	vii
1	**Bottled Houses: A Description**	1

Why 1
Who 3

2	**The Bottle and Its Closure**	5

History of Bottlemaking 5
The Relationship Between the Bottle and Its Contents 8
Bottle Characteristics and Qualities 8
Discovering New Bottles 13
Finding Old Bottles 18
Bottle Cleaning 24
Bottle Closures 26

3	**House Design and Modification**	29

Architectural Styles 29
Adapting an Existing House 37
Adapting a House of Your Own Design 39

4	**Building Tools**	51

Store-Bought Tools 51
Homemade Tools 58

5 Materials for Building   65

    Wood and Stone 65
    Paper, Modeling Clay, and Paints 69
    Wood Putty and Polystyrene Foam 71
    Plastics, Glue, and Cement 72

6 From Building Site to First Floor   74

    Mountain Building 74
    The Flat Building Site 75
    Structural Supports 78
    Flooring 79
    Wall Framing 80
    Windows 82
    Doors 84
    Wall Covering 85
    Final Steps 87

7 Above the First Story   89

    Roof Construction 89
    Balconies 93
    Chimneys 94
    Bay Windows 97
    Second-Story Walls 100
    The Main Roof 100

8 Building Nonwood Walls   104

    Stone and Brick Wall Construction 104
    Adobe and Stucco Wall Construction 106

9 Landscaping a House   111

    Foliage Materials 111
    Making Trees 112
    Planters 113

10 After Completion of the House   116

    Some Remaining Tasks 116
    Care of Your Bottled House 117

11 Regarding Bottling Ships   120

    A Description 120
    Some Clever Variations 121

12 A Few Types of Watercraft   127

    Work Vessels 128
    Recreational Vessels 138
    Historic Vessels 146
    Naval Vessels 152

13 Bottles and Materials   161

    Bottle Shape 161
    Glass Quality 162
    Types of Bottles 163
    The Closure 165
    Building Materials 166

14 Tools — 174
Store-Bought Tools 174
Homemade Tools 176

15 The Fold-Up Method of Construction — 179
Preparations 179
Construction 181
Insertion 189

16 The Sectioned Method of Construction — 194
Preliminary Steps 194
Construction 195
Mast Installation 201
Postscript 202

Appendix — 203

Glossary — 205

Index — 209

Acknowledgments

I am greatly indebted to and graciously thank Victor Crosby, master craftsman of bottled ships, for his technical advice and the use of his artwork; David Brierley, curator of the San Diego Maritime Museum, for his help and support; Bud Upton, builder of a bottled house, for original inspiration; Heritage Square, a collection of classic Victorian buildings, for enlightenment; Larry & Teri Brown; Duane & Noreen Dobratz; Richard & Joyce Heffrnan; Jon & Jan Knickerbocker; Carl Lane; Chick & Shirley McIlroy; Brad and Jeanny Merritt; George & Betty Michie; and Roscoe & Kathrine Roush.

Special appreciation must extend to my wife, Suzanne, and her animals for all their patience and encouragement.

Introduction

Undoubtedly, since the first clear-glass bottles were made, craftsmen have been intrigued with building structures within those confined spaces. A craftsman of artwork such as this must be equipped with a few tips and "secrets" enabling him to enjoy a generous measure of success. *Bottling Ships and Houses* is intended to instruct the beginning builder in the basic techniques required for successful completion of a bottled house or ship. Although step-by-step instructions are provided, an attitude of self-reliance and experimentation is encouraged. I also attempt to inspire the reader to strive for achievment and the self-satisfaction that comes with completing a worthwhile project.

Naturally, the bottle itself is a very important component of this craft. There are a multitude of bottles available, including antique, new, slightly used, custom-made, valuable, and not so valuable. Selecting suitable bottles from all these types is a major consideration. You need to know in what exotic locations some of these unusual vessels can be found. Glass quality and color must be carefully analyzed so you do not choose a bottle that might cause excessive eyestrain. Once a suitable bottle has been obtained, it must be properly cleaned and prepared for building. An appropriate bottle closure (cap, lid, or stopper) must also be selected, or designed and constructed.

Designing houses, ships, or whatever you intend to bottle requires a great deal of careful thought. A builder can design a house for a specific bottle or find a suitable bottle for a particular house design. Trying to choose from all the possible architectural styles of houses and kinds of boats and ships can be mind-boggling. Adapting a house design by stretching its proportions and recording these mental images on paper is an important exercise in planning.

The selection and proper use of particular tools, both store-bought and homemade, can be a great help in having success with this craft. In order to obtain some of these tools, you, the builder, must know the best sources in which to purchase them. Some tools required for this craft must be constructed by the craftsman himself. Although simple, these homemade tools perform a variety of important functions, without which this kind of craft would not be possible. You must also understand and know how to use these unusual tools.

There are thousands of building materials in this world, but only a select few of these may be useful for bottling houses and ships. They include: wood, stone, paper, modeling clay, paint, wood putty, cloth, plastic sheet, polystyrene foam, and adhesives. You should know where to obtain good-quality building materials. You should know which materials may be gathered for free, and which ones must be purchased.

Constructing a house or a ship in a bottle must include a number of important tasks. Through the use of written instructions, photographs, and diagrams, I have simplified these tasks into individual steps. The tasks required for bottling a house include preparing the building site, securing the foundation, laying flooring, framing the walls, making and installing windows and doors, applying wood siding, building second-story structures, making chimneys, and constructing roof structures. The tasks required for bottling a ship include constructing the parts of the ship, assembling and rigging the sailing ship, inserting the folded ship into the bottle, securing the ship's hull to the bottle glass, pulling up the masts and sails, setting deck features, applying water around the ship, and painting the waves onto the water. Ships and boats may also be bottled by assembling the vessel in sections, and inserting these sections into the bottle. This method requires extensive assembly inside the bottle after some very careful planning and preassembly tests.

By using these bottling techniques, almost anything can be constructed in a bottle. These methods are not limited to houses and ships.

Brick and stone masonry create the need for special attention. Mortar must be formulated and mixed; bricks must be made or purchased; stones must be collected and cleaned. The actual brick and stone wall construction is relatively simple, as long as effective planning has preceded the building. Although mortar trimming is a difficult task, it can be accomplished with special tools and a little patience. Adobe and stucco wall construction can also be achieved in a bottle.

Landscaping helps make a house look more complete and appealing. Bottled houses may also be landscaped. Utilizing a number of kinds of plantlike materials will add variety and realism. Planters also add charm and that "lived-in" look. Preparation and installation of miniature plants can be an extensive process, but well worth the effort.

Recognition of a few precautions will help ensure the longevity of a bottled house or ship. Although both require but little care, temperature, light, vibration, and shocks are elements which should be considered when displaying the artwork. Traveling can present some particular problems unless the bottle is properly packaged.

Although *Bottling Ships and Houses* is primarily written for the beginning craftsman, the advanced builder will benefit from many of the ideas and tips found throughout this book. Occasionally, this information will provoke, or at least encourage, the inventive builder to create improvements in the use of materials and construction techniques. Just as the bottled house shown here was the original inspiration for me to try bottling houses, it is hoped that readers of this book will be encouraged to build as well. If a builder is willing to take the time to think and plan carefully after studying the ideas and techniques in this book, he should be well prepared to experience numerous achievements resulting in the rewards of substantial self-satisfaction.

Fig. I-1. This bottled house, the first I ever saw, was built by Bud Upton of Catalina Island. It provoked many theories of how it came to be bottled and later inspired me to try the art in 1967.

1 Bottled Houses: A Description

Sometimes descriptions, both verbal and written, can be wholly inadequate. This chapter will serve as an honest attempt to describe the craft of bottling houses, nonetheless. A proper description will help a prospective craftsman to make an informed decision. After all, before beginning something which requires as much effort and time as artwork, a person should know exactly what kind of situation and commitment he is about to create for himself. The description of a bottled house requires a careful explanation. It is a miniaturization of a craftsman's creative fantasy, which has been painstakingly constructed within the confines of a narrow-necked, glass bottle. There are no clever, time-saving tricks to bottling a house. The entire house is constructed piece by piece and inserted through the neck of the bottle. Assembly takes place inside the bottle. Cutting the bottle in order to insert a fully constructed house model is "against the rules." There is little challenge in that! There are no pull-strings, as in some ship-in-a-bottle projects, to raise the walls. Since the inside bottom of the bottle is almost always too irregular, constructing the house entirely outside and then disassembling it only to reassemble it inside is not an effective technique. Each piece must be inserted, measured inside, removed, and trimmed several times until it fits properly. Then, it is again inserted and glued into place. The house is, for the most part, constructed just like a real house, sometimes including interior decoration and furniture. The house requires a foundation, floors, structural framing, exterior siding or masonry, doors, windows, and roofing almost exactly as a real house. Although the bottled house is built from the ground up, much like a real house, each level, or story, is completed before the next level is begun. Later, every small detail, including decorative moldings and wall vents, must be installed. After you have completed the entire house and its landscaping, the bottle is permanently sealed. Then, the bottled house remains unaltered and preserved in its own protective atmosphere for years. Considering this description with a proper perspective, you are now adequately informed in order to make a decision whether or not to pursue this craft. Although it is an undertaking which demands a great investment in time, effort, and patience, its dividends are great. **WHY.** Why would anyone want to build a house in a bottle? Although each builder must analyze his motivations and answer that question for himself, a number of good reasons are apparent. For the challenge, creativity, sense of accomplishment, buildup of one's confidence, personal relaxation, entertainment, a lasting legacy, and just plain fun are all possible reasons depending on your point of view. The value of each of these motivations will vary from person to person. What seems to be a valid justification to one person may appear to be meaningless to another. All these reasons concern primarily the builder. Magic and intrigue are also valid reasons to some, but they are associated mainly with the admirers of the art.

What may appear to be great difficulty and frustration in constructing bottled houses is actually a terrific and rewarding challenge. A challenging task remains interesting. Some creative endeavors become stale with time. Bottling houses is constantly challenging, however, and tests the abilities of the artist or builder. It is like creating your own crossword puzzle for your specific level of ability. Make it as easy or difficult as you wish. Design into the bottled house challenging engineering problems, and then set out to solve them. You can make this interesting art one of the most exciting and thought-provoking activities you can pursue. It is this constant challenge that keeps the craft alive.

The pride of expressing your own creativity is a marvelous reward in itself. While creating original house designs, artists of bottled houses become their own architects. There exists a warm feeling of personal satisfaction when you have created a carefully thought-out house plan and then watch your ideas come alive three-dimensionally during construction. Creativity is a very effective method of personal expression and can be developed and expanded from the most primitive of beginnings. Everyone has some measure of creativity. It just needs to be exercised and encouraged, much like a muscle in our bodies. Work the muscle of creativity, and it strengthens. Allow it to be inactive, and it will wither away.

Designing and constructing a bottled house is a remarkable undertaking, and completing one produces within the builder a terrific sense of accomplishment. It is such a great relief to finally cap the bottle for the last time. Thoughts of the long hours and hard work fade quickly with the completed project in view. When a bottled house turns out well, it just does not seem possible to even the builder that a house is really preserved inside the bottle. That is the magic of a completed bottled house. You have achieved what appears to be the impossible. Such feelings contribute to the pride of your craftsmanship and ingenuity and further heighten your sense of accomplishment.

Most people will agree that constructing a house in a bottle is no mere feat. As a gift, they are highly regarded, and seen as something very special. Anyone can begin to imagine the many long hours required to complete a bottled house, a fact that keeps such a gift from being relegated to the back of some forgotten closet. Children, especially, perceive a bottled house as an example of perpetual magic as they try to imagine how it came to be there. Such universal regard of a bottled house further strengthens the builder's sense of accomplishment and personal pride.

Completing such artwork also helps develop your self-confidence. Finishing even the most primitive of houses will encourage you to go on to attempt more difficult designs. As you gain experience and success in this craft, your increasing self-confidence may spill over into other challenges in your life. Once you begin to feel good about your successes in one area, you may be inspired to make improvements in other tasks.

This is why a hobby can help increase a person's self-worth. He likes the feeling that he has value by his achievements. If he can increase the frequency of that feeling by improving in other areas, he will experience the satisfaction all the more. When a person is rewarded handsomely for what he accomplishes, he will be compelled to repeat the achievement. Such are the benefits of a worthwhile hobby.

Continued technological advances free us from many tasks or shorten the time required to complete them. The result is more spare time and the need to fill that time with worthwhile recreation. Everybody deserves to enjoy the pleasures of a relaxing and entertaining hobby to fill their spare time. Many people believe they will live longer when they regularly participate in a hobby. The resulting relaxation can soothe away the tensions of the day. When they are deeply absorbed in a hobby, people can often forget the conflicts encountered throughout their workday. Such relief, resulting from relaxing with a hobby, lowers the heart rate, which especially benefits your health.

For some, bottling houses can be such a hobby. Further, a builder can work for hours constructing a house, while conversing with family and friends. It is gratifying to find and enjoy a hobby which does not detract from family time. It is only a matter of working in close proximity with the family rather than isolating yourself in a cold garage or restricted corner of the house. Likewise, you can be reasonably attentive to the television or stereo while constructing a bottled house. Fortunately, it is not such an intense craft that it requires total concentration all the time. The depth at which you absorb yourself into your work is entirely up to you. It is this marvelous versatility that is of great value to the craftsman.

Bottling houses is also a good form of mental and physical exercise. It requires careful thought and planning, as well as meticulous construction. The activity helps to develop and exercise hand/eye coordination. Proficient dexterity is a skill which almost every person can realize with a little practice. Practice is a key word here. As with most activities, a person must practice or keep in shape in order to continue the activity at the same level of proficiency or even to expect to improve such skills. We humans tend to become "rusty" without practicing for a time.

The hand/eye coordination, developed as you learn and practice building houses in bottles, is often handy in other areas of everyday life. The tasks may be sewing a dress, repairing the bodywork of a car, trimming a hedge, plastering a wall, or many other jobs requiring manual dexterity. How many times has a mechanic dropped a nut or bolt into a difficult-to-reach location in or around the engine and had to figure out how to retrieve it? A little ingenuity and some good hand/eye coordination can go a long way in solving some problems. Skills and coordination developed in pursuing one task may often be useful in accomplishing other chores.

Interesting artwork is a worthwhile legacy by which others will measure us after we are gone. The need to leave behind someone or something capable of declaring that we did indeed exist here at one time seems to be a trait of human nature. Leonardo da Vinci wrote, "Our lives must not pass without leaving some memory of ourselves in the minds of men." Although none of us will ever compare with da Vinci, we all could do well by following his advice. Our descendants and our patron's descendants are the eventual beneficiaries of the endeavors we achieved during our lives. An object of art which we have made with our own hands is much more meaningful to leave to our heirs than money or our faded photograph. It is not how much we leave behind, but rather the quality which will give a lasting impression as to our real character. A bottled house may express a great deal as to who we were, what we did, and perhaps how we did it.

A person really does not need a reason to practice a particular craft or hobby, although some of us have a need to justify the use of our time for recreation. Some of the justifications or reasons for bottling houses just mentioned may be more important to some people than to others. It all depends on the individual's own personal needs. Bottling houses has filled the needs of at least one person and may provide for the needs of others as well.

WHO

Bottling houses is a craft which will be great for some people, but not for others. Parents, for example, should exercise common sense when encouraging children to try this hobby. After all, glass bottles are breakable, and the clumsy builder should be especially cautious. Children from the age of 12 years should have no difficulty in developing the required skills, if their coordination is normal for their age. Dexterity-impaired adults should be cautious as well.

Time, patience, and common sense are the bases for this craft. If you have little spare time to devote to this hobby, you may be months or even years trying to complete your first bottled house. A minimum of 100 hours would be consumed in building even the most simple of houses. You must remember the unwritten rule, which states that the house must be constructed piece by piece inside the bottle, without cutting the bottle in any way. My first bottled house (Fig. C-1 in the color section) required at least 150 hours to complete, while the victorian house in Fig. C-2 required around 1800 hours. The rewards and enjoyment of completion may be delayed too long if you must stretch out the construction time over many months. Delays may diminish the motivation to complete the job.

More important than time is the patience required for such a craft. Frankly, this craft can be tedious at times, and you must recognize when an accumulation of frustration is about to "get the best" of you. You must know when to set aside the bottle and find some other activity to do for a while, returning later to continue the building. Common sense can be a great guide.

Everybody can at least attempt the craft of bottling houses without being harmed by the experience. Some individuals may even find such a hobby relaxing, as well as rewarding.

2
The Bottle and Its Closure

One impressive feature of a bottled house is the bottle itself. The bottle is responsible for conveying to the viewer the magnitude of challenge that the builder was required to meet. Its shape helps to indicate the amount of difficulty that was encountered during the construction of the bottled house. The bottle must be of suitable glass quality and color to permit easy viewing of the house preserved inside. The bottle's bottom provides a place for the builder's signature and the date of completion. Adequate space inside the bottle must be provided for building a structure. The bottle's neck must allow for a proper closure. The nature and quality of the bottle will contribute to or diminish the overall, aesthetic value of the completed house inside it. Only a vessel with specific features is classified as a *bottle*. A bottle must have a restricted opening, such as the one pictured in Fig. 3-1. A *jar*, on the other hand, has little or no restricted opening and lacks the challenge of a real bottle. A *bottleneck* is merely an extension of a restricted opening, as shown in Fig. 2-2. The more narrow the opening is on a bottle, the greater will be the challenge of constructing a house in that bottle. **HISTORY OF BOTTLEMAKING.** The history of bottlemaking is so interesting it justifies a few paragraphs. Without a proper understanding of the pains bottlemakers went through in order to form even the most primitive of early bottles, a builder may tend to take for granted the existence of the bottle. Glass was discovered several thousand years ago. Sand from beneath a campfire was found to have melted into a solid, translucent mass. Over the centuries this glass was refined to the often sophisticated quality we see today. Surprisingly, glass is actually a very slow-moving liquid! Windowpanes from very old buildings are found to be thicker at the bottom than at the top. The means that through time, the blass actually runs, or sags, from the downward pull of gravity. Bottles may be made of a very slow-moving liquid, but they sure break easily. About 2,000 years B.C., Egyptians realized they could make glass threads of varying sizes by pulling and stretching a lump of molten glass, much like pulling taffy. They later found that if they wound these glass threads around a wet-sand form, they could make containers and bottles. It should be noted that it would be "murder" to try to build anything inside these early bottles. These bottles were actually too small for building anyway, since they were containers intended for substances regarded as precious, such as body oils, perfumes, cosmetics, and ointments.

was permitted before it was dipped into the pool of molten glass. This process was repeated until a large enough bottle form was achieved. Metal and wet wood tools were used to form the bottle into the desired shape. Sometimes the glass bottle was blown into a wet wood mold to form it into a square or other geometric shape. A heavy metal rod was attached to the bottle's bottom with a little glass wad called a *pontil*, and the bottle was *cracked off* the blow pipe by scratching or filing a mark at the desired separation point. After a gentle tap on the pipe, the bottle, being supported mainly by the pontil rod, was released from the blow pipe. Then the bottle was reheated in order to smooth the opening's rough edge. Some neck shaping completed the piece. A small kiln or furnace was used to anneal

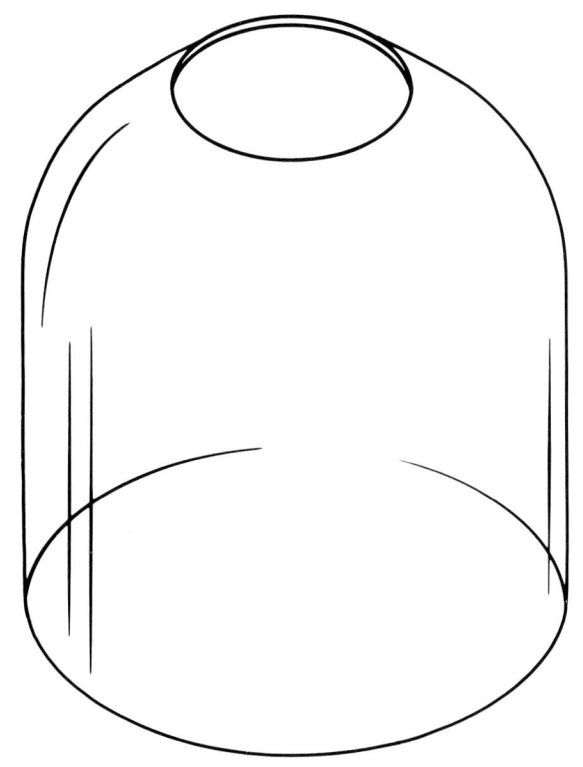

Fig. 2-1. If there is no neck, a bottle must at least have a restricted opening. Vessels with neither a neck nor a restricted opening are usually considered jars.

The Egyptians later discovered an improved method of bottlemaking. They found that if wet sand were packed into a wet leather or cloth bag, which was shaped similar to a bottle, it could be dipped into a hot, molten pool of glass. Removed from the glass pool quickly and allowed to cool slowly, a bottle was made which was superior to that made with the thread method. More bottles could be made in a shorter amount of time, and these bottles were of greater durability.

Classic glassblowing, using a long metal pipe, was invented in the first century B.C. by the Romans. The end of the metal pipe was dipped into a pool of molten glass, and it gathered a glob of glass, which was rolled on a rock slab and shaped into a manageable form. Next, the glassblower blew air from his own lungs through the pipe, expanding the glass into a thick-walled bubble. After reheating, the bubble was enlarged. Some cooling

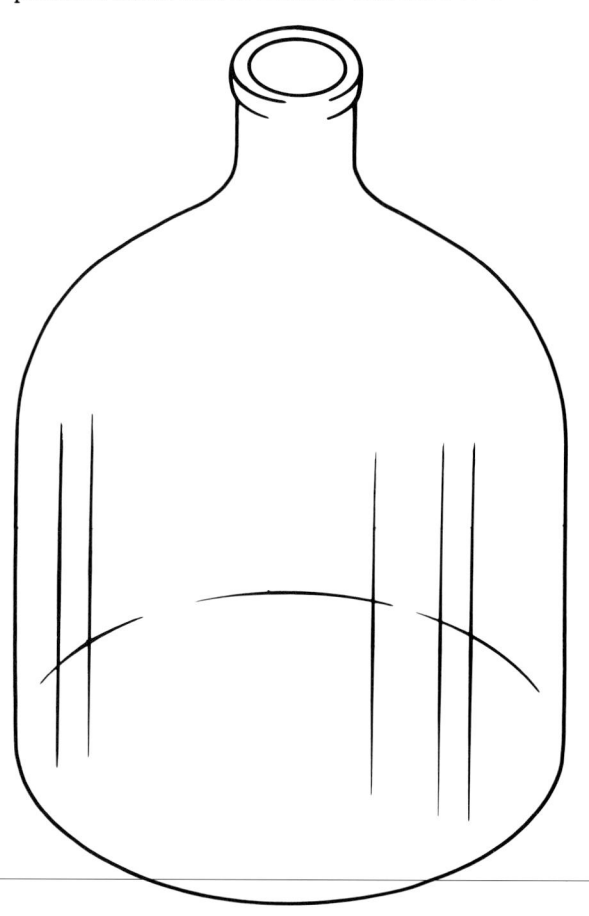

Fig. 2-2. The bottle's neck is an extension of its restricted opening.

the bottle. *Annealing* releaves any stress in the glass which will later manifest itself as cracks. The bottle was *tapped off* the rod by separating at the point where the pontil glass touched the bottom of the bottle. The bottle was set upright in the furnace for overnight annealing.

These hand-blown bottles were larger and more stable than the ones made by previous methods. The Romans often used such bottles for storage of cremation ashes. The tear holder seen in Fig. 2-3 is an example of early Roman glassblowing. Some art glass made currently throughout the world is formed using the same glassblowing techniques as invented by the Romans and is identified by the characteristic pontil mark found on the bottom of such work.

Around the turn of this century the automatic bottle machine was developed. It popped a molten glass wad into wood and later cast-iron, molds of varying shapes without a human ever touching the bottle. It even set the completed bottle on a conveyor belt to transport it through the annealing furnace. The conveyor belt later took the cooling bottle into the packaging area at the end of the production line. These bottles never varied unless another type of mold was used to make a different style of bottle. Most of today's bottles are made using a similar, updated model of the automatic bottle machine and can be identified by the characteristic, full-length, mold marks along the sides.

Fig. 2-3. This Roman tear holder is an early example of hand-formed glass containers. It is shown with a standard tennis ball to indicate comparative size.

THE RELATIONSHIP BETWEEN THE BOTTLE AND ITS CONTENTS

The bottle acts as a display case enhancing the image of the object contained within it. There always exists a relationship between the object contained inside and the bottle itself. Thoughtful consideration as to proper selection of a bottle which will harmonize with its subject is essential. You, the builder, may have a house design or plan for which you must select a bottle. On the other hand, you may have a bottle for which you must create a house design. Although planning and designing houses will be covered in Chapter 3, its mention is noteworthy for bottle selection purposes.

A study of the relationship between the bottle and its contents will be helpful. Some houses seem to "fit" their respective bottles very well. They appear to exist in aesthetic harmony with one another. The unoccupied space around the house is minimal, and the house and bottle seem to be well matched. On the other hand, some combinations are poorly suited for each other and appear as embarrasing mistakes. It can work both ways. A tall, stately Victorian house should be matched with a tall bottle which itself expresses a certain dignity and elegance. This has been achieved, more or less, by the bottled house appearing in Fig. C-2. Before construction began, some people commented on how "beautiful" or "handsome" the bottle alone seemed to be. The harmony would be diminished if the same house stood in some bulbous, free-flowing bottle whose shape failed to repeat the strong vertical lines of the house. Likewise, the thatched-roof "hobbit-looking" house and an old, barrel-shaped, root-beer bottle, pictured in Fig. 2-4, seem to be a pleasing combination. Conversely, the log cabin in Fig. 2-5 and its common, 1-gallon, apple juice bottle appear to be awkwardly teamed. Perhaps a shorter, more graceful wine bottle would have been more appropriate. You will to learn as you gain more experience.

There are literally millions of different kinds of bottles in this world. Some are common, some are rare. They can be new, slightly used, or valued antiques. Some bottles are machine-made, and others are hand-blown. They range in size from very small, as in Fig. 2-6, to very large, as seen in Fig. 2-7. They come in clear glass, or tinted in varying degrees and colors. Some bottles may be plain, while others are embossed with designs and letters. You must learn to screen the useful bottles from the rejects.

BOTTLE CHARACTERISTICS AND QUALITIES

The glass color or lack of color is an important consideration with which you must deal when choosing a bottle. Although it is a case of personal preference, common sense will indicate that the less color tint in the bottle glass, the easier it will be in which to build. Some builders may find some frustration with having to build in tinted bottles. Other craftsmen may survive building in even moderately tinted bottles. No builder, however, can effectively work in a bottle of darkly colored glass. Not only would such a bottle create unbearable eyestraining, but the image of the artwork constructed inside would be greatly diminished. The artwork simply could not be seen clearly. Tint colors include shapes and combinations of green, blue, brown, amber, and sometimes a rare form of red. You must decide for yourself how much of a tint, if any, you can endure.

There is an effective test you may wish to employ to help determine whether or not a tinted bottle is usable. Simply roll up a newspaper and stuff it partway down the neck. Leave enough of a paper "handle" outside the bottle to provide easy removal. The newspaper should be inserted far enough into the bottle's work area to be seen. Next, try to read the exposed words, as in Fig. 2-8. It should be apparent whether or not the bottle is worth the eyestrain, and this will be the determining factor. Again, common sense should rule the day.

The size of a usable bottle is less of a problem for the builder. A beginner should start with a bottle which seems comfortable to handle. It should be large enough to provide adequate working space. It is true that a small bottle may contain a smaller,

Fig. 2-4. An antique, barrel-shaped, root-beer bottle complements the charm of the thatched-roofed, Hobbit-looking house constructed inside.

Fig. 2-5. This log cabin, built inside a common, 1-gallon juice bottle, appears lost among the rocks scattered along the bottom.

less-detailed house, while a larger bottle should display a larger structure, requiring more detail. Although it is an option you must determine, a 1-gallon bottle is the recommended size with which a beginner should start.

The size of the opening of the bottle is another consideration worth some careful thought. If your little finger is all that can pass through the neck, a wise builder would select a more suitable bottle. Doors, windows, and other prefab parts must pass through easily. A small bottle neck will greatly increase an admirer's amazement, but will also increase the difficulty of building in the vessel. On the other hand, an excessively large bottle neck will greatly diminish the challenge and the magic associated with a bottled house. Building in a wide-mouthed jar will probably evoke a reaction of "So what!"

Glass distortion is usually considered an undesirable effect that often occurs to a greater or lesser degree in every glass bottle. Besides creating unbearable eyestrain, glass distortion causes the image of the object inside to appear deformed or misshapen. Although the artist has little control over this problem, it is advisable to avoid selecting bottles with excessive distortion.

Distortion is caused by variations in the thickness of the bottle's glass wall. Embossed designs and letters are the main contributors to glass distortion. Unless the amount of these designs and letters are prohibitively excessive, however, some of these distinctive effects may actually be desirable. An example is shown in Fig. 2-9. These identifying marks often add to the overall charm of a bottled house. Note, too, that some labels are in the form of painted designs applied to the out-

Fig. 2-6. Miniature bottles may also be useful to the bottler.

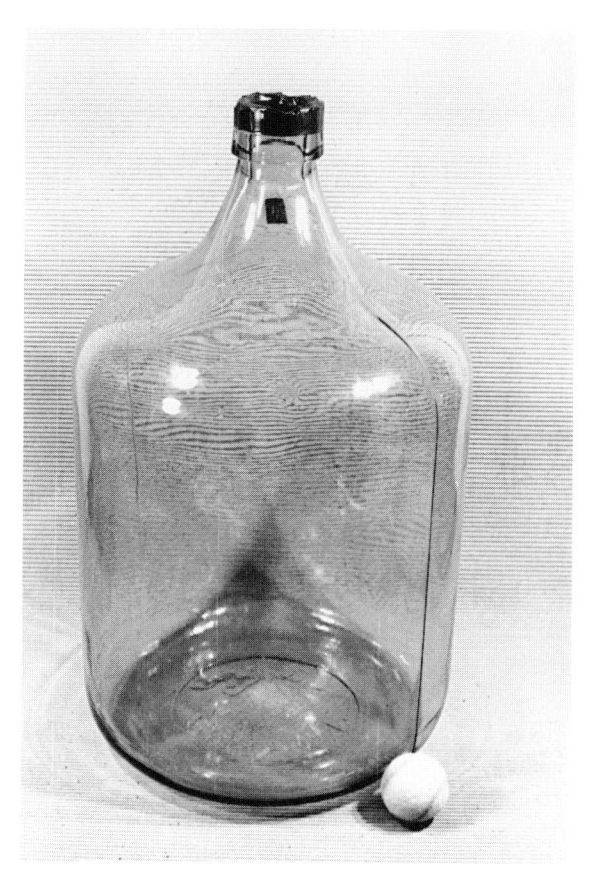

Fig. 2-7. A whole village could be constructed inside this 13-gallon chemical bottle.

melts, rather than wait overnight to allow the bubbles to escape. A few bubbles may be acceptable in a bottle, but excessive numbers will cause eyestraining while building, as shown in Fig. 2-10. From an admirer's point of view, many bubbles may appear as falling snow around the house. Too side of the glass. These, too, can be excessive and obscure the view of what is inside.

Bubbles within the glass wall of the bottle are another form of distortion. This problem occurs almost exclusively with hand-blown glassware. Bubbles in the glass are caused because the manufacturer fails to allow a newly mixed batch of molten glass to sit undisturbed long enough for the bubbles to make their way to the surface of and exit from the glass pool. This bubbling occurs when the batch of glass is being heated to the temperature at which the glass mixture will melt into a usable liquid. The heating is best accomplished by burning natural gas. The expenditure of such energy is an expensive one. It is less expensive, and therefore understandable, for a manufacturer to begin bottle production as soon as the new batch of glass

Fig. 2-8. Although the newspaper can still be read with varying degrees of difficulty, this tinted bottle would be unsuitable for building.

11

problem. Glass folding is inevitable in forming some glassware, but it causes distortion nevertheless. Sometimes it is caused by applying another layer of glass over an existing glass shape without smoothing or stretching it flat (Fig. 2-11). This kind of distortion is almost always undesirable, although it remains "in the eye of the beholder." What may be undesirable to one, may be regarded as charming to others.

Bottle *seams* or mold marks, are also considered forms of distortion. Seams are characteristic, vertical lines, usually located on opposite sides of the bottle from one another. They are not actually seams, but rather marks where the mold halves come together while the bottle is being formed. These mold marks are unique to machine-made bottles. They are considered objectionable because admirers sometimes think that the bottle was cut, the completed house model inserted, and the bottle

Fig. 2-9. Some glass distortion forms designs which add distinction to the bottle on which they are found.

much of this snow will obscure the image of the object inside.

Large bubbles may also be caused by the glassblower folding over part of the glass wall over another trapping some air between the two layers. Experienced glass blowers can usually avoid this

Fig. 2-10. Thousands of tiny bubbles cloud the glass quality of a Mexican, hand-blown bottle.

Fig. 2-11. Glass folds, such as the one located just below the neck of this bottle, can create serious distortion problems if they are situated in a prominent area of the bottle.

halves rejoined and cemented together.

Less serious distortions are the surface textures. They are irregular, pebble-textured areas usually surrounding the main body of a bottle. These textures are formed when the hot, molten glass comes into contact with the cold, wet wood or metal mold surface. This condition is produced by both hand-blown and machine-made methods of bottle making. The effect is more apparent in hand-blown bottles than with machine-made ones, however. In some cases, when the texture is severe, unbearable eyestrain can develop quickly. The bottle in Fig. 2-12 is such a bottle.

The preceding bottle characteristics should be considered carefully when you select prospective bottles in which to build. Haste or lack of thought in bottle selection may result in physical discomfort and possibly embarassing disasters. Such misfortunes may lead you to give up bottling houses and ships as a pastime. Spending a little extra time in choosing a proper bottle will help eliminate problems later.

DISCOVERING NEW BOTTLES

We are fortunate to be graced in this day and age with a great variety of new bottles that are being produced and available. Observation of all the things around you will be a great aid in finding a suitable new bottle in which to build. They seem to appear in the most unexpected places. Supermarkets, gift shops, department stores, wine-making shops, and liquor stores are a few examples of places in which new bottles may be obtained.

Art glass can be a good source of suitable bottles. They are noted for their unusual and aesthetic shapes. Often hand-blown, their glass quality can be extremely high; naturally, so can their prices. A good example of art glass appears in Fig. 2-13. Made by Blenko Glass of West Virginia, its distortion- free glass quality provides much better

Fig. 2-12. Distortion caused by textured glass imprints on the bottle's surface will create unbearable eyestrain for the builder.

specifications, if the compensation is seductive enough. The bottle containing a Victorian house in Fig. C-3 is such a bottle. These bottles are made of Pyrex glass tubing, which is very tough and durable. This is an excellent, but expensive, way to obtain new good-quality glass bottles.

Beverage and material containers are also a terrific way of obtaining new bottles. Not only are they usually inexpensive, but a great variety of bottle shapes are available. Being observant will most certainly result in some surprising finds.

The local liquor store is an obvious warehouse of good bottles. Although I would never intentionally promote the solitary emptying of spirit bottles, there may be ample cause for celebration with friends and relatives after discovering a worthy bottle. The 1-gallon, Jim Beam bourbon bottle in Fig.

Fig. 2-13. This bottle, made by Blenko Glass of West Virginia, is an example of excellent-quality art glass.

than average comfort for the eyes. A mining village was constructed in a Blenko bottle and is pictured in Fig. 2-14.

Sometimes hand-blown, Mexican glass can be purchased in gift shops and department stores. It is usually characterized by the bubbly glass quality. A simple Victorian house was built in such a bottle and appears in Fig. 2-15. That particular bottle is square, rather than round, having been blown into a square, wooden mold. Some people may find objections to the many large as well as tiny bubbles, while others may find such a characteristic charming.

Another possible source of good-quality bottles is scientific glass-instrument manufacturers. These businesses make laboratory apparatus and may be talked into constructing a glass bottle to your own

Fig. 2-14. A mining village was constructed in this 2-gallon Blenko bottle. Notice how little glass distortion obscures the image of what is inside.

Fig. 2-15. A Victorian house is preserved in an unusual square hand-blown bottle from Mexico.

is by looking at the unobscured, neck area above the liquid level, the distortion problem is another story. Pick up the bottle and turn it so you can look through the bottle without interference from the label. Even if you are looking through the darkest of the wines or liquors, when moving the bottle across the image of a window or light, the amount of distortion should become relatively apparent. Likewise, running your fingers across the surface of the bottle will permit discovery of embossed designs and letters, which contribute to excessive distortion. These maneuvers may be employed anytime bottles contain relatively transparent liquids. Materials or liquids which are not transparent require more examination, depending on their color. Sometimes such purchases are a real gamble, but often they are worth the chance. After all, there may be some consolation in enjoying the contents of some of these bottles.

The supermarket is a worthwhile place to

2-16, is such a prize. On the other hand, Fig. 2-17 shows a bottle selected after such a celebration had begun. It is sorrowfully inappropriate for reasons which are readily apparent. In contrast, the unusual, 1-gallon Scotch bottle in Fig. 2-18 is in the form of a rectangular solid. This size Scotch bottle may be difficult to locate. Currently, wineries are marketing their products in much more attractive, 1-gallon bottles such as seen in Fig. 2-19 (now rare) and the popular, but slightly smaller, 3-liter, wine bottle in Fig. 2-20, rather than the typical, 1-gallon jug, Fig. 2-21, available in the past.

A few words of caution are in order at this point. It is very difficult for even the most alert person to make good judgements as to the glass quality of a bottle while it still contains a substance. Although you may check how darkly tinted the glass

Fig. 2-16. This 1-gallon, Jim Beam bourbon bottle would someday contain a 2-story, western-styled saloon.

15

Fig. 2-17. This unusual, machine-made wine bottle is a highly improbable choice for any kind of building.

shelves. It is only a matter of being observant and discovering them.

Another great source is a wine-making shop. These businesses often sell a variety of new bottles for the purpose of fermenting and storing wine. A large 6-gallon bottle with a screw-on cap and similar in shape to a common, 5-gallon water bottle is occasionally available through these shops. Sometimes good-quality, 1-gallon bottles are available as well.

In metropolitan areas, industrial-container manufacturers and distributors may be located. Some of these companies handle glass chemical bottles for storing acids and other substances, such as seen in Figs. 2-25 and Fig. 2-7. A telephone call to a business of this kind may lead to some pleasing bottle discoveries. Bottles made for such uses are almost always heavy-duty in order to ensure durability, which may mean thicker glass walls and more distortion.

The preceding sources of new bottles are, without a doubt, not the only ones existing today. The

discover suitable, new bottles. There is a greater variety of bottled goods being marketed in the larger stores. Again, being observant can pay off. Manufacturers seem to delight in marketing their products in distinctive bottles. Fruit juices are often sold in bottles worthy of consideration. Figure 2-22 shows an apple-shaped, 1-gallon bottle, and another style of apple-juice bottle appears in Fig. 2-23. Some juice producers continue to use the standard, 1-gallon jug as seen in Fig. 2-21. The jug is a good, inexpensive bottle in which to experiment with different construction techniques.

Both distilled and drinking water occasionally come in interesting glass bottles such as the unusual form pictured in Fig. 2-24. There may be a number of supermarket products being marketed today in suitable bottles which have yet to be discovered by "bottle scavengers." As manufacturers change packaging methods, even more distinctive and worthwhile bottles will appear on the market's

Fig. 2-18. This interesting, rectangular-shaped Scotch bottle is badly flawed with glass distortion.

Fig. 2-19. This modern 1-gallon wine bottle and others similar to it are being replaced by the wine industry with new 3-liter bottles.

Fig. 2-21. Many juice bottles are still being made in the 1-gallon size and remain among the best of quality for building.

Fig. 2-20. The new 3-liter wine bottle is slightly smaller than the older, 1-gallon one, but will substitute just as well for building.

Fig. 2-22. This distinctive, apple-shaped juice bottle is rare but still seen in junk stores and swap meets.

17

Fig. 2-23. This 1-gallon, juice bottle can be found in many supermarkets across the United States.

telephone book may provide leads to other possibilities. Try looking under the headings "Bottles," "Containers," "Glass Containers," and "Industrial Containers." It still boils down to being observant of what is around you. The more deliberate looking and investigating you do, the more discoveries you will make.

FINDING OLD BOTTLES

A long history of bottlemaking has provided us with a multitude of antique bottles of varying quality and size. Although there are many more modern bottles—those not old enough to be considered antiques—than antique ones, enough "oldies" still exist to make it worthwhile to search for them. Many people who collect old bottles feel that antique bottles are more desirable than the new ones. The antiques are usually found to be constructed with greater durability in mind. Today bottles are made more inexpensively, using less glass and resulting in thinner, more fragile walls than the antique ones.

Many people prefer the old-fashioned bottle

Fig. 2-24. This unusual 1/2-gallon water bottle can also sit vertically like most bottles.

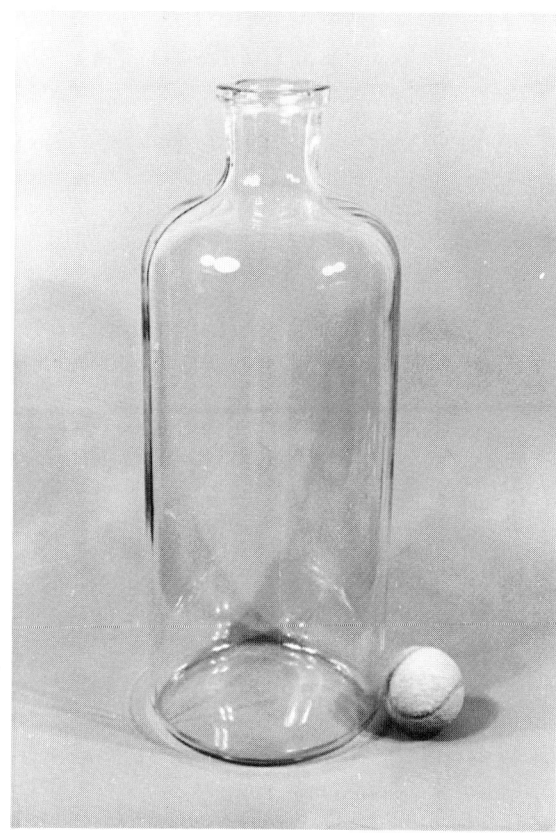

Fig. 2-25. Bottles such as this laboratory vessel may be difficult to obtain, but their quality makes them worthwhile.

designs and embossed labeling of the antiques as compared with the modern shapes of today. There is much to be said for the old designs. So much charm is apparent with formal moldings lining the edges and embossed, Gothic lettering across the bottle's face. Lacking the mechanical, screw-on closures of the modern bottles, the antiques are usually capped with corks or glass stoppers, further adding to the charm. The only disadvantages are the purchase price and the relative condition of the bottle after the ravages of time. Chipped rims, scratches, cracks, and mineral deposits are some of the possible defects which might be encountered. Cleaning and restoration will be covered later.

There may be a question of values or ethics when using a rare and possibly valuable antique bottle for use with a bottled house. This is a consideration every builder must think about carefully. If an antique bottle is very expensive, the price may be a signal to you that the bottle is perhaps too rare to alter permanently by building in it. Avid antique-bottle collectors will agree that nobody should diminish the value and charm of rare and valuable bottles. Leave them for the collections and museums.

A number of unusual and interesting places sell old bottles among other things. Looking in the right places may well be the secret of locating such antiques. Check at garage sales, antique shops and shopping malls specializing in antiques, swap meets and flea markets, junk shops, ghost-town dumps, and gift shops. These sources may be plentiful or scarce, depending on the region in which you live. Some of these sources are "limited-time-only" sales, such as the swap meets and garage sales. Once the opportunity passes, it is gone forever. Often advertisements in the newspaper, specifically in the classifieds section, will reveal where and when these sales occur. Try to arrive early in order to find the best selection of goods.

Sometimes antique bottles are found at garage sales. Call them yard sales, moving sales, patio sales, or garage sales, these market places are organized by an individual or groups of residents for the purposes of cleaning out garages and homes and, more importantly, to make some extra money. Occasionally these sales are not advertised in the newspapers but are instead found by chance. Cardboard signs on utility poles are their only announcements. Great bargains can be had, since the sellers are eager to rid themselves of unwanted possessions, rather than have to find storage for them again. Buyers should know a little about the object they are about to buy. It is a "buyer beware" market. Admittedly, antique bottles are not found that often at these sales, but when they are, terrific deals may be made.

Swap meets and flea markets are among the very best sources of antique bottles. These grand sales are organized by a producer, possibly a drive-in movie or school booster club, and weekend sellers flock to its location along with many regularly attending buyers. Some of these sales specialize in antiques and are worth real attention. Most swap meets occur every week, while others are held only monthly. Some sellers buy objects on speculation, hoping to resell them the next week at a small profit. One of the very best of these swap meets is the monthly flea market at the Rose Bowl in Pasadena, California. Literally thousands of sellers appear each month, selling everything imagineable. All kinds of antiques are sold there, and old bottles are often among them. The buyer should, again, be knowledgeable about what he is trying to buy, for some swap-meet prices are a little inflated. On the other hand, many fantastic bargains can be struck. It can work both ways.

Junk shops are loosely organized markets, often filled to the ceiling with a seemingly unmanageable collection of used treasures. Although it is often a hazard to walk through the narrow aisles between stacks of objects, some marvelous surprises can be discovered and rescued for a song. Antique bottles are almost always found in junk shops. These bottles may not always be in great condition, but their prices are usually attractive.

Abandoned garbage dumps are occasionally a source of old bottles in the western United States. Many bottle collectors make their most cherished finds while digging in ghost-town dumps. Most of the refuse has already decomposed, leaving the more durable pottery and glassware waiting to be unearthed. Although many of the bottles discovered in a dump may be too small or badly broken for use with bottling houses, with a little luck a worthwhile piece or two may be rescued. Be prepared for long hours of hard work without finding anything of value. Such are the risks involved in searching for "freebies." A number of books are available which accurately pinpoint the locations of ghost towns, including maps of the streets, prominent buildings, wells, mines, and dumps. Caution should always be exercised because many dumps are located on private property, and trespassers may be apprehended and prosecuted. Dangerous insects and reptiles may also inhabit such areas, further increasing the hazards of such searches. A wise bottle hunter should make local inquiries, as well as search cautiously.

On rare occasions, antique bottles may be found in gift shops. Some shops owners combine a variety of antiques with their usual gift items in order to create or improve the atmosphere and charm in their establishment. Some of these antiques may be for sale if the compensation is great enough. If this fails, pleading and begging may have to be employed along with the cash before the shopkeeper will consider relinquishing his little treasures.

Antique shops are among the very best sources of old bottles. These shops seem to be located in almost every town or city and specialize in vintage things of all sorts. Although prices are usually high in such places, bartering may occasionally seal a good bargain. Bottles may not always be available, but as popular a collectible as they seem to be these days, most dealers should know where to direct you to them.

A phenomenon of growing popularity is the antique mall. This clever arrangement consists of a large building containing many small antique shops or booths, each managed by an absentee family, partnership, or individual. It is usually a cooperative organization in which the booths are looked after by a management team. Sales are transacted at a central cashier's desk after the item to be purchased has been removed from its booth. It is a great way to see a large number of individual antique shops without having to drive from shop to shop. It is like a swap meet of antiques with the business hours of a supermarket. One real disadvantage does exist, however, in that the seller is rarely on hand to barter with freely. All the prices are marked usually without compromise. The prospects of worthwhile bottle-hunting are excellent in these malls. Considering the large number of dealers seen at one time, at least a few good bottles must be available. The unusual variety of bottles in Figs. 2-7, and 2-26 through 2-28 were discovered on a single day in The Memory Lanes Antique Mall in Harbor City, California. A single-day's hunting is not always this productive at every mall, but should be satisfying nevertheless.

which to build a house, as indicated by the example pictured in Fig. C-4.

A liquor store display bottle is an example of giant proportions. These bottles are often two or more gallons in size, similar to the one appearing in Fig. 2-9. These bottles were never intended to be filled with liquor, but were used as a promotion of the product they represented. In the case of the Gordon's Gin bottle, it is a 3-gallon replica of the shape and color of the smaller sizes of Gordon's bottles, complete with paper lables and closure. The glass quality of this one is good, although the embossed lettering adds some distortion. The closure pictured with this particular bottle is not original, but complements the dignity of this piece of art.

Another bottle found in plentiful numbers is the 5-gallon water bottle. Many sellers of drinking water had bottles made especially for their particular company. Each company had its own trademark and labels embossed into the glass. The water companies could then keep better track of their own bottles. In recent years, however, the companies

Fig. 2-26. Bottles such as this 5-gallon one are often found in antique shops and swap meets.

Some types of bottles are found more often than others and should be mentioned here. Your own bottle hunting may very well encounter these at one time or another. It may be helpful to be equipped with some knowledge of what they are.

The demijohn bottle seen in Fig. 2-27 is often found in shops and swap meets. This one had at one time a wicker covering, which has long since deteriorated and fallen away. *Demijohns* were originally used for wine and were sealed with a cork. The glass often has a slight texture from the mold used to form the demijohn. The characteristic mold marks are also visible. The unusual oval shape is the real attraction of this piece. The glass quality is not that great, since the distortion is rather prominent and the glass slightly tinted with green. In spite of these problems, this is a fine bottle in

Fig. 2-27. This antique wine demijohn can hold around 6 gallons.

Fig. 2-28. This beautiful wine decanter is probably too valuable in which to build.

have started using standard, unlabeled bottles to save money. Some have even resorted to using plastic bottles rather than the heavy glass ones. The glass quality is usually pretty poor because of so much distortion, as seen in Fig. 2-26. It should be noted, however, that some of these water bottles are easier to work in than others. Builders should delay buying a water bottle until they find one with the least distortion and the lightest color tint in the glass. The Victorian house seen in Fig. C-2 was constructed in a relatively rare, 2-gallon, unlabeled water bottle.

Appearing more often these days are the 1-gallon liquor bottles, such as the one shown in Fig. 2-16. These are still being made and are actually filled with spirits. They often come with pumps for easy dispensing. Such bottles are heavy-duty and constructed to endure grand parties, at which they are often seen. Some of the older ones are now being found in antique shops and swap meets. They are machine-made, but their glass is sometimes badly distorted.

Large chemical bottles similar to the one in Fig. 2-7 are occasionally available in some antique shops. These monsters are very heavy-duty and are designed to contain 12 to 13 gallons. They are machine-made and usually slightly to moderately tinted gray-green. A bottle this large would be difficult to work in, although with a few tool modifications, grand things are possible. Imagine a whole village or even a merry-go-round constructed and perhaps electrified to rotate on its own. A combination of lively imagination and these big bottles can create a wealth of impressive possibilities.

Some antique bottles from Europe are making their way into shops in America. They are probably liquor or pharmacy bottles, the larger marked *3L* for three liters. One such interesting bottle appears in Fig. 2-29. Notice the formal lines and decorative moldings.

One of the strangest bottle shapes is the "Camp Minnow Trap," pictured in Fig. 2-30. It is a 1-gallon container which is submerged into a pond or. stream. Its three cone-shaped entryways allow the minnows to swim inside. Once they enter, the minnows cannot find their way back out. Later, the trap

ever, may well be one of those rare and unusual bottles which should not be diminished in value by building inside of it. It is a decision to ponder.

The unusual square decanter in Fig. 2-28 is a worthwhile subject. It was hand-blown into a wooden mold. Even its closure is handmade. Although it may be too short for most buildings, this bottle could be used with a modified, one-story dwelling which has predominantly horizontal lines. The glass quality is excellent with little distortion, while the color remains clear throughout.

Large light bulbs, such as the one pictured in Fig. 2-32, can be used in this craft as well. A large light bulb can be used for houses but is especially well-suited for containing ships. The bulb's shape seems to lend itself to use with a yacht under sail. Although a special stand must be constructed to hold the bulb with the threaded end up, the

Fig. 2-29. The pleasing lines and shape of this bottle give it distinction and value.

is hauled out of the water and the screw-on top removed to allow the minnows to be poured out. Although the glass distortion is relatively severe, the unusual shapes may provide some interesting construction problems and many intriguing challenges. Even without building inside, it is a fine conversation piece.

Another fascinating piece is the "Fulton Straight Whiskey" bottle. It is a 1-gallon container which is capped with only a cork. What is unusual about this bottle is its color. Since the bottle was made prior to 1917 when zinc was eliminated from glass-making formulas, the glass has turned purple from lengthy exposure to the sun. The tint is very subtle, but attractive just the same. This bottle is pictured in Fig. 2-31. Although its glass has been permanently stained by mineral deposits, the bottle is still very appealing and useable. This, how-

Fig. 2-30. This strange vessel is not really a bottle but rather a glass minnow trap from Checotah, Oklahoma.

Fig. 2-31. The glass of this antique whiskey bottle has become tinted from prolonged exposure to the sun.

tique bottles. There are many more kinds throughout the world, but they have to be discovered. People who are willing to search in the right places will find those exceptional bottles.

BOTTLE CLEANING

It is a triumphant achievement to discover a marvelous bottle, but still another to find an effective method of cleaning it. Extreme frustration can result from being unable to properly clean a beautifully shaped, but filthy, bottle. The trauma may continue, if some of the residual deposits remain behind after hours of tedious cleaning attempts. Some recommendations on how to effectively restore a soiled bottle will save the prospective builder hours of misplaced effort.

The residue can appear in a variety of forms. Some bottles have been found to contain the dried fascinating effect of a house or ship in a light bulb is well worth a little extra effort. The one pictured is a Westinghouse 120-volt, 1500-watt bulb. They are occasionally seen in store liquidations, junk shops, and antique malls. Entry is gained by chipping away the black, ceramic insulator found just below the threaded brass holder. It is not as difficult as it appears. After enough of the ceramic insulator has been removed, the interior glass tube holding the wires and filament can be removed. A metal rod is inserted, pushing aside the interior wires. A wrenching action at an angle will snap the glass tube free. Remove it from the bulb and begin building. The inside of the bulb should not require any cleaning. This can be a fun and challenging vessel in which to build a variety of structures.

The preceding examples have been described in order to point out the remarkable variety of an-

Fig. 2-32. A large 500-watt light bulb would make an excellent container for a house or ship.

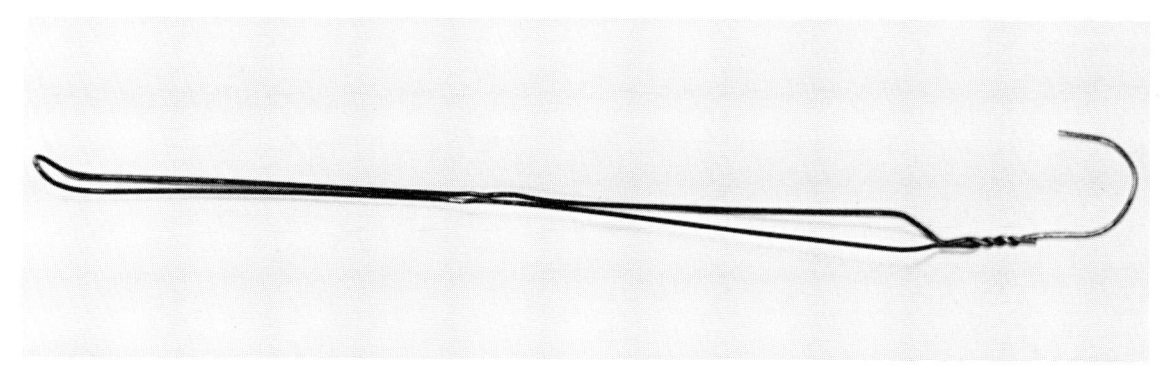

Fig. 2-33. A standard coat hanger is altered to this shape in order to make a bottle scrubber.

remains of used engine oil. Others have contained ugly colors of paint, while mineral deposits are often among the most frustrating challenges found inside of a bottle. Equal parts of earth and pancake syrup also make for interesting, cleaning fun. Dust and bugs are about average, however. Be prepared for all kinds of bottled surprises.

Sometimes a good tool can be of great help in the cleaning process. A simple, but adjustable, scrubbing tool can be constructed from a standard coat hanger. Start by bending the hanger into the shape pictured in Fig. 2-33. Next, wrap a long strip of rag around the loop opposite the hanger's hook, and wind the cloth with several layers up the wire to a point 3 or 4 inches from the bottom, as shown in Fig. 2-34. Secure the end of the rag by taping it to the wire handle. This scrubbing tool can be adjusted by bending it into a infinite number of shapes in order to accommodate the contours of each bottle shape; so hard to-reach areas of the bottle can be cleaned as well.

An effective cleaning solvent can be a tremendous aid in bottle cleaning. First, try the universal solvent: water. Many residues can be dissolved by a good soaking in water. Failing this, a stronger cleaner must be mixed. A solution of 1/2 cup household ammonia and 1/2 cup tap water poured into the bottle will begin to break down a variety of oil-based substances. Read the caution label on the ammonia container. Cap the bottle securely with a cork or a wad of paper covered with a plastic sandwich bag. "Shake, rattle, and roll" the bottle to properly agitate the solution. Pour out and rinse several times with tap water. One last rinse with distilled water will complete this first cleaning attempt. Turn the bottle upside down in an empty

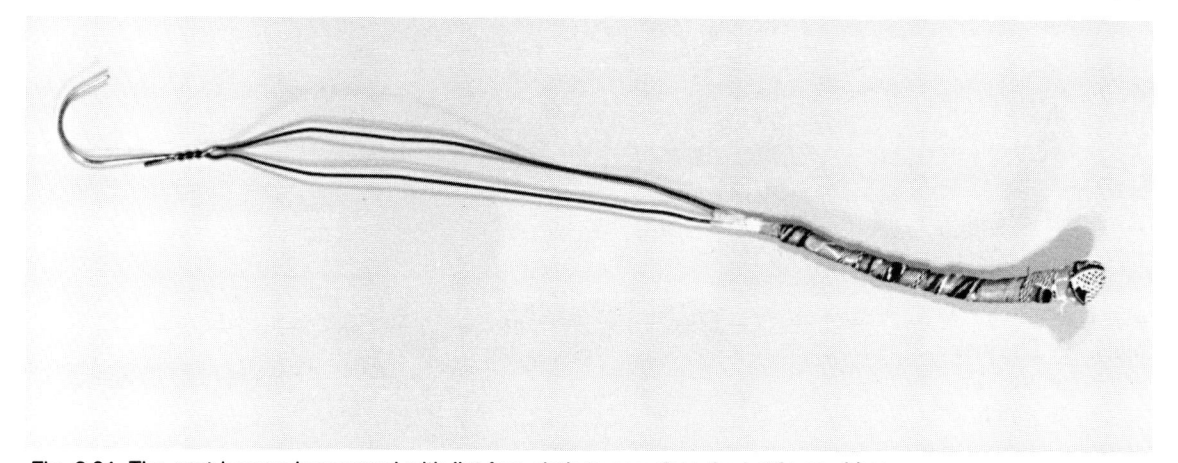

Fig. 2-34. The coat hanger is wrapped with lint-free cloth to complete the bottle scrubber.

flower pot to drain until completely dry.

Some mineral deposits or residues may reappear when the glass finally dries. Mark these remaining spots with a grease pencil to provide a scrubbing target. Examine the bottle under a variety of light sources. Mark any other hard-to-see spots. Then refill with the cleaning solvent and scrub vigorously with the scrubbing tool. Repeat the rinsing process until you are convinced that this method has cleaned to the best of its capabilities. These efforts should remove most dust, debris, and many residues. With a little luck, all will come clean. If you are not so lucky, proceed with "Plan B."

"Plan B" employs the use of even stronger solvents. Paint thinner, alcohol, acetone, lacquer thinner, and vinegar are just a few of the effective solvents useful for bottle cleaning. Even a wedge of lemon used as a scrubbing pad or tied to a coat hanger will help clear away some mineral deposits. Whenever volatile solvents are used, always read the caution labels. Employ the same scrubbing techniques with the stronger solvents as with the ammonia water. Some of the stronger solvents may leave behind their own residues. Try using the ammonia water to remove them, and always finish by rinsing with distilled water.

The use of abrasive cleaners should be avoided, if possible, since they can permanently scratch the surface of the glass. These abrasives range from common household powdered cleanser to coarse river sand. Even the smallest particle can mar the glass surface. You should never use abrasives with the scrubbing tool. An abrasive should always be used with water in order to diminish the harsh effects. One effective technique is to fill a large bottle with sand and water and then proceed to roll the bottle, if it is round, across the lawn. This technique provides a great scrubbing action. This method was employed to clean the 13-gallon chemical bottle in Fig. 2-7.

These bottle-cleaning techniques have evolved through trial and error. They are by no means the only approach to the problems of bottle cleaning. Someone may very well have or develop a better idea. By employing good common sense and creative inventiveness, another builder may be quite capable of developing other, more effective, methods of cleaning. Analyze the challenge, considering the risks and what the positive results may be. If the idea is logical, it should be tried. Nobody can know the results until the idea is tested.

BOTTLE CLOSURES

A *Closure* is an object which closes and seals a vessel. The main concern here is with aesthetics. How will a particular lid, stopper, or cap appear in relation to the bottle it is to seal? What additional statement should it make while performing as a closure? A good example of this consideration is pictured in Fig. C-5. The subject is a Western storefront building constructed in an antique bottle. It was decided to use an old, rusty, dented, screw-on cap rather than a cork. It appears to complement the rustic building very well. The dilapidated cap corresponds to the deteriorating, ghost-town structure inside.

Older bottles, specifically those without screw-on caps, are good candidates for corks as closures. Corks are made of the outer, thick-bark material of a species of oak tree. Corks may be purchased in drug and hardware stores. Some art supply stores and ceramic suppliers sell corks which still have the dark, outer bark attached to the lighter cork material. This feature gives a much more rustic look, which adds a lot of charm to the right combination of bottle and building. An example of this kind of cork seals an old mining village in a hand-blown bottle in Fig. 2-14.

Stately and more formal-looking, wood closures add a feeling of real dignity to the right bottled house. Notice the closures on the bottled houses pictured in Figs. C-2, through C-4. Exotic woods from far-away places are especially effective in providing the "classy" look required. These are shaped with a router after being cut out and sanded, but a stopper can be hand-carved in any shape you desire. If a craftsman has access to a wood-turning lathe, many outstanding shapes can be created, such as shown in Fig. 2-9.

It is an easy task to shape a closure using the

ing saw, which is shown in Fig. 4-3. A power tool called a *band saw* works even better.

To start, use a compass to mark a circle, the diameter of which should relate to the bottle's shape. Circle the compass point with a pencil in order to find it again later. Cut out with a saw and sand the edges until almost furniture-smooth. Cut out a second disk which will slide snugly into the neck of the bottle. The neck disk is first used as a handle to securely hold the larger wood disk while using the router. Refer to Fig. 2-35. Drill a 1/4-inch-diameter hole through the neck disk, as shown in the illustration. Next, drill a 3/16-inch-diameter hole only halfway through the large disk from the bottom. Aim the drill bit at the circled compass point. Assemble with glue by inserting a 1/4-inch-diameter wood screw 1 1/4 inches long. You may countersink the bottom side of the neck disk for a neater screw-head fit, but this step is optional. Tighten the screw for a secure assembly. Study the illustration. Clamp the entire assembly in a bench vice or other holding device. See Fig. 2-36 for proper arrangement. Run the router around the top, sand, and rub with furniture wax. The formal closure is now ready for sealing a bottle.

Other closures are also effective. If you are skilled with the knot-tying art of macrame, a rope router. Three parts are required and include one disk for the top, another disk to slide into the neck of the bottle, and one wood screw. A 3/4-inch-thick wood piece is cut into a round shape using a cop-

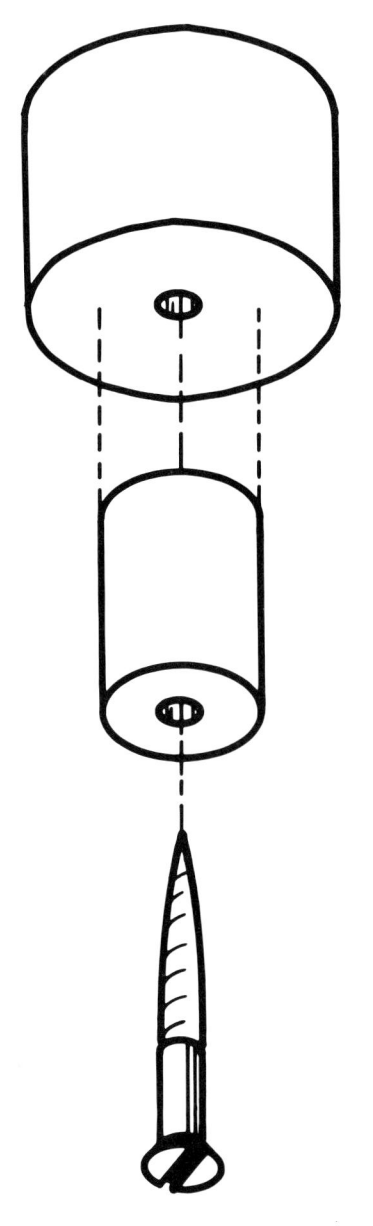

Fig. 2-35. The decorative wood closure is composed of three parts: the top disk, a bottleneck disk, and a wood screw. Countersink the bottom side of the neck disk before gluing and assembling.

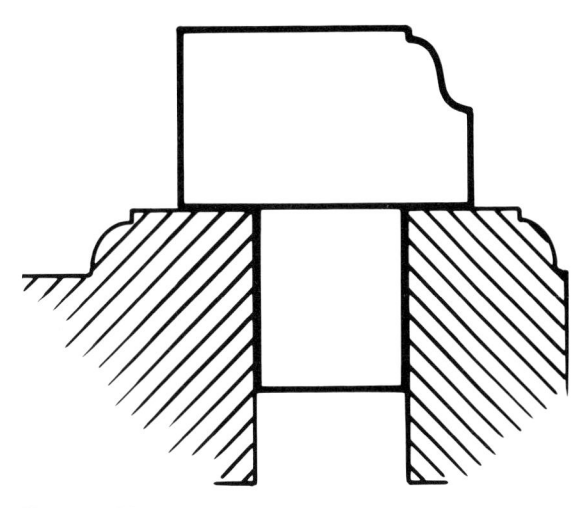

Fig. 2-36. Make sure the jaws of the vise securely grip the closure assembly before proceeding with the routering process.

or cord closure can be fashioned to cover the rim of the bottle. Ships in bottles are often sealed in this way. Another kind is the antique glass stopper. These closures were primarily used on old pharmacy bottles many years ago. If some are discovered in the antique shops or flea markets, purchase only those which fit snugly into the bottles being used. Ceramic closures could be made by hand through sculpturing them or by forming them on the potter's wheel.

There may be a number of other types of closures not considered here. Creative people are good at inventing solutions to problems. Thinking and experimentation can go a long way in finding solutions. The first step is a matter of getting started.

3

House Design and Modification

The house design is a very important factor in the success of a bottled house. A simple box of a house may seem boring and hardly imaginative, leading the admirer to think of how great it could have been. On the other hand, a house design combining a variety of geometrically shaped architectural forms into a pleasing composition will create enchantment, magic, and continued interest for years. It is not just the architectural style, but rather the composition of shapes and forms, which bring a design out of the ordinary and into the exceptional. Combining cylindrical, cubic, triangular, and rectangular shapes with the proper roof peaks and valleys can create a more pleasing and charming arrangement in the overall design. It may be helpful to play with blocks of wood in the shapes to be used in the preliminary house design. Arranging and rearranging these blocks help the mind's eye begin to imagine and select pleasing compositions. While analyzing each arrangement with a critical and aesthetic eye, decisions can be made as to which combinations look balanced and interesting and which look funny. Most everyone has the ability to recognize awkward-looking things, as well as those which are attractive and pleasing. We are constantly making these aesthetic decisions when we choose a car or a piece of furniture we wish to buy. There is a streak of artist in every one of us, whether we develop such an ability or let it lie fallow. Perhaps the Edsel was discontinued for that very reason. Planning a house which will fill most of the space in a bottle is a must. Care should be exercised to avoid constructing a house in only the lower portion of the bottle, leaving a larger, empty space toward the top like the one seen in Fig. 2-5. The result looks like a very awkward mistake. Fortunately we usually learn from our mistakes. A house that consumes the lower 2/3 or more of the bottle's interior space, leaving only 1/3 or less empty, is much more pleasing to the eye. The rule of thirds is a valuable law in the art world, and it works very well! Towers, roof shapes, and chimneys, which seem to stretch upward near and even into the bottle's neck, help create more charm and magic in a bottled house. Careful thought and planning will help produce a house properly scaled to fit the bottle. **ARCHITECTURAL STYLES.** The architectural style selected for the bottled house is also an important consideration. The decision on the style of the house is usually made by the builder or by the prospective buyer/owner. It is merely a matter of personal preference. Once the decision has been settled and the style established, however, that style should be maintained to completion. Otherwise, an incompatible, architectural mix may result, looking strange and awkward.

Fig. 3-1. Examples of Victorian-styled architecture may also be found constructed of stone, like this one discovered in Los Angeles.

Fig. 3-2. This Victorian house is made almost entirely of wood. It is one of several located in Heritage Square, a park dedicated to the preservation of outstanding architectural and cultural buildings rescued from around the Los Angeles area.

31

Fig. 3-3. Another Heritage Square Victorian sports a classical mansard roof.

Research may be necessary in order to develop a house design which will maintain the accuracy of a specific architectural style. The local library usually has a wealth of information in the form of drawings, photographs, and written descriptions of a wide variety of architectural styles. See also the Appendix.

Some useful styles may be exemplified by old homes and buildings located in your area. These examples can provide great ideas for the house-planning process.

The *Victorian* style, often referred to as the Queen Anne Style, is an excellent example for bottling. The charm and beauty of this architectural style is hard to rival. Although tedious and time-consuming to build, Victorian houses relate well to the strong, vertical lines of most bottles. The house's round towers and turrets repeat the cylindrical shape of round bottles. The delicate *gingerbread*, or decorative filligree, often in the form of miniature, individually lathe-turned and hand-carved parts, amaze and delight many admirers. The beautiful, fancifully decorated windows and doors further charm and enchant devotees. Tall, stately chimneys heighten the vertical theme. These characteristics contribute to making the Victorian style one of the most suitable for construction in a bottle. Some excellent examples of this style are pictured in Figs. 3-1 through 3-3. Bottled replicas are found in Figs. C-2, 3-4, and 2-15.

Another architectural style worthy of consideration is the *Tudor* style. Being an intermittently popular transplant from Europe, it is often referred to as the *Tudor Revival* style. It provides a very warm and charming effect, justifying its popularity. The roof is characterized by steeply pitched forms on which real slate tiles are laid. Sometimes thin wood shingles are substituted. The walls are defined by heavy, exposed, dark-colored timbers between which plaster, stucco, or a brick pattern may emerge. The windows are usually tall and narrow, with many individual panes of glass. Often leaded-glass shapes are also included in the window's opening, further enhancing the house's fairy-tale charm. Chimneys are usually of brick or a combination of brick and stone, presenting a form of textured sculpture atop the roof. Some examples appear in Figs. 3-5 through 3-7.

The *Cape Cod* style may also be adapted to building in a bottle. It is usually characterized by painted or naturally dark wall-shingles, or *clapboard*, siding which contrasts in color with the window and door trim. The exposed roof rafters generally appearing below the eaves. A popular color combination includes medium blue siding or wall shingles and prominent white trim. Cape Cod houses are much less complicated and formal than Victorian homes, although both make use of similar materials. The windows may vary in size; the large ones are defined with many individual panes of glass in a standard grid arrangement. The roof is almost

Fig. 3-4. An exaggerated two-story tower and a rounded front porch help bring a greater degree of Victorian flair to an otherwise simple farmhouse.

33

Fig. 3-5. The decorative exposed wood timbers identify this home as an example of the Tudor Revival style of architecture.

always shingled with wood or composition shingles in either natural-wood or dark gray colors. A white picket fence sometimes accompanies the Cape Cod house. This style can be very appealing and is worthy of being considered as a subject for bottling. Some West Coast versions of the Cape Cod style are pictured in Figs. 3-8 through 3-10. A bottled example appears in Fig. C-6.

Tall brick tenements, occasionally referred to as *brownstones*, are great for bottling when stylish. Their basic shape relates very well to most tall bottles. Colorful bricks contrasting with the white mortar and weblike fire escapes clinging to the outside, upper-floor walls create interesting moods. Figure 3-11 shows a West Coast tenement. A bottled brownstone is pictured in Fig. C-7.

Despite their simplicity, a common *tract home* may be included as a possible subject in a bottle. No matter how plain and simple a house may be, the bottled version can be of real sentimental value to its owner. A completed bottled house showing a tract home in the process of being constructed is shown in Fig. 3-12.

Castles can be very effective subjects. Castle designs may be traditional or styled from your imagination. You can create all kinds of clever possibilities as far as shape, form, and features are concerned. Towers, gates, arches, walls, battlements, drawbridges, and parapets are just a few features of a castle which can be designed and arranged into a pleasing composition. A bottled castle constructed of polystyrene foam bricks is pictured in Fig. 3-13, while a simplified one made of pebbles appears in Fig. C-10.

The *Mission Revival* and *Spanish* architectural styles are chiefly characterized by their red tile roofs. The tiles are shaped like cylinder halves which are laid in an interconnecting arrangement, alternating upside down and right side up. Walls are usually thick and covered with painted plaster or stucco. Although windows are usually small and wood-framed, larger windows do exist in this style.

Fig. 3-6. The steeply pitched, sculptural roof of this house is a stylized departure from the usual slate-covered Tudor style.

With their massive facades arching skyward, the Mission Revival style appears much like The Alamo, a former mission in Texas. These facades sometimes repeat the shapes of decorative floor tiles. In both the Spanish and the Mission styles, some windows are shielded by a decorative, wrought-iron grille. In the Spanish style, lathe-turned wood railings adorn the balconies protruding from the upper-floor walls. Both styles are truly majestic forms of architecture and are worth considering as subjects for bottled houses. Some grand examples are pictured in Figs. 3-14 through 3-16.

Adobe or *Pueblo* structures can be interesting subjects of bottled art. This form of architecture evolved in regions where the only practical building material is mud. Heavy clay walls, thicker at the base than at the top of the wall, are coated with plaster for durability. Fireplaces and chimneys are usually round, graceful, cone shapes which are exposed on the outside of the walls. The roof is flat or recessed and supported by round timbers, the ends of which are exposed through the wall to the outside. The windows and doors are usually small and unimposing. A heavy, timber lintel supports the adobe wall above the windows and doors. Real pueblos are characterized by the interesting effect created by the composition of stacked rectangular solids in a variety of pleasing relationships to one another. This style is pictured in Fig. 3-17.

Other architectural styles are often remarkably adaptable to bottling. Mountain cabins, bottled in Figs. 3-18 and 3-19, and a thatched-roofed Hobbit house (Fig. 2-4) can be very effective. Whole villages may be designed and constructed in a bottle with impressive results, as seen in Fig. 2-14. Many architectural styles found in foreign countries

Fig. 3-7. This Tudor fantasy is a real residence located in Beverly Hills, California.

can be easily adapted. Monuments to wishing wells may be effective subjects with the use of a little imagination. Even a long, skinny, mobile home or trailer could be constructed in a tall bottle and then displayed on its side. Lighthouses (Figs. 3-20 and 3-21) are also worthwhile subjects. Being observant of the world around you will help you discover an effective subject for bottling.

Architectural structures are not the only subjects which can be adapted and designed to be constructed in a bottle. Almost any object in which you may be interested can be altered and bottled. For example, a model of an antique automobile would be a terrific subject. The techniques and logic outlined in this book can be adapted to accommodate many unusual objects. Even mechanical gadgets, often classified as kinetic sculptures and powered by small electric motors, can be constructed in bottles, as indicated by Fig. 3-22. The additional engineering challenges of making a number of individual parts move in harmony with one another can be entertaining, as well as a great mental exercise. A favorite piece of furniture would be effective as well, as seen in Fig. 3-23.

Using practical, common sense as a guide is sage advice in selecting an architectural style or unusual subject for bottling. Although your own imagination can often compose marvelous designs, it can be like suntanning. Avoid overdoing it at first.

Some conflicts between the shape of the bottle and the shape of the house can cause great difficulties. For example, if a bottle has been selected and it is the only possible candidate, then the house shape as well as the style must be adapted to fit that particular bottle. If a real, existing house is to be duplicated in a bottle, searching for the right bottle should continue until the best possible, shape can be obtained. It comes down to choosing a bottle for a particular house design or choosing a house design for a particular bottle. If a patron of the bottled-house arts should ever wish a particular house design, shape, and style constructed in a particular bottle, the possible resulting conflicts could cause madness and trauma in the builder.

ADAPTING AN EXISTING HOUSE

Extensive preparation is the key to successfully adapting an existing house's design for construction in a suitable bottle. The builder must go to and observe the existing house. Freehand sketches must be drawn of the front, each side, and the rear of the house. (See Fig. 3-24.) A top view indicating the roof configuration will also be helpful, although it may be difficult to see the actual roof shapes from ground level. If good vantage points are not available, try to imagine the overall roof shape after taking into account the shapes of the roof areas that are visible. Include in the sketches as much information as possible, otherwise additional trips to the existing house will be necessary. Observe and indicate colors of paint used and the kinds of building materials making up the structure. Notice what kind of roofing materials and exterior wall coverings were used on the house. Indicate the window construction and consider how it can be effectively miniaturized. Describe the landscaping along the house walls. Draw detailed sketches of hard-to-see areas of the house. Close-up views of decorative moldings and other intricate parts are a great help as well.

Next, photograph the existing house. As with the freehand sketches, each side, the front, and the rear of the house should be photographed using straight-on views rather than angular shots. Com-

Fig. 3-8. Although this beach house is a bit small, its shingle siding, dormer (roof) windows, roof pitch, and basic shape are typical characteristics of the pure Cape Cod style.

Fig. 3-9. Although the roof shape of this house is a variation of the Cape Cod style, its blue clapboard siding and white trim are often regarded as typical characteristics.

pare the accuracy of the sketch in Fig. 3-25 with the one in Fig. 3-26. Straight-on views help determine accurate wall proportions and shapes, while angular shots are often misleading. Unlike freehand sketches, photographs are good about "remembering" all details. On the other hand, the sketches will help reveal areas of the house where there is a poor field of view because of the presence of trees or other buildings. Written notes can be added to the sketches, but they are not possible on the slick-surfaced photos. Both sketches and photos have their own particular value to the builder.

After all the research materials depicting the existing house have been collected and prepared, and a suitably shaped bottle has been obtained, the final planning may proceed. Study the bottle and note the shape of its interior space. Actual measuring of the interior's dimensions may even be helpful to some builders. You can measure by inserting small sticks into the bottle using the needle-wire tool which will be studied extensively in Chapter 4 to manipulate them into position. Remove the sticks and, if necessary, shorten by cutting off a section or lengthen by gluing on a small section of stick. Continue this process until all the necessary dimensions have been obtained. These measuring sticks will help you visualize the bottle's interior space.

Next, consider the true proportions of the house's shape, while using your imagination to stretch or shorten those proportions in order to fit the house into the interior space of the bottle. Begin sketching those altered proportions in both straight-on and bird's-eye view drawings. (See Fig. 3-27.) Inch-by-inch dimensions of the house's proportions are not necessary unless you find them helpful in arranging the bottle's interior space. "Eye-balling it" (guessing) seems adequate usually.

Only after every aspect of the planning has been completed, should the actual construction

Fig. 3-10. This is another stylized version of the Cape Cod style.

begin. Later, as you gain experience in planning and constructing bottled houses, some of these preparations may be abbreviated. The result of such planning for a bottled house adapted from an existing one is pictured in Fig. 3-28 and C-4.

ADAPTING A HOUSE OF YOUR OWN DESIGN

Adapting a design from your own imagination to fit a specific bottle is much simpler than adapting an existing design, as well as creative. Major design changes may be made even in the middle stages of construction. Such changes will result in few complaints, if any, since the design is your own. After you compose a final house design, including structural shapes and architectural style, measure the bottle's interior space. Imagine how the house will look inside that particular bottle. Alter the proportions of the house's shape as required for proper fit. Stretching and shortening the proportions of the house to conform with the bottle's shape and dimensions must be carefully thought out. Sketching a bird's-eye view drawing will again be helpful at this point. Drawings of details and some straight-on views may be required as well, depending on the complexity of the shape and architectural style. Measuring and estimating processes are the same as with the planning of the existing house. After most of the basic planning has been completed, actual construction may proceed. Small details may be planned and incorporated into the design during construction.

The importance of careful planning cannot be overemphasized. It can be so frustrating, as well as embarrassing, to near completion of a bottled house and have to leave off the roof and chimney because of poor planning.

Fig. 3-11. This West Coast tenement is similar to, but no comparison to, the classic New York brownstones.

Fig. 3-12. A Borden's milk bottle contains a tract house under construction. Although this bottled house is finished, its intrigue comes from the attempt to build it according to the Los Angeles County Building Code.

Fig. 3-13. A castle, designed from fantasy and made of polystyrene foam bricks, is contained in a 1-gallon juice bottle.

Fig. 3-14. An excellent example of Mission Revival architecture is located in Fullerton, California.

41

Fig. 3-15. The grand old Mission Revival homes often become boarding houses, but their stately dignity lives on.

Fig. 3-16. This variation on the Mission Revival style is especially majestic.

Fig. 3-17. This is just a portion of the interesting composition forming the famed Taos Pueblo in northern New Mexico.

Fig. 3-18. A mountain cabin clad in hand-split cedar siding is contained in a 1-gallon juice bottle.

Fig. 3-19. Mountain cabins allow for ample use of the builder's imagination in their design.

43

Fig. 3-20. The Point Fermin Lighthouse, located near San Pedro, California, would make a worthwhile subject for bottling.

Fig. 3-21. The Point Loma Lighthouse, located near San Diego, California, is considered a classic form.

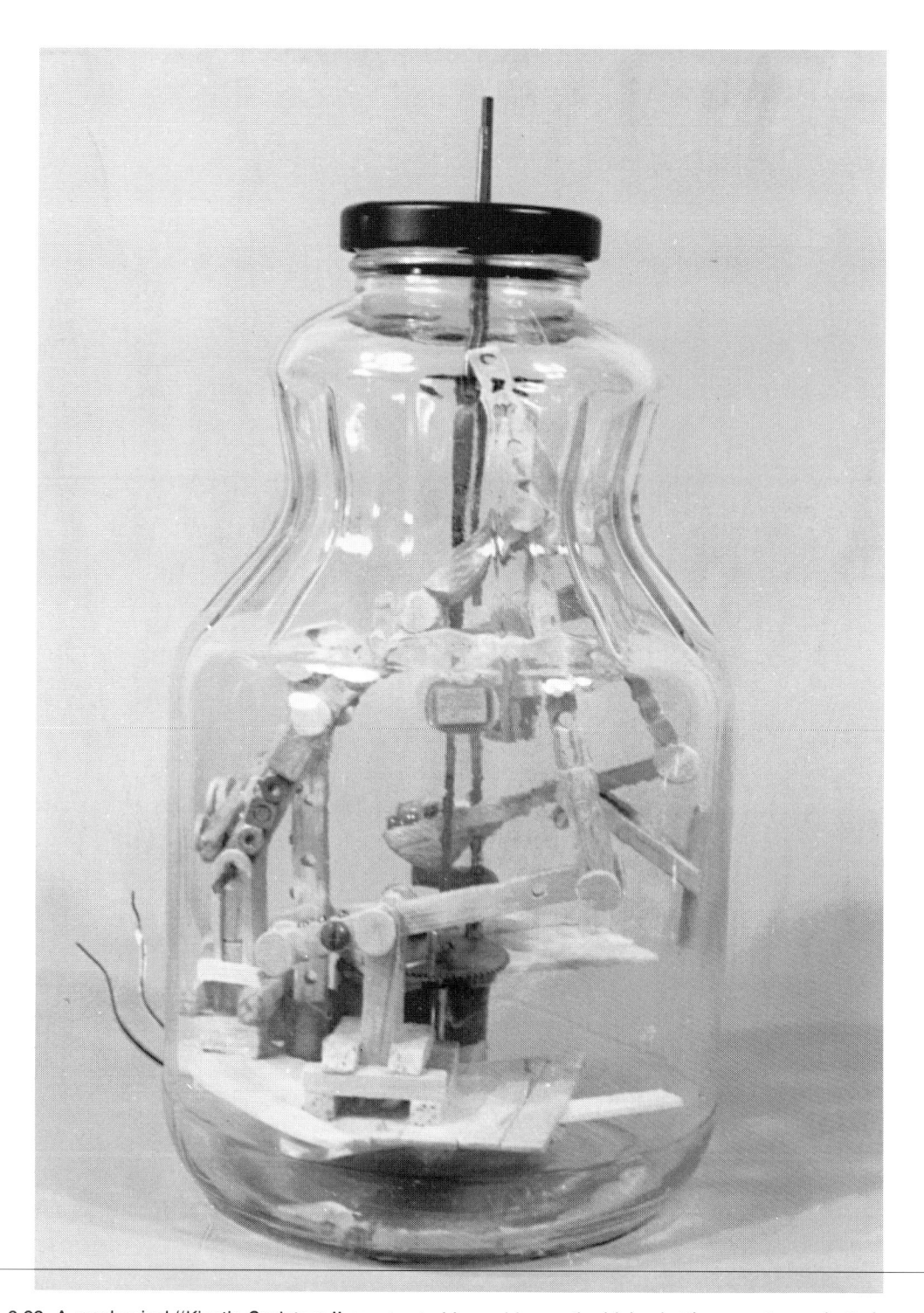

Fig. 3-22. A mechanical "Kinetic Sculpture," constructed in a wide-mouthed juice bottle, operates on batteries.

Fig. 3-23. A rocking chair, which actually rocks, was constructed in a 1-pint bottle by an unknown craftsman. It was purchased as an antique from a swap meet.

Fig. 3-24. This freehand sketch of an existing house shows a straight-on view of true proportions.

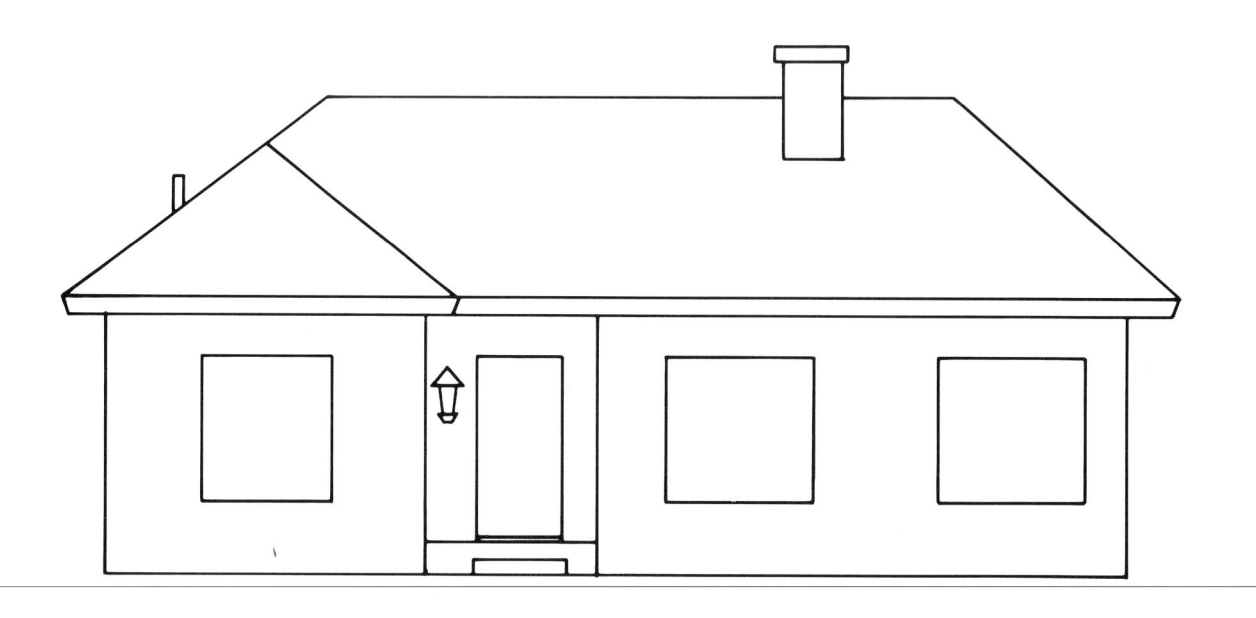

Fig. 3-25. A correct angle of view for a straight-on photograph reveals accurate placement of architectural features.

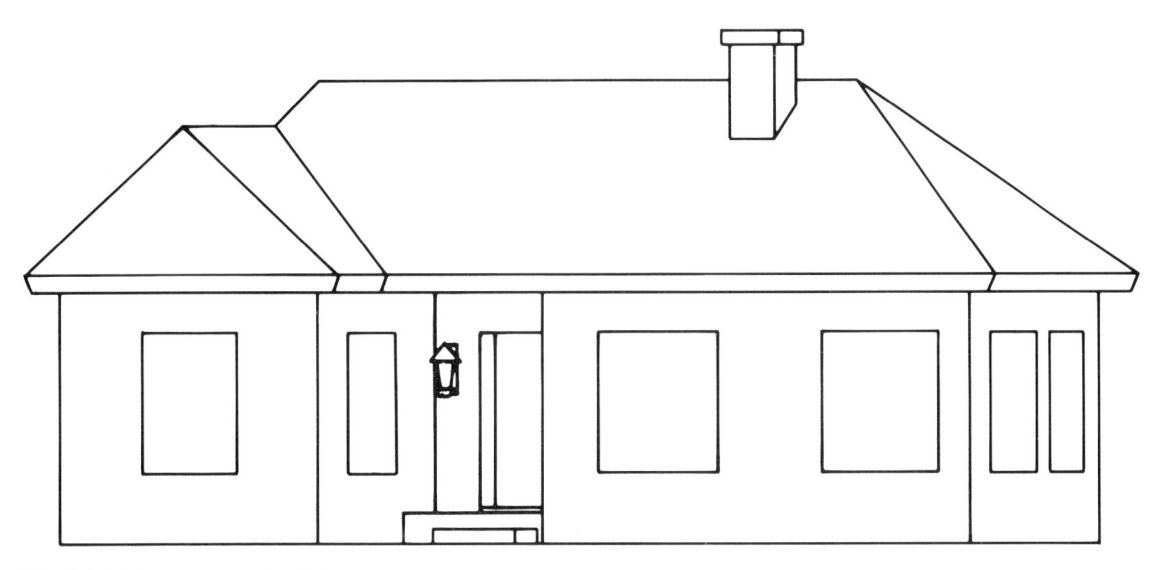

Fig. 3-26. The wrong angle of view for a photograph shows misleading proportions.

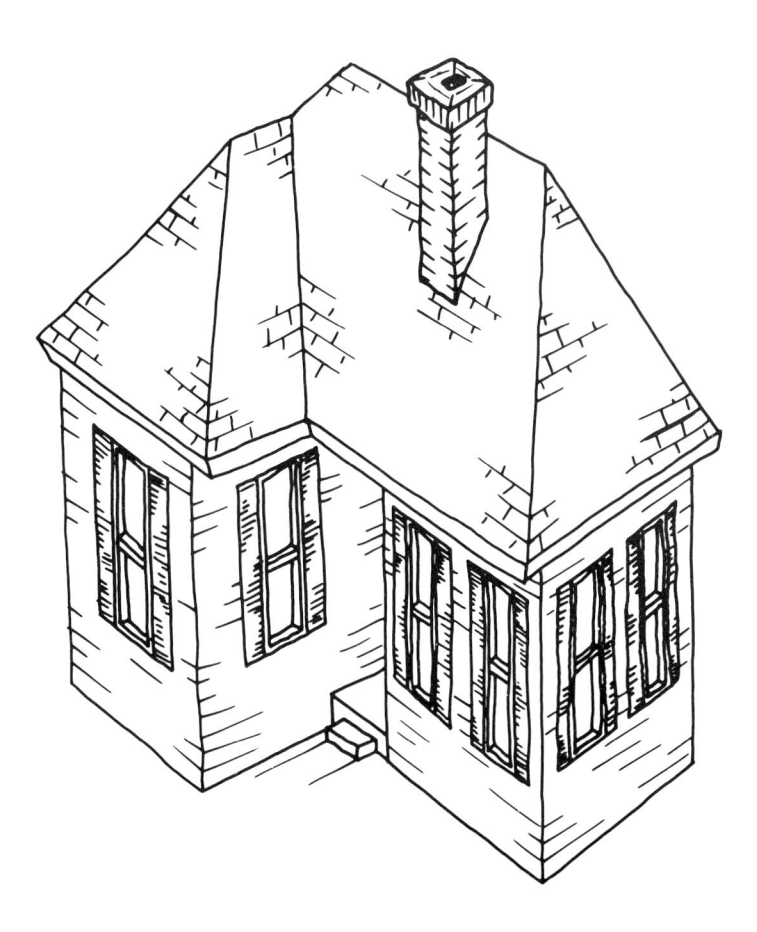

Fig. 3-27. This freehand sketch shows a bird's-eye view of a house whose proportions have been stretched to accommodate the bottle.

49

Fig. 3-28. The Dutch Colonial beach house, from which the design for the bottled house in Fig. C-4 was copied, is located in Hermosa Beach, California.

4

Building Tools

Tools profound-
ly contribute to
man's mechanical a-
bilities by functioning as
marvelous extensions of his hands
and mind. Man is set apart from other animals,
not only by his abstract thinking and problem-solving
capabilities, but also by his persistent use of tools. Most of
man's great accomplishments would not have been possible without the
extensive use of simple, as well as complex, tools. Clever, new tools are constantly being developed as man faces new and difficult challenges. It is doubtful that
this condition will ever change. **STORE-BOUGHT TOOLS.** Tools may be classified into two
distinct groups: store-bought and homemade. *Store-bought tools* are those which can be purchased ready-made from a great variety of sources. It is astonishing to consider all the different
kinds of stores which sell tools. As expected, hardware and auto parts stores carry the most complete line of tools, although some machinery shops specialize in certain types of power tools and
machines. What is surprising is how many other kinds of stores also sell a fair variety of tools.
Department stores, hobby shops, drugstores, supermarkets, art-supply stores, and some kitchen-
supply shops also carry tools of one kind or another. Although drugstores and supermarkets sell
less-expensive and lower-quality tools than the others, some of these tools are adequate for the
novice craftsman. Hobby shops and hardware stores tend to carry a higher-quality line of tools.
The only problem is that you must learn to select at least medium-quality tools and leave the
cheap ones for the bargain hunters. The store-bought tools can be divided into two important
groups; power tools and hand tools. One particular power tool worth mentioning is the Dremel
Moto-Tool, available at some hardware stores and many hobby shops. It appears in Fig. 4-1.
This tool consists of a hand-held, motorized machine capable of grinding, polishing, engraving,
sawing, drilling, and sanding. The chuck or tool holder can also grip a short dowel of up to 1/8
inch in diameter for making miniature wood turnings. Some of the turnings appearing on the
Victorian house in Fig. C-2 were shaped in this way with the aid of small files. Although it is
an expensive piece of equipment, its quality is excellent. It is amazing how many tasks this tool
can handle. Store-bought, hand tools make up the bulk of the tools required for bottling houses
and ships. Each one helps perform a specific task and should be described in detail. Note that
some other, often less-expensive tools can sometimes be substituted for the ones outlined here.
Carving wood is perhaps the most time-consuming task involved with bottling houses and ships.
Since so much time is spent laboring over this process, it is wise to select and use good-quality

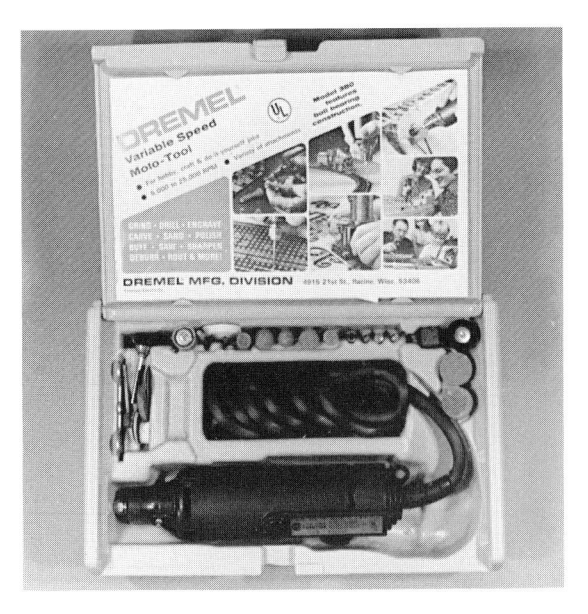

Fig. 4-1. The Dremel Moto-Tool is a handheld, electrically operated machine capable of cutting, grinding, polishing, drilling, engraving, sanding, carving, deburring, and many other functions. It performs these tasks on a variety of materials, including metal, wood, plastic, glass, and ceramics.

tools whenever possible. Although a common pocket knife will substitute in a few cases, a good set of wood-carving tools are made by X-acto. Figure 4-2 shows several X-acto knives and a few of the many blade shapes and gouges available from most hobby shops. The No. 11 blade and the small-diameter blade holder/handle seen with the cutting board in Fig. 4-4 seem to be the most versatile, although it is a matter of personal preference which of the blades are selected. *Gouges* are bladelike attachments used to hollow out material and shape relief carvings into the wood surface. They come in large and small *U*- and *V*-shaped gouges. Working with a combination of these tools will provide you with maximum, wood-carving capabilities.

Sawing wood is an important and often precise process. In order to perform this task efficiently, only good-quality saws should be used. Poorly made saws are too difficult to control. A great variety of hand saws are available in most hardware stores. While some saws are designed to cut across the wood grain, others are made to rip along the grain. Still others are for cutting in both directions. Fig-

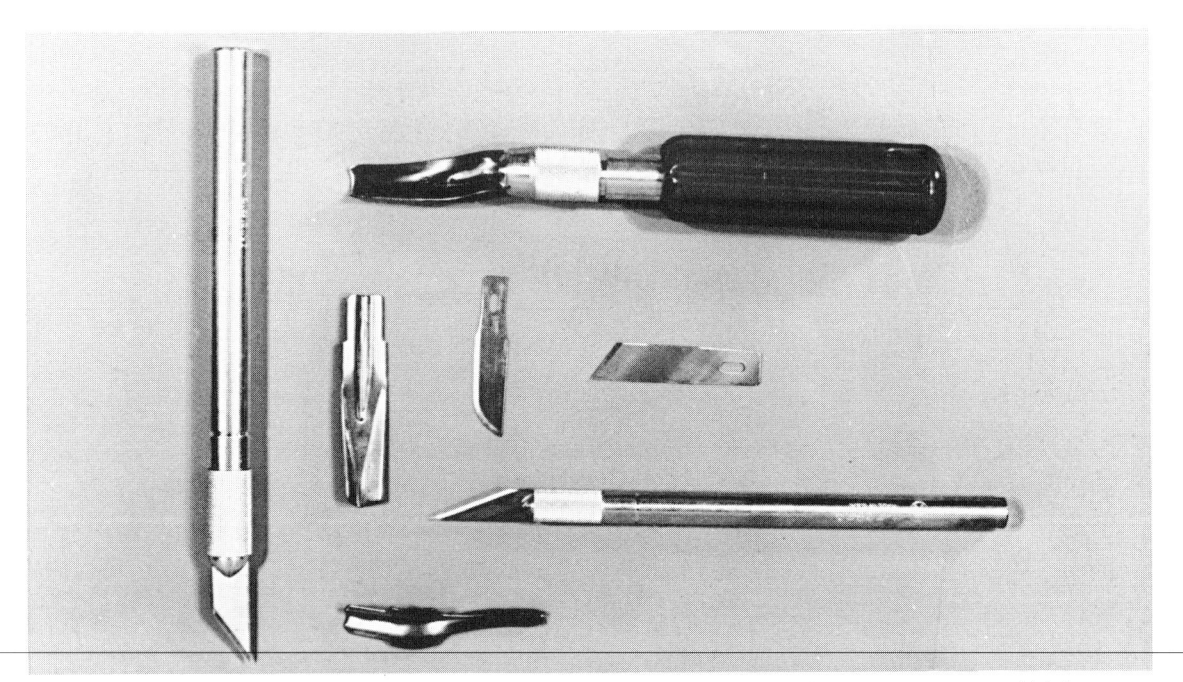

Fig. 4-2. These X-acto knives are composed as individual blades and separate handles, an arrangement which increases convenience as well as capability.

ure 4-3 shows a variety of useful saws. For cutting sharp corners and curves in material of medium thickness, the *coping saw* is the best tool to use. Coping saws are also available in most hardware stores and some hobby shops. A very precise and convenient saw is the X-acto #35 *box saw*. It is used to cut cross-grain and miter-cut small pieces of wood. This X-acto saw is available at most hobby shops. A saw similar to the coping saw, but smaller, is the *jeweler's saw* in Fig. 4-3. Its saw blade may be as thin as a horse's hair. Although it is primarily used for cutting soft metal, it works very well for cutting delicate, incised designs in all types of wood and plastic. Using one or more of these saws will effectively solve almost any sawing problem.

Slicing, cutting, chopping, and sawing should always be done over a cutting board. The cutting board protects tabletops, work benches, and any other vulnerable work surface. The board also provides an elevated, cutting surface from which chips of materials being cut or sliced may be brushed. A good-quality kitchen cutting board made of a plastic is pictured in Fig. 4-4. This kind of cutting board will not dull the knife blades as quickly as wood boards. The plastic cutting board's surface will not deteriorate and chip away as wooden boards do. Plastic cutting boards are usually available in kitchen supply shops, department stores, some supermarkets, and some large drugstores.

A simple block of hardwood 6 inches × 6 inches and 1 or 2 inches thick will make an adequate cutting board. Maple, birch, and oak are hardwoods which make reasonably durable boards. Some store-bought chopping blocks and cutting boards will do, but it is a real shame to spend so much money on something which will deteriorate so quickly with heavy use.

Clamping, grasping, and holding together

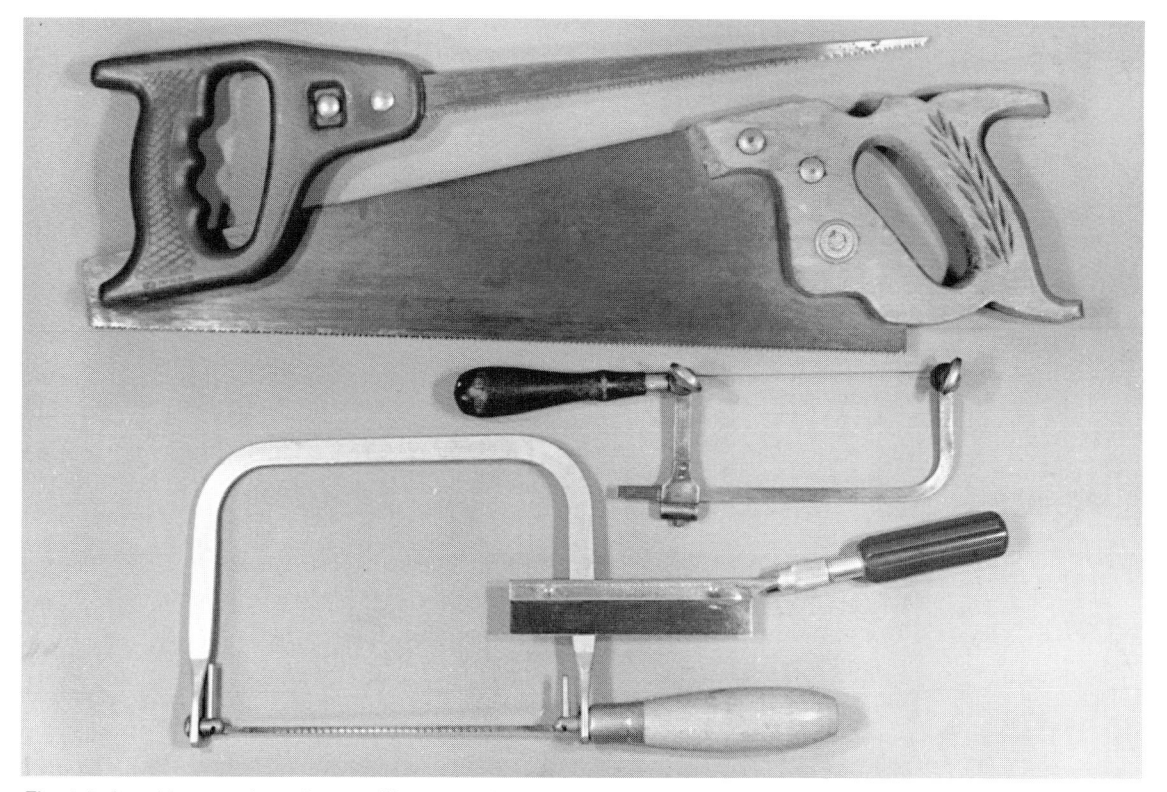

Fig. 4-3. Acquiring a variety of saws will prepare the craftsman for most wood-cutting problems. From top to bottom are a keyhole saw, a basic ripsaw, a jeweler's saw, a hobby saw, and a coping saw.

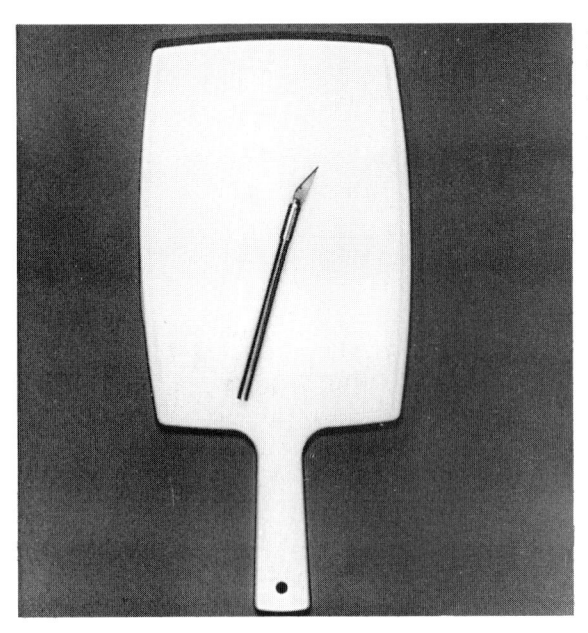

Fig. 4-4. A common kitchen cutting board, made of a type of plastic, will help keep blades sharp and protect work surfaces.

pieces of wood have always created problems for woodworkers. Figure 4-5 shows a number of inexpensive clamps available in hobby and gift shops and even in some supermarkets. The *metal clamps* are made by X-acto and afford the greatest flexibility. The *clothespins* are often used to hold tiny pieces to dry after painting with the help of straight pins, as shown. The *miniature clothespins* are useful in clamping laminated wood, plastic, and cardboard. Surgical clamps are useful as well and can be purchased in hobby shops, at swap meets, and through some mail-order houses.

Scissors, tweezers, and pliers are also helpful with this craft. Scissors are used for cutting cloth, thin wood veneers, and paper products. *Pointed tweezers* are also helpful, especially when picking up small pieces of wood and applying them to glued areas of assembled parts. *Wire-cutter pliers* are great for cutting and bending coat-hanger tools and wire tools, mentioned later in this chapter. Pointed tweezers are found in hobby shops, drugstores, and some art-supply stores. Wire-cutter pliers are found

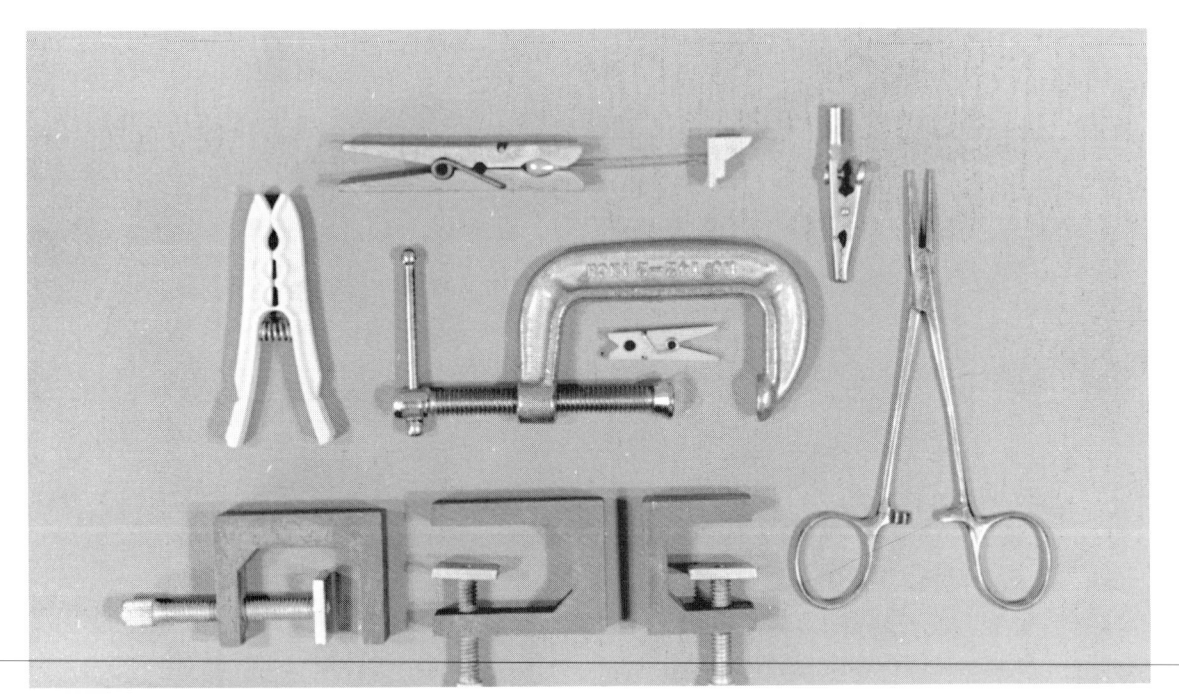

Fig. 4-5. This collection of clamps was acquired from a number of places and form the basis for another set of hands. Although not all of them are required all the time, individually they can be real lifesavers.

in hardware stores, hobby shops, and at some supermarkets.

Sandpaper is used to smooth the surface of a number of materials. It is available in a variety of textures, identified by a number on on the back of the sandpaper sheet. The smaller the number, the larger the particles of sand will be. Most hardware stores carry a plentiful supply of different types of sandpaper ranging in coarseness from 80 to 600. The 600 is a very fine-textured "wet or dry" paper used for final *sanding* of plastics and metals prior to machine buffing. You should have a wide variety of sandpapers handy for whatever special need may arise.

Another tool with which you should be well equipped is the *paintbrush*. Sizes of paintbrushes range from those with brushes smaller than a single grain of rice to some which are 4 inches wide and 1 inch thick. The brushes on the smaller end of the scale are the most useful in this craft. Pictured in Fig. 4-6 are a few brushes worth acquiring. They are found in hobby shops and art supply stores. Select brushes which can be used in enamel as well as water-based paints.

Hat pins are also useful. A single pin is stuck in the bottom or back of a wooden part that must be painted. After paint is applied, the pin is clamped in a clothespin and set on a shelf or other protected area to dry. The clothespin provides this assembly with stability, keeping it from falling over. It also keeps the painted part up in the air, allowing it to dry without sticking to a flat surface. Hat pins are available in the notions department of yardage shops, department stores, and some large drugstores.

It is literally suicide for the eyes to work without a proper *work light*. Eyestrain is a constant adversary in this craft and should be minimized

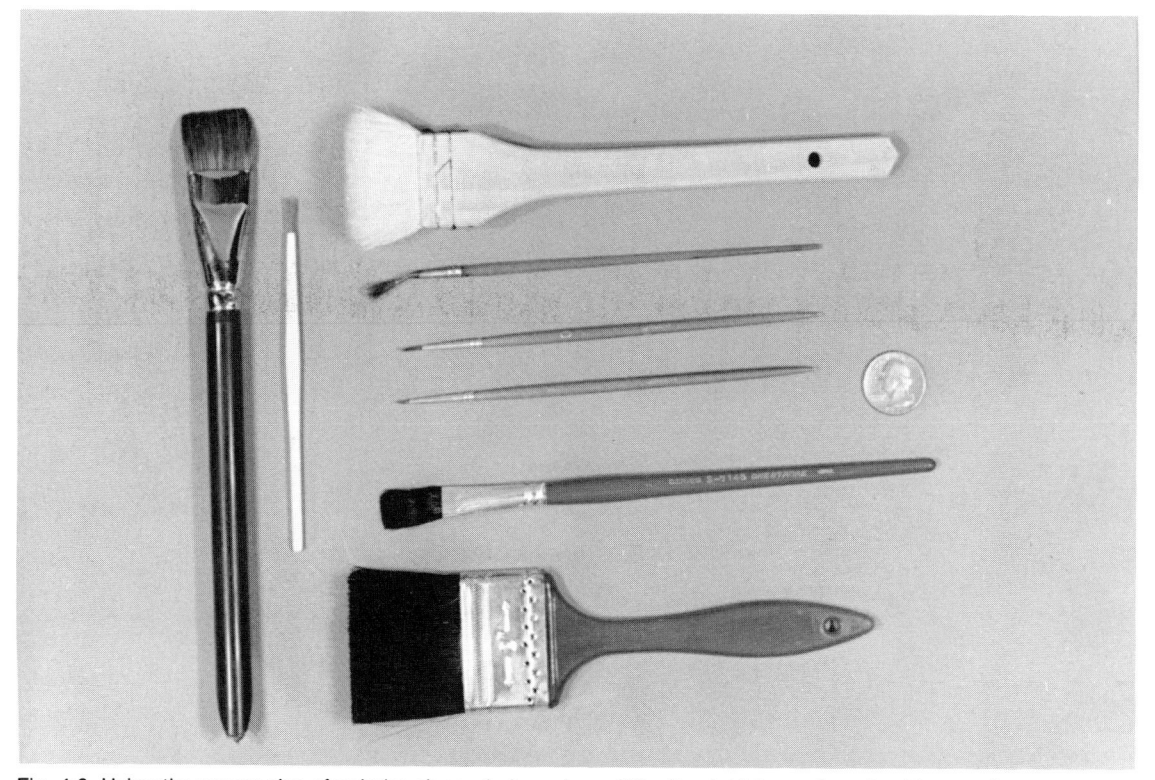

Fig. 4-6. Using the proper size of paintbrush can help make a difficult paint job much easier. The smaller sizes of this group are the most useful.

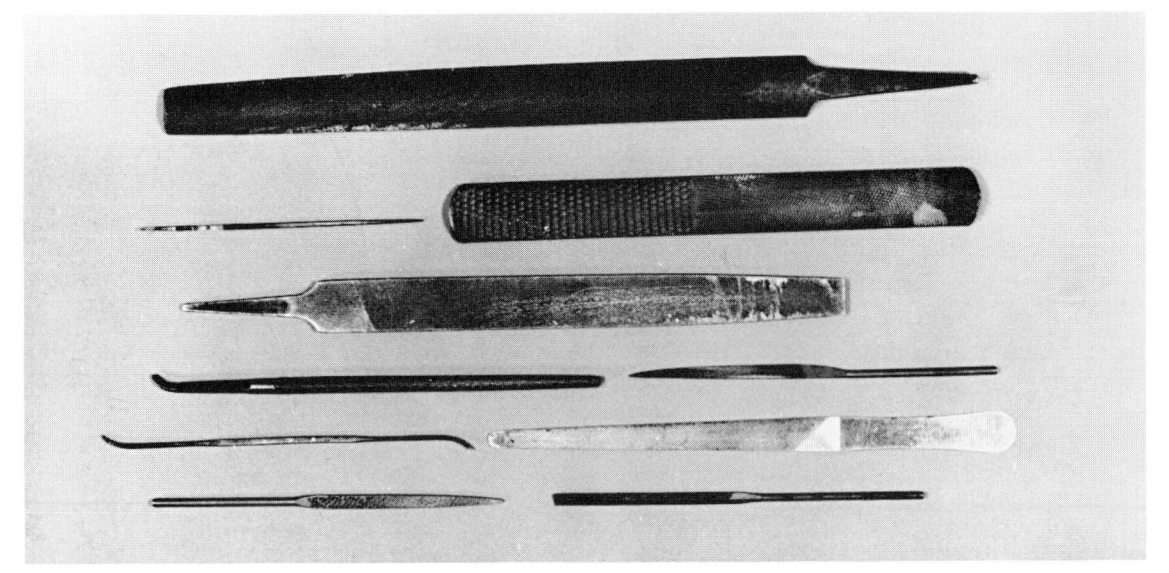

Fig. 4-7. Files and wood rasps make an important contribution to the total craft capability package. Some work with both metal and wood, while others can shape only wood.

whenever possible. An effective work light will help greatly. One of the best and most effective work lights is the adjustable-position drafting lamp. A system of springs and counterbalances allow this type of lamp to be set in seemingly limitless positions and remain until moved. Light is provided by either an incandescent light bulb or a fluorescent tube. The fluorescent-tube type is superior because it is cooler and provides a more uniform distribution of light over a wider area. The fluorescent-type lamp is available in either single-or double-tube arrangements. A circular tube wrapped around a magnifying glass is another popular lamp.

Most drafting lamps clamp securely to a table or bench. This is an important consideration when choosing a work table or bench. An average television tray would obviously be unacceptable for use with such a lamp, since the lamp's weight would topple the entire work area. Drafting lamps are usually available in art supply stores, office furniture shops, drafting supply stores, and some hobby shops.

Desk lamps, both small and large, may also help limit excessive eyestrain. Small goosenecked lamps, often called Tensor Lamps (a brand name), are popular and seem to be available almost everywhere. The old-fashioned, single-bulb desk lamp will also help light the work area. Any one or a combination of lamps arranged to suit you will pay handsomely by reducing eye fatigue.

After a wooden part has been cut out, further refinement or shaping may be necessary before completion and painting. One method of refining is to remove unwanted, wood material with an abrasive tool called a *file*. A set of small jeweler's files is a great asset to the craftsman's tool chest. A set consisting of round, square, flat, and triangular-shaped files (Fig. 4-7) provides you with almost unlimited shaping combinations. Each shape of file is usually available in a number of sizes and textures. Such files are sold individually or in sets in most hobby shops and art supply stores, as well as some hardware stores.

A clever, automobile repair tool called *mechanical fingers* (Fig. 4-8) can often be very handy when you are bottling houses. Its four, steel fingers open with a push of a button and close when released. This tool can tightly grasp rocks when "building a mountain," the results of which are seen in the bottles appearing in Fig. 3-13 and C-10. These mechanical fingers also have the capability of ripping out mistakes in wood framing from in-

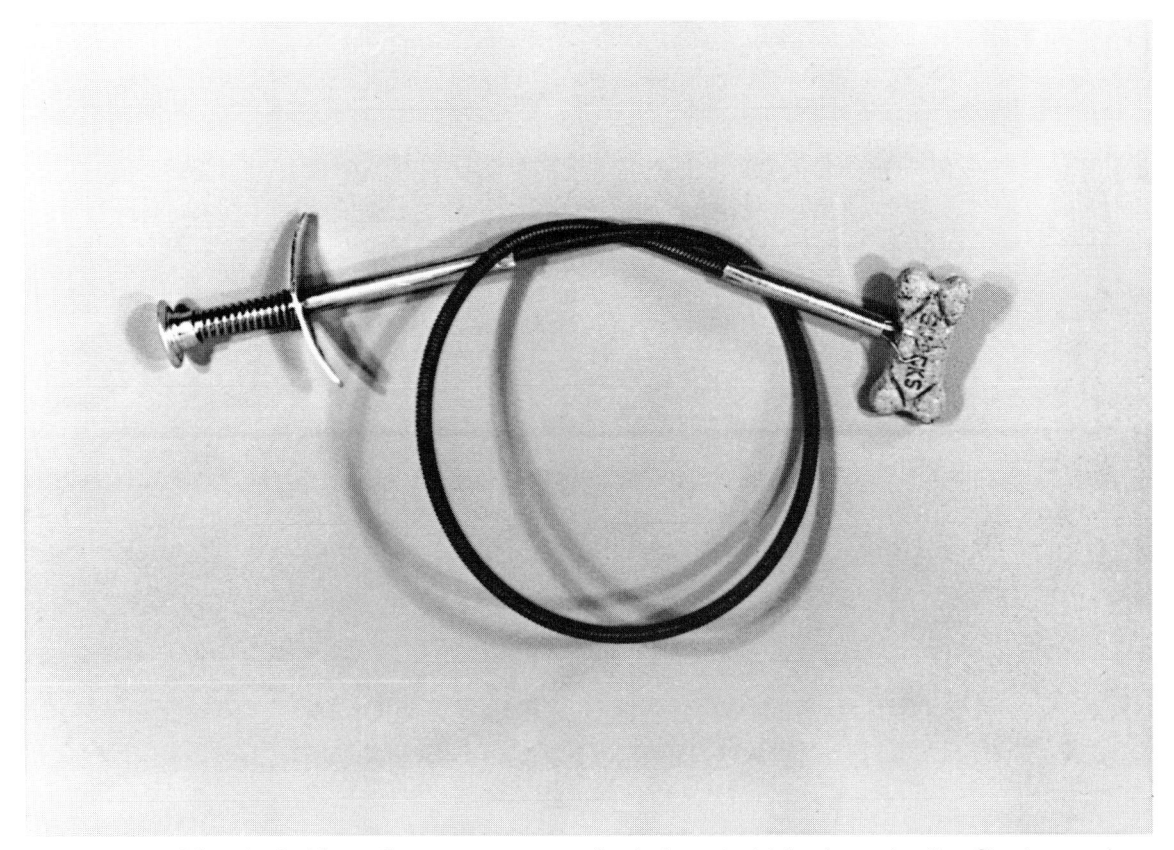

Fig. 4-8. A set of "mechanical fingers" are very easy to use for ripping out mistakes in construction. Simply press down on the plunger extending from the handle to open the grasp of the fingers. Release to close the fingers around an object.

side the bottle. Whole walls can be removed one piece at a time from the bottle. As marvelous as this tool may be, it should not be used in the actual construction of the house, since it will not provide the delicate control required in manipulating the individual parts used in construction. Mechanical fingers are usually sold in auto parts stores and hardware stores.

A few other useful items, pictured in Fig. 4-9, complete the collection of tools found in the well-equipped craftsman's tool chest. One such tool is the *compass*, which is used for drawing circles on paper and wood. Another tool that is often necessary is a small 45-45-90-degree *drafting triangle*. This 6-inch-long tool is an effective aid in laying out pencil lines on wood, plastic, or metal prior to cutting out with a saw. The *protractor*, also seen in Fig. 4-9, determines the number of degrees of an angle. It can be very handy when working with irregular shapes in a precise manner. A small *carpenter's square* is another valuable tool used for laying out cutting lines on a variety of materials. *Pencil* and *paper* must not be forgotten. Sketching ideas, making notes for remembering thoughts, and drawing final plans are some of the uses for these two. It is said that a serious artist carries a sketchbook and pencil wherever he goes, recording ideas and thoughts as they come to him for future reference.

Occasionally, other tools may be useful to some builders. Every person is an individual and will develop his own techniques for accomplishing a particular task. Often, a divergent method requires the use of tools other than those which have been recommended. A little common sense will help you determine which tools should be selected and used.

It is always advantageous to be inventive and clever whenever possible.

It is not uncommon for even the most knowledgeable craftsman to misunderstand the proper function or capabilities of some new or unusual tool. There are a number of helpful books available in libraries and bookstores. They present revealing diagrams and photographs, as well as explanatory text. See also the Appendix.

HOMEMADE TOOLS

There are times when store-bought tools are not adequate for all tasks. It is at this point that the craftsman's ingenuity begins to create "hybrid tools" capable of meeting the challenge of unusual problems. A little imagination, tempered with some common sense, will help visualize and develop complex as well as simple devices which will manipulate objects into achieving the specific task you desire.

During the process of bottling houses, some of the specific tasks which interest the builder include: inserting, measuring, withdrawing, locating, gluing, and securing objects within the confines of a bottle. One simple tool may be capable of achieving all of these tasks. Not only must it grasp and move the object while inserting it into the bottle, however, but it must also release the object at the desired time. These are additional requirements to be designed into the tool. In this case, just one tool should be used to complete all functions, rather than two or three. This analysis is tedious but necessary for determining what form the homemade tools will take. The only remaining examination is that of the

Fig. 4-9. Useful drafting and layout tools include, from left to right: 45-45-90-degree triangle, carpenter's square, protractor (for measuring angles), compass, and 30-60-90-degree triangle. Not shown is a T-square used to base the triangles and draw parallel lines.

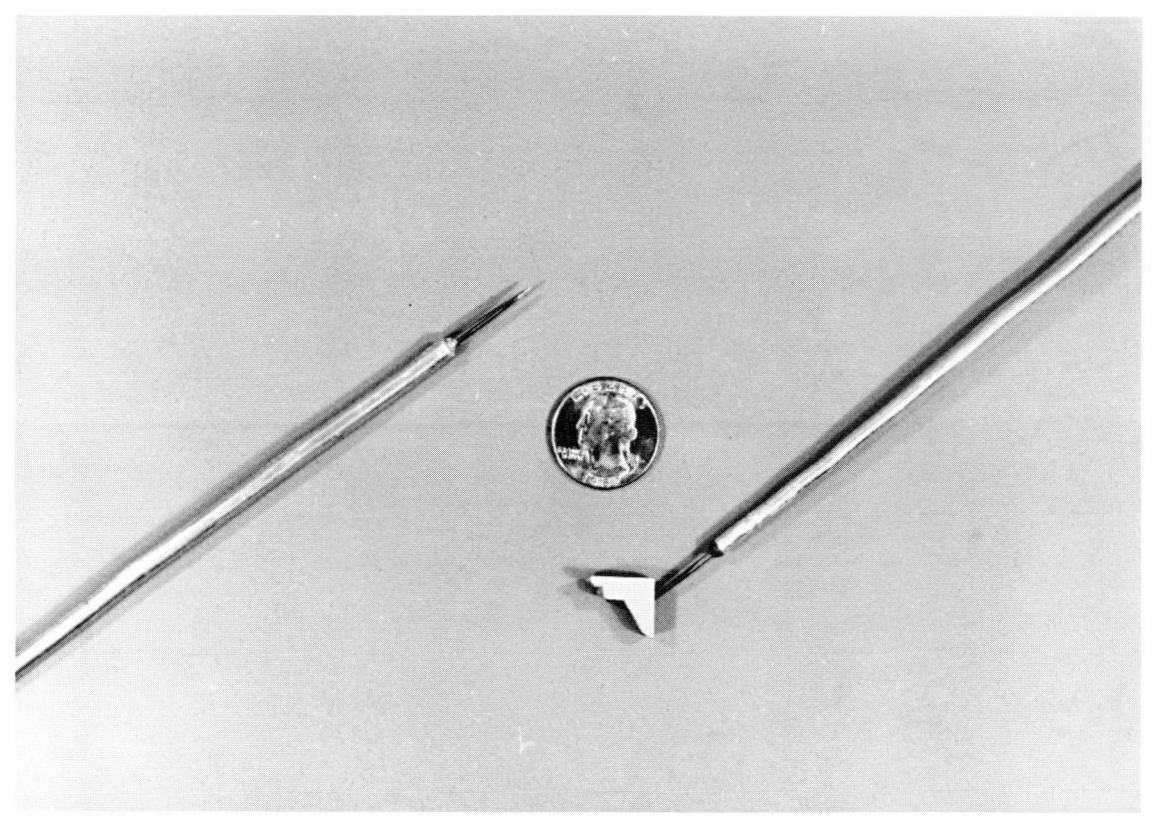

Fig. 4-10. Used more often than any other tool in bottling houses is the needle-wire tool, shown here holding a wood part.

object to be manipulated. If the object being inserted into the bottle is made of a soft, penetrable material, one type of tool will have to be developed. On the other hand, another tool approach will have to evolve for objects made of hard, inpenetrable materials. What works for one type will not work for the other type.

Needle-Wire Tool

For soft objects such as wood, paper, and polystyrene foam, the basic tool will be in the form of a sharp needle, as shown in Fig. 4-10. A heavy-duty sewing needle, purchased in a fabric shop or the notions section of most department stores, is attached to a flexible, 1/8-inch-diameter aluminum wire. The aluminum wire can be easily bent into many convenient shapes, depending on where the target is located in the bottle. Variations of this tool are pictured in Fig. 4-11.

The construction of the basic, needle-wire tool is simple.

☐ First, purchase the 1/8-inch-diameter (3/16- to 1/4-inch diameter will do) aluminum wire in a hardware or art supply shop. Aluminum wire may be difficult to find sometimes; so other kinds of wire may have to be substituted. Keep in mind that steel or copper wire of the required diameter will be more difficult to bend. Cut off a section 18 inches long and file both ends flat, as shown in Fig. 4-12.

☐ Next, obtain a heavy-duty sewing needle of a maximum diameter of .045 inch. The average paper clip, measuring .035 inch in diameter, is a good guide. Then, drill a hole lengthwise into one end of the aluminum wire to a depth of 3/8 to 1/2 inch. The

59

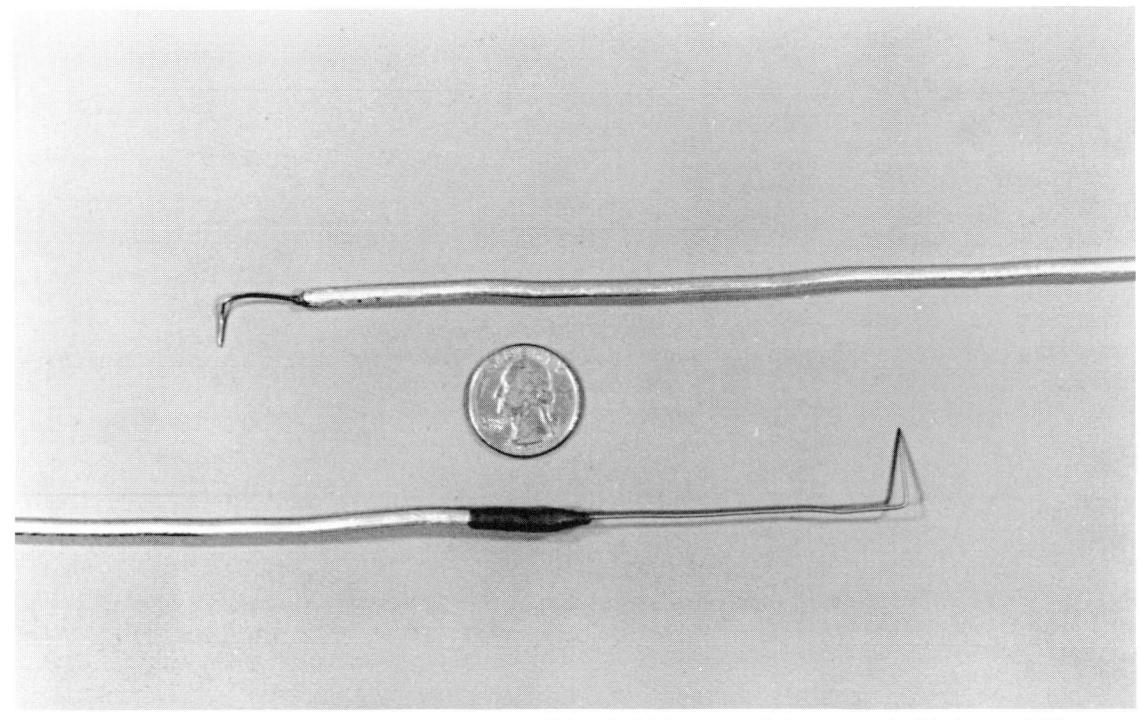

Fig. 4-11. The bent needle-wire tool is another very useful tool which can vastly improve a builder's capabilities.

diameter of this hole should be large enough to allow a sloppy fit of the needle, as indicated in Fig. 4-13. If a .046-inch-diameter needle is being used, a hole of a diameter of .056 or so should work fine. The seemingly poor fit allows for cement. Tiny drills are available in hardware stores, some hobby shops, and machine-tool supply shops.

☐ Mix a small amount of epoxy cement. *Epoxy cement* is the kind which comes in two tubes, "A" and "B." Equal amounts of both tubes are mixed and used immediately. Using a straight pin, insert some of the cement into the hole in the end of the aluminum wire. Then, smear more cement on the needle shaft opposite the point.

☐ Using a twisting action, insert the broken end of the needle into the hole, allowing the excess cement to ooze from the hole. Continue to twist and push the needle into the hole until it will penetrate no further. Wipe away some of the excess cement, but leave a small amount around the end, as shown in Fig. 4-13.

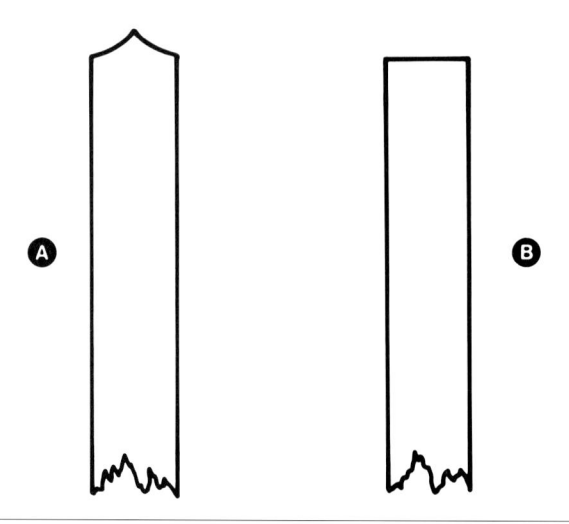

Fig. 4-12. After the aluminum wire has been severed with wire cutters, its raw end appears as "A." "B" shows the end after being filed flat.

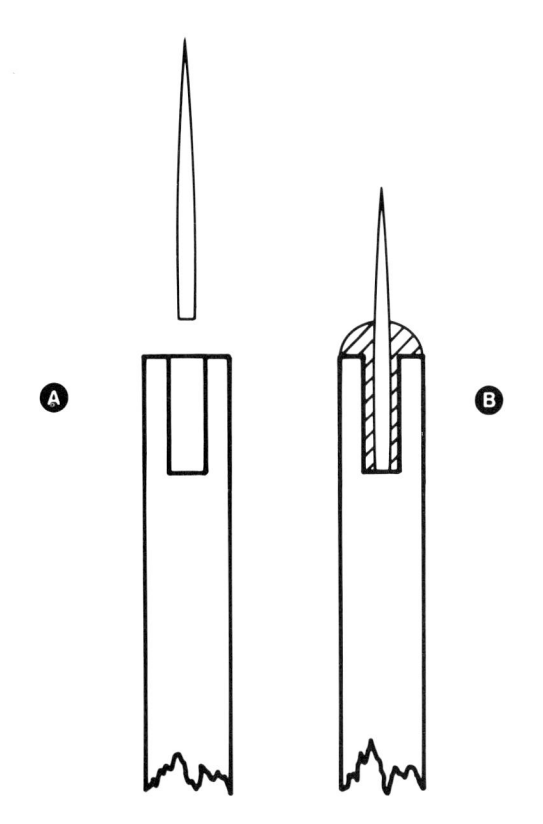

Fig. 4-13. "A" shows the needle tip and the drilled end of the aluminum wire prior to assembly. "B" reveals the completed needle-wire tool assembly after setting the needle in epoxy cement.

- [ ] Clamp this tool assembly to a shelf or table with the needle pointing up and allow the cement to dry a full 24 hours without disturbing it.

This construction technique will also work when building the other various needle-wire tools, examples of which appear in Fig. 4-11. For safety, attach a needle to only one end of each wire tool.

The needle-wire tool operates very easily once some experience has been gained in working with it.

- [ ] First, gently pierce the wooden part to be installed in the bottle with the needle-wire tool. Insert the needle only deep enough into the wood so that the part will remain attached without falling from the tool's grasp.
- [ ] Hold the tool by grasping the handle at a point along the long shaft where it feels balanced and comfortable.
- [ ] Practice turning the tool by rolling it between the fingers.
- [ ] Making use of a "dry run," insert the tool and its attached part into the bottle.
- [ ] Practice setting the part down onto its proper location and detaching the tool by twisting it from the grasp of the wooden part. The release should occur easily unless the needle is stuck too deeply into the part. Twisting, wiggling, and tapping are maneuvers which will help detach the wooden part from the needle. If all else fails, insert another wire tool into the bottle and push the part off the needle's point. Keep in mind that the glue will help pull the part from the needle as well.

The "business ends" of three bent-wire tools are pictured in Fig. 4-14. Tool A and A-1 is a simple, straight version with one end filed flat or rounded slightly. Modeling clay attached to the end of the wire tool, marked "A-1," is capable of grasping a pebble, inserting it into a bottle, and releasing it atop a new stone wall. The walls of the castle in Fig. C-10 were constructed in this manner. Tool B is a bent end formed by bending a 1/4-inch-long length of the wire end a full 90 degrees. Also shown is a modeling clay attachment used to grasp pebbles and other parts. Without the clay this tool is especially effective in applying glue to exact areas in the bottle. It can also be used to manipulate loose parts to their proper location prior to gluing. Tool C is a variation of B. By bending a 3/4-inch end 90 degrees, it can also be used to manipulate loose parts and apply glue in some hard-to-reach spots.

Other Homemade Tools

A plastering trowel, pictured in Fig. 4-15, may be constructed by attaching a dull #11 X-acto blade to the bent end of an aluminum wire tool. Bend the wire end into a curved arc and cement the blade to the flattened, wire end using epoxy cement. The blade can also be welded to the bent end of a steel rod that is the same diameter as the aluminum wire. Stainless steel blades cannot be welded to aluminum. A plastering trowel is used for applying and smoothing the wood dough of stucco and adobe walls.

Sometimes, roof shingles, placed on a circular or conical-shaped form, tend to curl uncontrollably when they are first installed and glued. An easily made tool for dealing with this problem is the *shingle press* pictured in Fig. 4-15. This tool is made of coat-hanger wire with the aid of wire cutters and pliers. Basically, the main wire is wrapped around another, forming a stylized *Y*. The wrapped area is mashed with the pliers so that the arms of the *Y* do not flop around. The rigidity of this tool will determine its effectiveness. The tool is inserted into the bottle, and the arm tips are placed against the shingle's curling corners or its bulging middle. Apply the press while the glue becomes tacky to secure the whole shingle at the same time. In a minute or two the press is removed, leaving the shingle neatly wrapped around its structural support.

Sandpaper boards (Fig. 4-16) are effective tools for shaping and smoothing the surface of parts made of various materials. The sandpaper boards function much like files, but often with greater convenience and capabilities. Sheets of sandpaper are held perfectly flat by cementing them to sheets of plywood or particleboard. Narrow sandpaper boards of various coarseness levels are used as files,

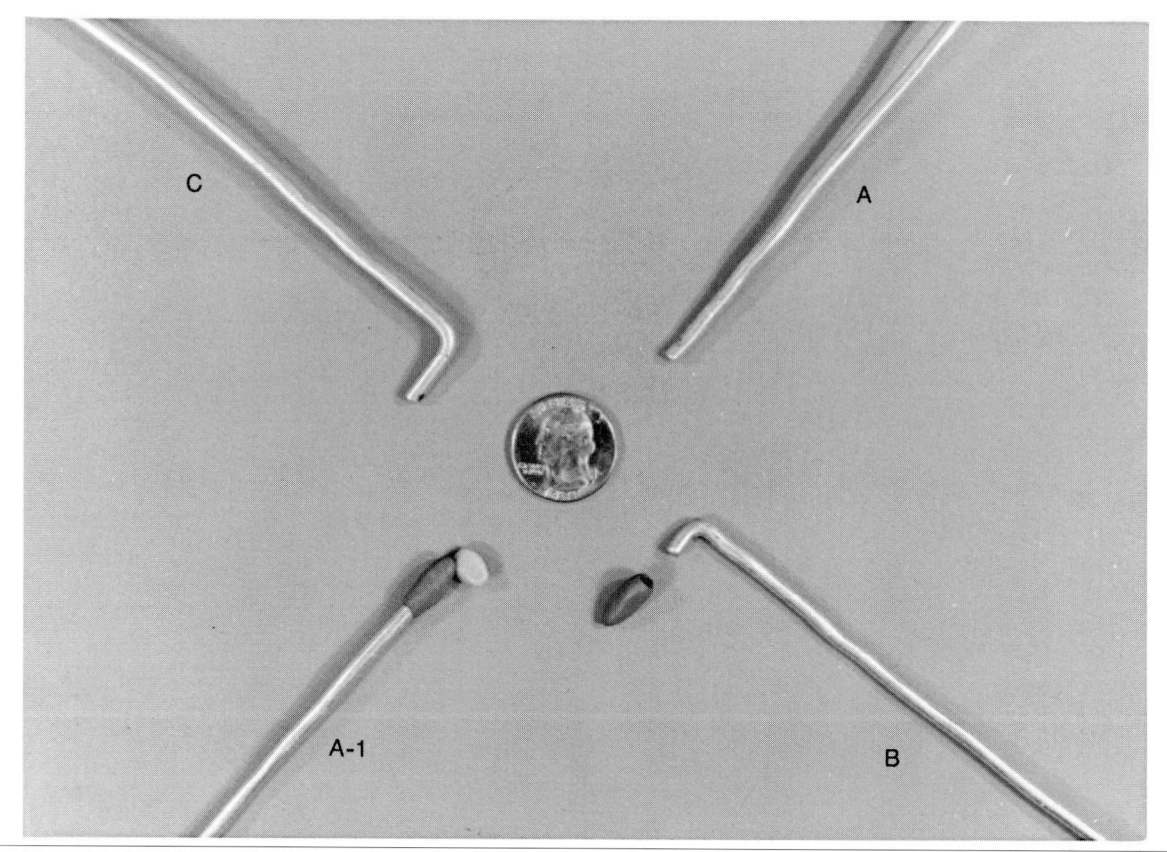

Fig. 4-14. Straight- and bent-wire tools are handy for applying glue, installing small parts, and maneuvering parts into position. After adding a small wad of modeling clay to the end of the wire, the tool can pick up and set into place stones and other hard-to-place parts.

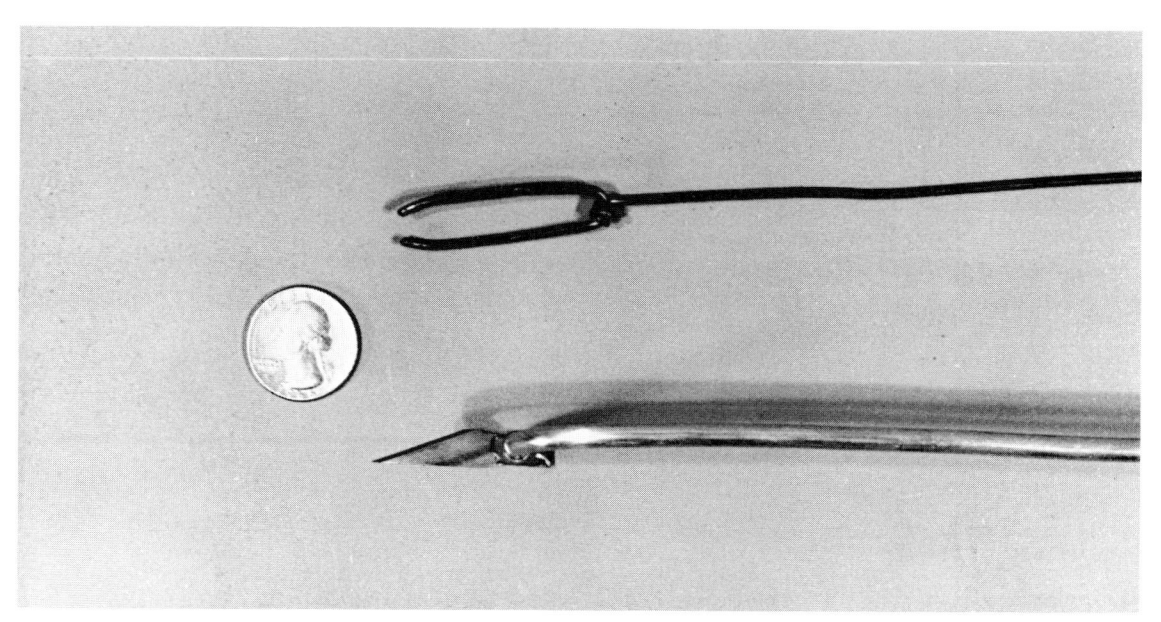

Fig. 4-15. A forked shingle press, made from a coat hanger, will hold a shingle flat on a curved subroof. The plastering trowel is made by cementing a knife blade to the end of a bent-wire tool.

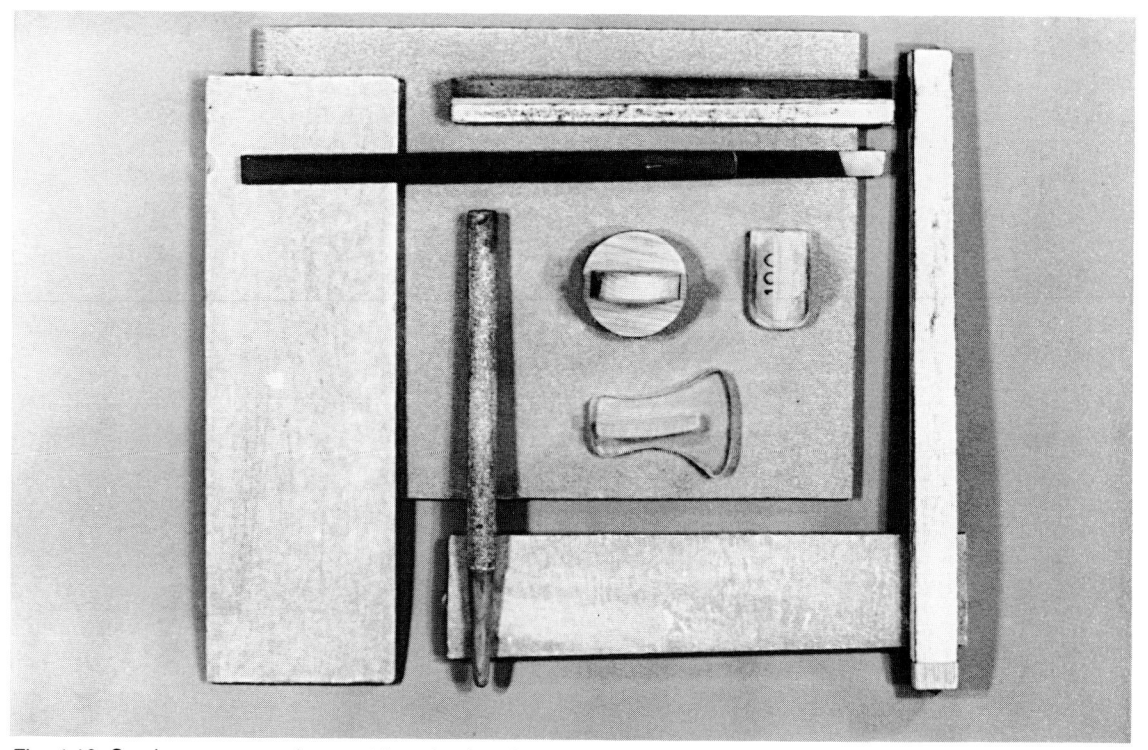

Fig. 4-16. Sandpaper wrapped around boards, dowels, and other objects comprise another set of files which are very handy for shaping hard-to-work objects. Sanding boards are usually made as they are needed.

63

while the large flat sanding boards are operated by skimming the part across the surface, with the board remaining stationary. The narrow sanding boards are made by applying contact cement to the back of the sandpaper as well as the connecting surface of the board. After allowing the cement to dry dust-free for 1/4 to 1/2 hour, the sandpaper is wrapped carefully around the board, taking care to sharply crease each fold. These tools last for years.

Some of these homemade tools may be constructed using different and more efficient techniques and materials. Such inventiveness is always encouraged. It is a worthwhile challenge to seek more effective methods of accomplishing a task. Naturally, however, this search for efficiency can be taken too far. It would be so much easier to cut the bottom off a bottle in order to insert a fully assembled house. Although that method is much more efficient, the challenge, magic, and charm of a bottled house would be destroyed.

5

Materials for Building

Without quality building materials, the effects of efficient tools, marvelous craftsmanship, and exciting creativity are rendered almost useless. Great works of art cannot be expected to endure the tests of time if they are constructed of less than the best quality materials. If Michaelangelo had sculpted his masterpiece *David*, from marble containing too many flaws, it might have crumbled into rubble long ago. Furthermore, had he, instead, carved it from limestone, the effects of modern-day pollution would have caused much serious disintegration of the statue's features. Perhaps a like result might have us see *David's* features more like those of the *Hunchback of Notre Dame!* Although few today are capable of sculpting with the same mastery as that of Michaelangelo, the point made here is universal. Substandard materials cannot be expected to last as intended. It is a consideration worth pondering. As far as constructing bottled houses is concerned, selecting only high-quality materials is worth the extra effort. For example, if it lacks the proper glue or cement, the house may deteriorate and fall apart with the passing of time. Consider the embarrassment it would cause if the house became detached from the bottle's bottom and bounced around inside. Think of the disappointment of watching the house's paint fade year by year. Such problems could be avoided with a little care in selecting proper materials. There are a number of building materials required for bottling houses. A few recommendations of some materials may be helpful. Although strict adherence to these recommendations is not necessary, substitutions should be of equal quality. Included among these recommended building materials are: wood, stone, paper, modeling clay, glue, cement, paint, wood putty, polystyrene foam, and plastics. Most of these items are not difficult to obtain, although it is a matter of keeping your eyes open. Observing things around you can often lead to the effective use of other materials not previously discovered or considered **WOOD AND STONE**. Wood is probably the most frequently used building material for bottling houses and ships. It is readily available in a number of convenient shapes from a great number of sources. The wide variety of kinds of wood also contributes to its value as a building material. The most useful wood shapes now available include beams, blocks, planks, sheets of plywood, paperbacked veneers, decorative moldings, dowels, and other forms (Fig. 5-1). Wood products such as these are available in lumberyards, doll house and miniatures shops, hardware stores, and hobby shops. Hobby shops seem to carry the best-quality, model building wood. Many hobby shops sell wood products prepared by Midwest Products Company. The sizes are all in inches and include:

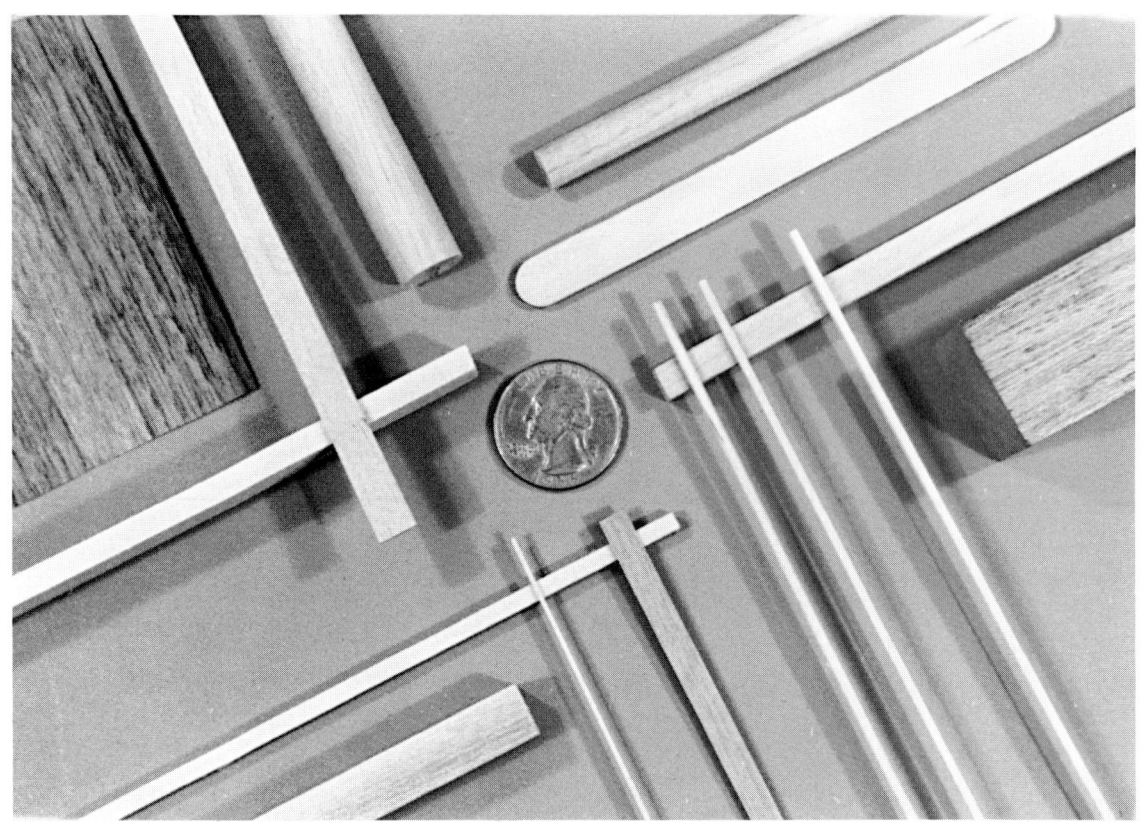

Fig. 5-1. Purchasing a wide variety of wood building products will greatly aid you in the construction of windows, doors, wall siding, roofing, floors, structural framing, and bottle closures.

- ☐ 3/8 × 3/8 × 24
- ☐ 1/4 × 1/2 × 24
- ☐ 1/4 × 1/4 × 24
- ☐ 3/16 × 3/16 × 24
- ☐ 1/8 × 1/8 × 24
- ☐ 3/32 × 3/32 × 24
- ☐ 1/16 × 1/8 × 24

Sheet sizes include:

- ☐ 1/4 × 3 × 24
- ☐ 3/16 × 3 × 24
- ☐ 1/8 × 3 × 24
- ☐ 3/32 × 3 × 24
- ☐ 1/16 × 3 × 24
- ☐ 1/32 × 3 × 24

What is surprising is the variety of wood available in these sizes, including mapel, basswood, walnut, cherry, pine, teak, and mahogany.

Hardware stores and lumberyards often carry paperbacked wood veneers which are great for house siding and roof shingles. One manufacturer, Roberts Consolidated Industries, distributes a flexible, wood-trim veneer called *Weldwood*. The veneer is available in walnut, mahogany, pine, maple, oak, cherry, and other woods. Douglas fir blocks of wood, required at a size of 1 × 1 × 6 inches, will have to be milled at a lumberyard, unless you have the tools and abilities to cut them yourself. These blocks are for chimneys and foundation blocks at 1 × 1 × 3/4 inches. Wood dowels, made of birch or maple, are almost always available in hardware stores and lumberyards. Diameters range from 1/8 to 1 inch; lengths are usually 36 inches.

Incredibly small-scaled wood moldings are found in doll house and miniatures shops. Usually made of pine or spruce, these moldings are around 24 inches in length. Such moldings are available in a variety of contour designs. Decorative moldings are added to any house structure where a more finished and sophisticated look is desired.

A few words about balsa wood are in order. This wood has been omitted because it has not proven to be consistantly strong enough to be used in bottling houses. During the construction process, the bottle is often turned upside down in order to shake loose any fallen parts. The stress created by inverting the bottle can destroy a house under construction, especially if it is nearly completed. Delicate railings are very susceptible to breakage if made of balsa. Beyond that, knife blades must be kept very sharp; otherwise, the soft balsa wood will be crushed rather than cut. Finishing with paint is another problem, if paste wood fillers are not used first to fill the grain openings. Considering these disadvantages, balsa wood should be left to the less stressful crafts.

Some bottled houses require the use of stones and pebbles in their construction. Mountaintops are constructed by cementing similar stones atop one another as in Figs. 2-14, 3-13, and C-10. Such stones should have similar coloring and texture. Rounded stones (Fig. 5-2) tend to look weathered and more realistic. Of course, the most important consideration is the need for each stone to fit through the neck of the bottle. A fascinating illusion is created with stones which narrowly pass through the bottleneck. Once inside, they appear as though they never could have slipped through. Their image seems to be magnified by the bottle glass. This

Fig. 5-2. Rounded stones, used for mountain building and landscaping with bottled houses, are often found along riverbanks, beaches, and streams as well as in some nurseries and building supply yards.

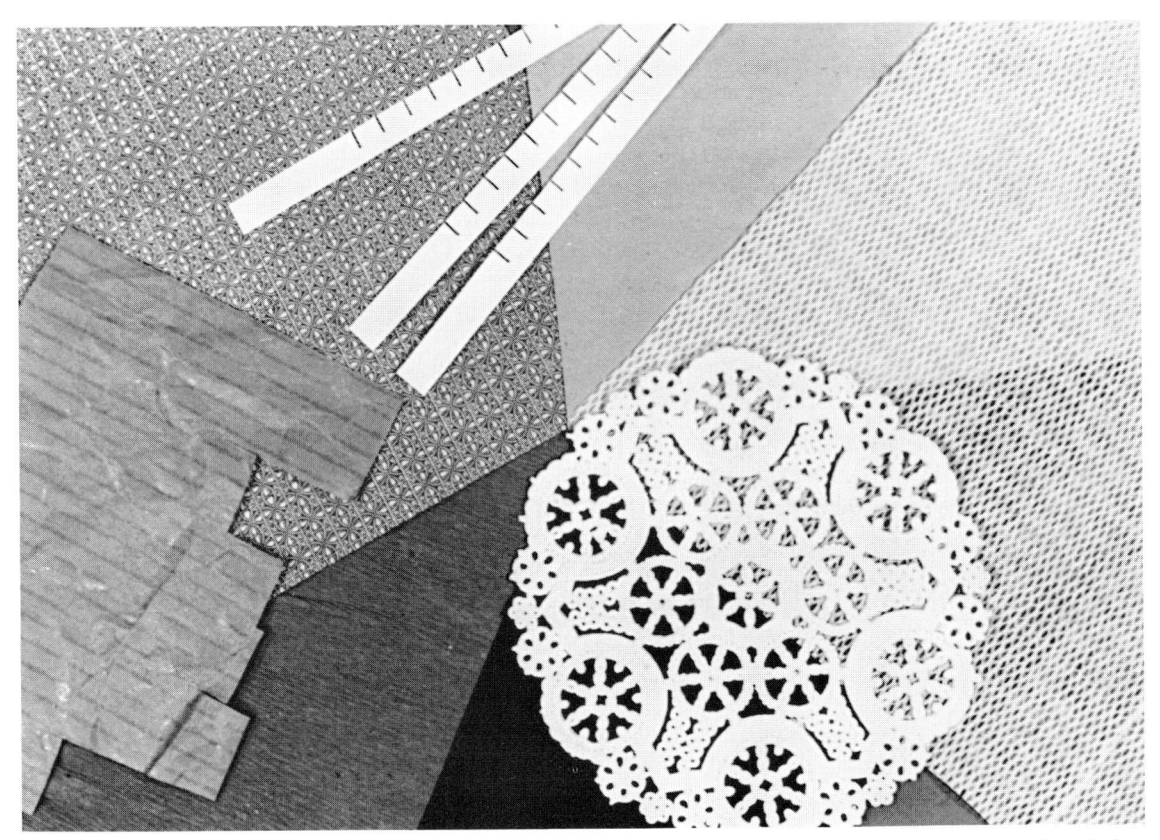

Fig. 5-3. It may take many months or even several years to collect a variety of paper products to be used for window curtains, wall coverings, and some types of roof shingles.

phenomenon adds to the magic of the bottled house.

Useful, rounded stones seem to be everywhere. They can be found in creek bottoms, along river banks and sea shores, as well as in many other places. Caution should be exercised because swiftly moving water can be very hazardous. Abandoned quarry pits are specially dangerous and should be avoided. Rounded stones are found almost anywhere water action has been strong enough to toss the stones around. This agitation results in chipping away rough places on each stone. If prolonged, the wearing of the stone's surface will smooth the rock until its shape is rounded.

In some regions of the country, whole parcels of land are littered with these rounded rocks after being deposited there by some formidable geological event. Although the sizes of these stones will vary greatly, enough rocks for a bottled "mountaintop" will be available. These locations are much safer for rock hunting than water locations, although any rock expedition should be wary of unfriendly reptiles and insects. Gravel pits, operating in various locations, often sell bucketfuls of selected rocks. This is by far the safest way of gathering suitable rounded rocks. The only problem may be in finding a gravel pit selling rounded rather than chipped stones. The cost is very minimal. Purchasing packaged, rounded rocks is the easiest and safest method of all for obtaining what is required; however, the prices are usually excessive.

Small pebbles are often used in chimney and wall construction. Figure C-10 shows a stone castle whose walls are constructed of selected aquarium gravel, while a Hobbit house with a stone chimney made of larger, rounded, aquarium gravel appears in Fig. 2-4. Aquarium gravel is available in a number of stores. Tropical fish shops and pet supply stores usually sell "natural," undyed aquarium gravel in bulk form for convenient examination. A number of rock sizes are also available. Almost any department store having a pet section will also sell aquarium gravel; however in these places gravel is usually packaged in plastic or in cartons which contain only one size of stone. Avoid the stones which are dyed in gaudy colors. Select the packages of undyed stones. Watch out for the packaged gravel in which each pebble is covered with a glossy-finished, plastic coating; these will appear especially artificial and tacky.

Of course, an eccentric builder could go the trouble of tediously picking out tiny pebbles from dry beach or river sand. I spent the day at the beach one time with a girl, picking out a few dozen black pebbles required for a project. Although we managed to do a lot of talking, I am sure this girl thought I had gone completely mad. I kept cautioning her about the hazards of "sun sickness."

PAPER, MODELING CLAY, AND PAINTS

Strange as it may seem, paper is also used in the construction of bottled houses. In fact, there are a number of uses for a variety of papers in this craft. Some are shown in Fig. 5-3. For example, newsprint, the paper on which most newspapers are printed, often works well as old, yellowing, window shades. Occasionally, buff-colored, department-store shopping bags come with a distinctive, striped, watermark design. The resulting window shade made adds class and variety to any window. Another example is that of a paper doily. The intricately incised and embossed designs are similar to lace used in old Victorian curtains. Paper doilies are sold in party supply shops, some department stores, and occasionally in supermarkets. Parts of antique greeting cards are sometimes also used for curtains. Whole antique greeting cards in good condition should not be destroyed merely to make a window curtain or two. They may be too valuable.

Black paper or cardboard may be used to form baffles for the interiors of the houses. Baffles are used to obscure the view through open windows and doors of a bottled house. When undesirable interior features are visible through these openings, black paper or cardboard baffles can block or restrict the view of them. A baffle can be made by simply darkening a single 3-x-5-inch recipe file card with a black, felt-tipped pen. Recipe file cards are also cut into tiny, square "shims" which are used to build up and level off vertical support members in preparation of setting horizontal beams as level as possible. File cards may also be cut, colored, and used as shingles on the roofs of appropriately styled houses. As you gain experience in bottling houses, you may find additional uses for paper products. It is surprising how such a seemingly insignificant material can come in so handy sometimes.

Modeling clay is an important material, without which some building techniques might not be possible. It is used as both a tool and as a finished part of the image of the bottled house. As I mentioned in Chapter 4, a small wad of modeling clay is wrapped around the end of aluminum wire and used as a tool for picking up and inserting small impenetrable parts, such as pebbles, into the bottle and depositing them in just the right location. The modeling clay can be made to hold a part just long enough to transport it to its proper destination and then release it. Without such valuable holding qualities, walls and chimneys of real stone could not be constructed inside the bottle. The modeling clay makes this tool an irreplaceable contribution to the art of bottling houses.

Modeling clay is used to simulate the ground on which the house is to be constructed. This building site must be built up to a suitable level, keeping in mind the image of proper aesthetics. Without this building site, the house might appear to float or stand atop the bare glass in the bottom of the bottle. Colored modeling clay is used to bring a little more realism to the site and its landscaping. Toy stores and some hobby shops sell modeling clay in a variety of colors. Select yellow, red, green, and blue to mix the desired earth color. In some stores brown modeling clay is available. Mixing a new color is achieved by squeezing and smearing two or three store-bought colors together. While working the clay in the hands, it will warm up and become easier to mix. Continue this procedure until the resulting color appears pure and free of streaks. Equal parts of green and red and a smaller portion of yellow will create a warm brown color fit for simulating earth. Liberal experimentation is encouraged. Avoid mixing red and blue clay, because a useless, bright purple will result. Bright purple earth is unnatural unless you still live back in the psychedelic 60s. The store-bought brown can be made to have more variety by mixing with it very small portions of each of the other store-bought colors. Once several different tints of brown have been obtained, they can be inserted into the bottle to provide an interesting, variegated brown earth. (See Figs. C-2 and C-8.) Some observers may feel that the variegated earth is more desirable than a single-colored one. Perhaps it is all in the eye of the beholder.

Selecting paints can be among the most confusing of all the decisions you will have to make, especially when you consider all the different kinds of paint. There are water-based paints, oils, enamels, aerosol sprays, temperas, acrylics, wiping stains, and glossy-and flat-finished paints. Although it is actually a matter of personal preference, enamels (oil-based), temperas (water-based), and oil wiping stains seem to be the most convenient to use and are shown in Fig. 5-4.

A wide variety of enamel paints are available in hobby shops, most large drugstores, and some supermarkets. Two major hobby-paint manufacturers are Testors and Pactra. Both companies produce an incredible number of colors in both glossy-and flat-finished paints. Small bottle containing 1/3 fluid ounce or 2/3 ounce make it convenient to purchase a number of colors inexpensively. Spray enamel paints are also available, although their color variety is not as extensive as with the small bottles. Once dry, the colors are very stable. The only disadvantage to using enamels is that paint thinner must be purchased and used for cleaning up, especially to preserve the life of the paintbrush. When you are mixing colors, Testors paints should be combined only with Testors paints. The same is true with Pactra paints. It seems that when the two brands are combined, the resulting mixture soon turns hard and unusable. Paint thinners are involved in a similar situation. The paint thinner of one brand cannot be used with the paint of the other brand. Despite these minor concerns, the paints of both companies are of excellent quality and convenience.

Water-based tempera paint is also convenient to use, especially at clean-up time. Tempera is available in art supply stores and some hobby shops, but only in flat-finished textures. The colors are usually bright and must be combined with other colors in order to provide a wider variety. Black, white, and the primary colors of red, blue, and yellow are designed to be mixed into almost any color and shade imaginable. Care must be exercised when thinning with water to avoid making the paint too thin. Tempera quickly looses opacity when water is added. Lack of opacity allows the underpaint features to show through after the paint is dry. Several additional coats may be required to eliminate this problem. Another disadvantage is that if the painted surface somehow becomes wet, it begins to dissolve and smear. Even body oils and perspiration on the fingertips will cause smearing. On the other hand, one great advantage is that cleanup of tempera paint is achieved with just soap and water. Dried paint on any washable surface will clean up with gentle scrubbing. The Victorian house in Fig. C-2 was painted entirely with tempera

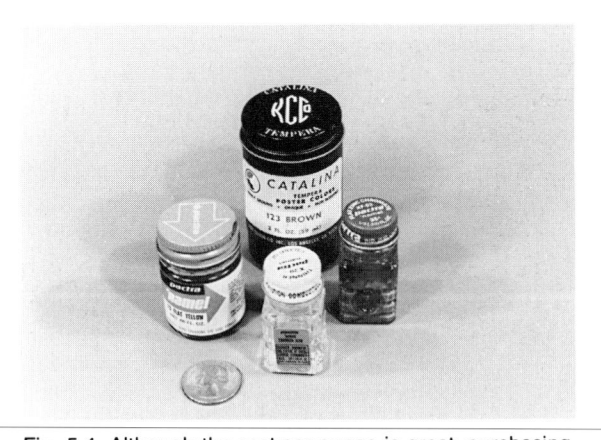

Fig. 5-4. Although the cost per ounce is great, purchasing these small containers of paint provide you with color variety and convenience.

Fig. C-2. A Victorian house, designed from a fantasy, was constructed in a 2-gallon water bottle and required 19 months to complete.

Fig. C-1. Requiring 2 months for completion, my first bottled house was constructed in a 1-gallon, apple juice bottle.

Fig. C-3. A custom-made Pyrex bottle was used to preserve this mahogany-paneled Victorian house.

Fig. C-4. This Dutch Colonial beach house was copied from an existing dwelling and constructed in an antique wine demijohn.

Fig. C-5. Although the glass distortion is considered excessive, this 40's era, 1-gallon beverage container was selected for a western storefront.

Fig. C-7. This brownstone tenement building was constructed in an antique pharmaceutical bottle. Glass microscope slides were used as window glass and set in wood frames.

Fig. C-6. A house in the Cape Cod style was constructed atop stones in a wide-mouthed juice bottle.

Fig. C-8. Although the glass distortion in this bottle may seem excessive, it complements the miner's cabin constructed inside.

Fig. C-9. The walls of this stone castle were constructed one pebble at a time in a square, antique bottle.

Fig. C-10. A tugboat was constructed and completed outside the bottle and later sliced into pieces for easy insertion into this liquor bottle.

Fig. C-11. A 1-gallon juice bottle was used to display the square-rigger *Columbia*, which I constructed at age 16.

Fig. C-12. A monkey shoving a ship into a bottle is the subject of this bottled ship constructed by Vic Crosby.

Fig. C-13. A pint bottle holds the figure of a man struggling to pull his ship through the narrow neck. Vic Crosby was the builder.

Fig. C-14. A quart-sized liquor bottle was selected to hold a man and his shipbuilding project. The figure represents Vic Crosby, the builder.

Fig. C-15. Vic Crosby built this man constructing a plank-on-frame ship's hull in a pint-sized Pinch bottle.

Fig. C-16. Miniature people are seen building the privateer *Virginia*, another plank-on-frame ship by Vic Crosby.

Fig. C-17. Although this is not a bottled ship, it is a very detailed coach and horses composition from Charles Dickens' story, *David Copperfield*. The artist, Vic Crosby, is a stickler for detail.

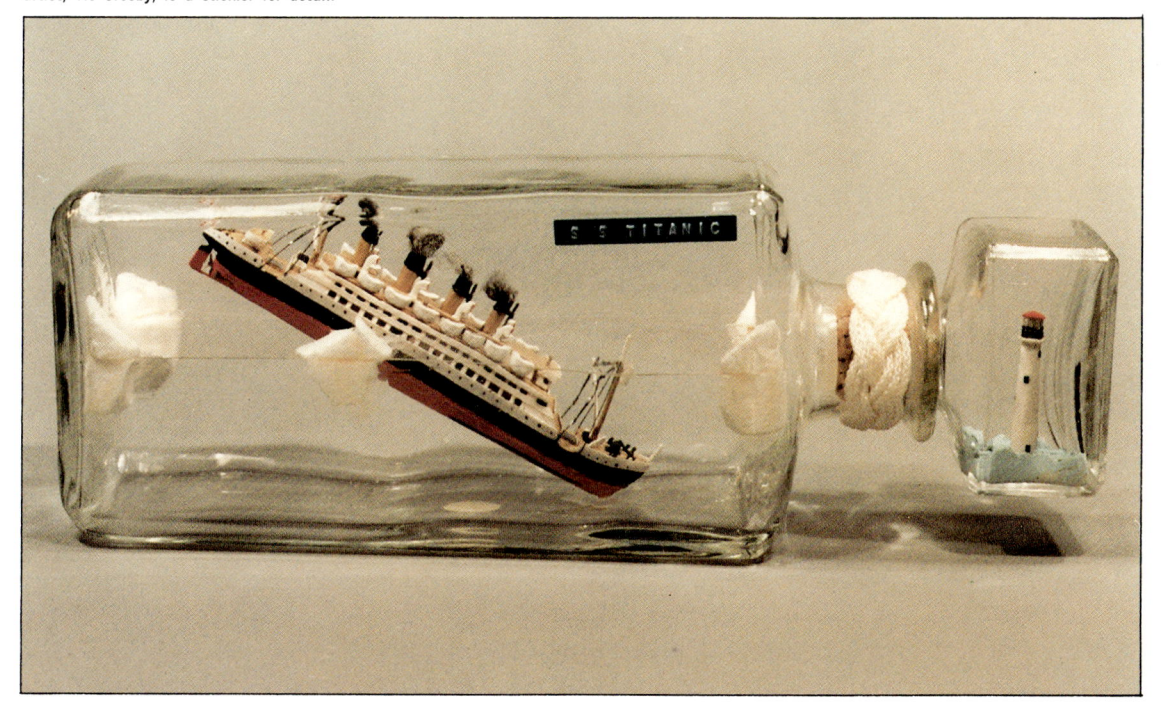

Fig. C-18. Vic Crosby's S.S. *Titanic* in a bottle is accurate even to its sinking.

Fig. C-19. This harbor dredge, constructed by Vic Crosby, can actually be manipulated to work using the lines provided.

Fig. C-20. The Seattle, Washington, fireboat *Alki* is a highly detailed work, constructed by Vic Crosby, one of its early fire fighters.

Fig. C-21. An Arabian dhow, bottled by Vic Crosby, required extensive research prior to construction.

Fig. C-22. Hornblower's Flotilla graces the inside of a quart-sized liquor bottle and was constructed by Vic Crosby.

Fig. C-23. Vic Crosby's bottled galleon is made almost entirely of bone.

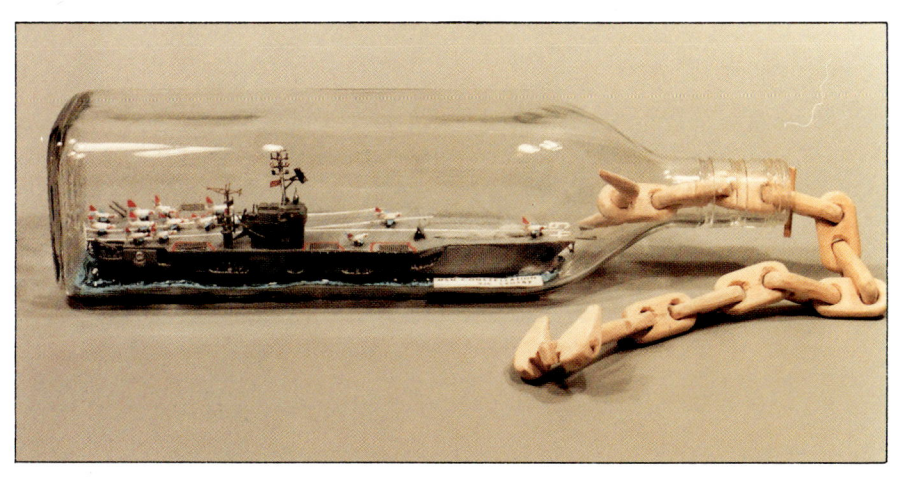

Fig. C-24. The aircraft carrier, U.S.S. *Constellation* built by Vic Crosby, sails through a liquor bottle.

Fig. C-25. The fishing boat *Sina* was once the command of Vic Crosby, who later constructed this bottled version.

Fig. C-26. A liquor bottle holds the ocean liner S.S. *United States*, constructed by Vic Crosby.

Fig. C-27. A United States quarter reveals the actual size of a miniature scene of a man and his son building a bottled ship. It was constructed by Vic Crosby.

Fig. C-29. The racing sloop *Intrepid* sails on dauntlessly in a well-chosen liquor decanter. Vic Crosby is the builder.

Fig. C-28. A 500-watt light bulb holds the Gloucester schooner *Bluenose*, while an old cork fishnet float secures the base. Vic Crosby created this interesting piece.

Fig. C-30. A vertical-standing wine bottle holds the ghost ship *Mary Celeste*, by Vic Crosby.

paint. With a little extra care, the use of tempera paint can be a very convenient way to maintain the desired coloring of almost any object. The selection of tempera paint would be a wise one.

Oil wiping stains are used to color but not cover the grain of some woods. Stains are found in paint stores, hardware stores, and in some lumberyards. House doors, floor planks, and some trim are often stained for use in bottled houses. After the wood has been shaped and assembled to its final construction, the oil wiping stain is applied liberally and later wiped off with a rag. The stain accumulates in open-grained wood and textured or carved areas of the wood's surface. This is a very effective method of bringing out the grain of the wood, as well as making doors, windows, and floor planks appear old and well used. Cleanup requires the use of paint thinner. Any drips or splatters of stain will remain permanently in clothing. Colors of oil wiping stain range from charcoal through warm brown tones, lightening to grey. A combination of stain with a subsequent dry-brush application of tempera or a flat-finished enamel can make a door appear extremely old and abused. *Dry brushing* is a technique by which a brush of paint is wiped on paper until it barely sheds any paint. Then, by brushing over the features of a door, a controlled formation of streaks of color will appear on the higher surfaces. The result of using flat-finished black, white, and light-colored tan enamel paints is a very old and dirty-looking door. If you allow it to happen, a real art of painting and finishing can begin to develop. It merely requires some occasional experimentation.

WOOD PUTTY AND POLYSTYRENE FOAM

The search continues for that perfect ground for the building site which is more realistic-looking but still easy to use. Modeling clay is only moderately adequate because its surface yields an undesirable shine from the oils which compose the clay. Granted, the control of color is excellent with clay, and the ease of inserting and spreading it in the bottle is superb. The modeling clay's glossy-textured ground, however, is difficult to accept as earth when you are striving for perfection. Experimentation with other materials can sometimes result in discovering a superior substitute.

Such a substitute is wood putty, which goes by the name *Wood Dough* if made by Duratite or by *Wood Patch* if made by Darworth. There are other brands of putties as well. The attractive features of using wood putty are its dull, almost stoney texture after drying, its natural-looking color, and the ease with which it is inserted and spread in the bottle. The nature of the texture is a welcomed one. Finally a rough-textured, realistic-looking material has been discovered. A number of colors are available, which further adds to its value to the builder. Although its purpose is to match a variety of woods, some colors of wood putty appear much like some types of soil. These colors range from a sandy color (a light oak) to a light-brown earth, or dark walnut.

Wood putty is not any more difficult to insert and spread inside a bottle than modeling clay. An olive-sized lump of putty is dropped through the neck, and a wire tool is employed to manipulate the lump to its desired location and mash or spread it flat. Starting in the center of the bottom and working toward the outer edge, the putty is inserted, positioned, and spread into a flat, interconnecting form, lump by lump. Using the small end of the bent-wire tool, the wood putty is tamped flat as possible. The entire bottom should be filled at one time with little delay, otherwise unequal drying and shrinking will cause cracks to develop.

Mild shrinkage and a few minor cracks can be expected and are the only disadvantages to using wood putty. It is sold in hardware stores and lumberyards and is available in small and large resealable cans. Cleanup requires acetone, lacquer thinner, or fingernail polish remover.

Another worthwhile building material is polystyrene foam, sometimes better known by the trade name Styrofoam. Polystyrene foam has many uses, including for insulation, packaging, and surfboards. As far as bottled houses are concerned, foam is used as building blocks for walls and towers. The bottled castle pictured in Fig. 3-13 was constructed with bricks of polystyrene foam. It is a strong material and is very stable. The foam is very easy to cut, and unlike some woods, it is quite uniform in its composition. Use a sharp-bladed knife for carving and slicing because a dull one will merely crush the soft foam. Polyvinyl glue, known to most craftsmen as white glue, is used in securing the foam blocks. Polystyrene foam can usually be obtained free among packaging materials. Many electronics products are packed in protective foam. It is not often that such a convenient building material can be obtained without any cost.

PLASTICS, GLUE, AND CEMENT

There may be times when you will strive to be as accurate and complete as humanly possible. This may mean using real glass in the windows. Although glass may be used, as in the window seen in Fig. 5-5, in which microscope slides fit neatly into the window frames, clear plastic sheet is more convenient and practical. It is easily obtained and cut. Plastic sheeting can be obtained from inexpensive, loose-leaf page covers or from plastic roll stock, both of which are available at many art supply and stationery stores. Plastic sheet can be cut with household scissors or a sharp X-acto knife. White glue seems to work well for holding the plastic securely in the window frames. Plastic appears to be an acceptable solution to the problem of constructing realistic looking windows. Colored plastic sheet will pass for stained glass windows if you have enough patience to cut and fit many tiny pieces.

Using the proper glue is the key to building ease and success, as well as long-term durability. If the wrong glue is used when constructing a bottled house, the building process may be even more tedious and time consuming, if not impossible. Glue which requires too much time to hold effectively may allow pieces to collapse or at the least drift apart. Additionally, a glue which dries out and releases from parts cannot be expected to hold together a bottled house for any length of time. After all, these bottled houses are intended to last for at least several lifetimes. No one knows for sure which particular glue or cement will successfully shoulder such a heavy responsibility. For now, however, builders must be content with a glue which is reasonably easy to work with while constructing complicated projects. Considering these long-term expectations, a builder may never know if he selected a durable glue for sure. So far, common white glue, a polyvinyl plastic, seems to be very successful. My first bottled house (Fig. C-1) was constructed in the summer of 1967, traveled with its new owner to New York, and at last report is still intact. Polyvinyl glue is available under the tradenames of *Glu-Bird,* made by Wilhold Glues, Inc. and *Elmer's Glue-All*, made by The Borden Company. There are a number of other brands which are equally good. Plastic bottles of these glues are available in a number of sizes from a few

Fig. 5-5. Extremely thin panes of real glass—microscope slide covers—were used in the construction of the windows of the tenement building appearing in Fig. C-7.

ounces to a full gallon. Some of the smaller bottles are equipped with a dispenser tip, providing additional convenience. The glue may be applied directly from the dispenser nozzle to the part being joined. Another application method is to pour out a nickel-sized pool of glue onto a small piece of paper, and apply the glue with a toothpick. This is an especially effective technique for fine, intricate gluing.

Epoxy cement is another valuable adhesive for this craft. Epoxy cement will adhere relatively well to glass, while polyvinyl will not. This feature is important when you are first beginning a bottled house, when the foundation posts must be secured to the bottle's slippery bottom. Epoxy has been found to accomplish this step with few failures. Follow the instructions carefully. Once a small amount is mixed, it must be used immediately; otherwise it will harden rapidly, becoming useless. The Borden Company manufactures a very effective epoxy cement under the trade name, *Elmer's*. Other quality brands are also available. Epoxy cement is available almost everywhere. Supermarkets, hardware stores, some hobby shops, drugstores, and even the hardware sections of some department stores sell this popular adhesive.

There may very well be many other building materials just waiting to be discovered. They may be of real value to the art of bottling houses. Although it may sound like a broken record, gaining experience and some inventive experimenting will uncover other useful materials. Likewise, being observant and staying informed will also encourage beneficial discoveries.

6

From Building Site To First Floor

Happily, that great day—the one you have been waiting for—has finally arrived. After all the reading, studying, bottle cleaning, house designing, tool buying, and material gathering, the actual construction of a bottled house is about to begin. Despite the increasing excitement and the excessive adrenaline pumping through your body, a cool head and clear thinking must prevail. It is now that you must make another decision. You, the builder, must decide whether to build your house on a flat building site or on one which is built up with stones forming a mountain. This decision must be made now because a different foundation system is used with each type of site. **MOUNTAIN BUILDING.** If a mountain site is desired, suitable stones must be obtained. Once they are, the first step in building involves inserting the stones into the bottle. Lowering the stones into the bottle requires special attention. You cannot simply drop the stones in without causing potentially serious damage. Furthermore, the rocks cannot be expected to arrange themselves into a believable, mountain-top formation, no matter how skillful a bombardier you may seem to be. Stones must be lowered into the bottle and positioned into their proper locations one at a time. A clever tool called Mechanical Fingers is very effective in delivering and positioning most medium-sized stones. The larger stones, which just squeak through the bottleneck, must be lowered into the bottle using a sling or basketlike device made of thread or string. Sometimes masking tape tied to a string will work as well, although the risk of premature release is always a real danger. Experimentation is encouraged in order to discover an effective delivery technique. Once the stone has been passed through the neck, it is lowered and set on the bottom of the bottle. Next, the stone is manipulated from the grasp of its delivery device and maneuvered to a spot near its intended permanent location. Epoxy cement is applied to the glass area by scooping the cement onto the bent-wire tool and inserting it into the bottle. Smear the cement onto the glass area intended for the rock's location. Continue this process one stone at a time until the entire bottom of the bottle is covered with a layer of stones, as illustrated in Fig. 6-1. This formation of stones must be allowed to dry, or *cure*, overnight. The successive layers of stones may be glued into place using white glue, but again, allow each layer to dry overnight. To place the next layer set each stone on the bottom area of the formation and apply glue to the contact points of the surrounding stones of its intended location, as seen in Fig. 6-2. Then, pick up the stone again with the mechanical fingers and set it in its sticky spot. Continue this building process until the desired

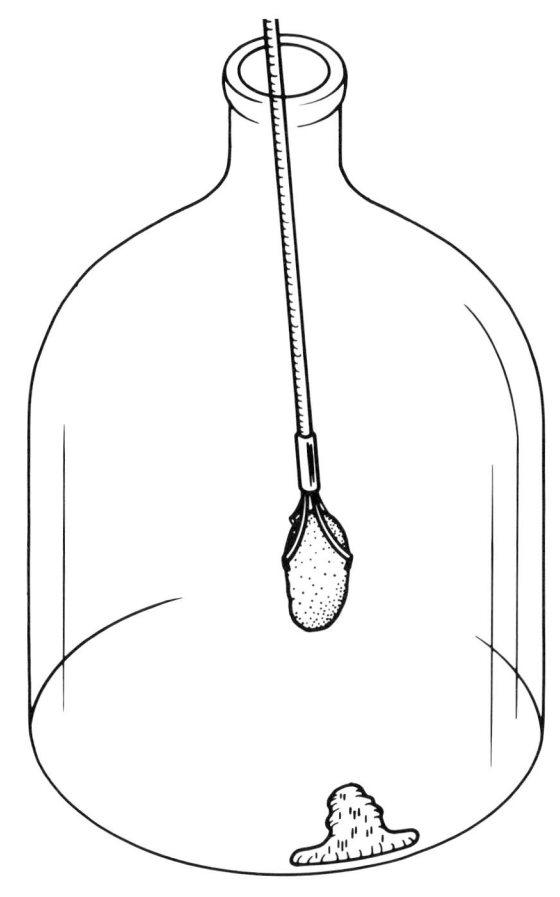

Fig. 6-1. The mechanical fingers are used to insert the stone through the bottleneck and set it in the pool of cement waiting for it.

mountain form has been completed, and allow to dry an extra day to ensure a secure bond.

Foundation posts must be prepared next. Apply walnut-colored stain to a foot or so length of square beam, the thickness of which is at your discretion. Although it depends on the scale being used, a 1/4-inch-square beam might be regarded as about average. Cut 1/2-inch lengths of the stained beam and shape one end to conform to the contours of the stone's contact point.

Glue each foundation post in a vertical position among the rocks along imaginary, horizontal lines representing the outer walls of the house. These foundation posts will later support the entire house structure and should be arranged accordingly.

Study Fig. 6-3. Additional sections of beams must be glued atop the foundation posts in order to provide a level system of supports. From this point on, the construction techniques will continue in the same way as on a flat building site.

THE FLAT BUILDING SITE

Construction of the flat building site moves much faster than that of the mountain site. First, on the outside bottom of the bottle, lay out lines with a grease pencil to represent the exact locations of eventual foundation posts (Fig. 6-4). These lines

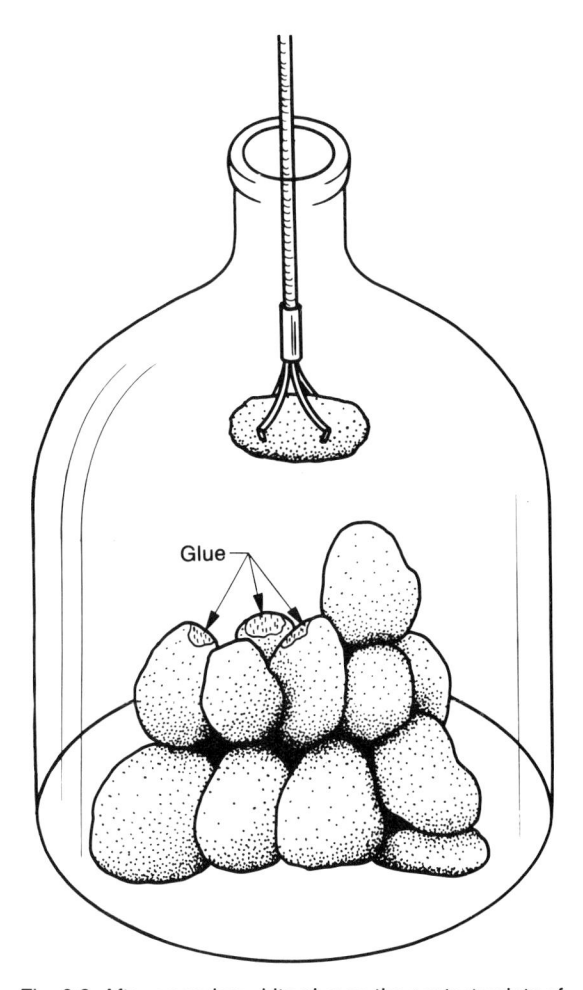

Fig. 6-2. After smearing white glue on the contact points of the surrounding rocks, the selected stone is set in place with the mechanical fingers.

Fig. 6-3. Wooden foundation posts are glued into a vertical position after you contour one end to fit its particular stone.

may be more extensive in order to help indicate the intended location of the house walls, much like a house's "footprint." The best and most secure arrangement is that of a square. These first foundation posts must be more concerned with providing a strong bond to the glass rather than with following the irregular "footprint" of the house. An X, marking the exact location of each post, will serve as a target over which each post will be cemented to the glass.

Now, the foundation posts are cut and shaped. Use any 1-inch square, or round, wood stock, each of a length of around 1/2 inch tall. The recommended dimensions are $1/2 \times 1 \times 1$ inch. Since smaller posts have less surface area across which to be bonded onto the glass with the epoxy cement, they will be less secure and are not recommended. A contoured shape should be carved across the bottom of each post accommodating the curvature of the glass. An example is pictured in Fig. 6-5. This contour does not have to be perfect because the cement will fill in any gaps between the wood and the glass.

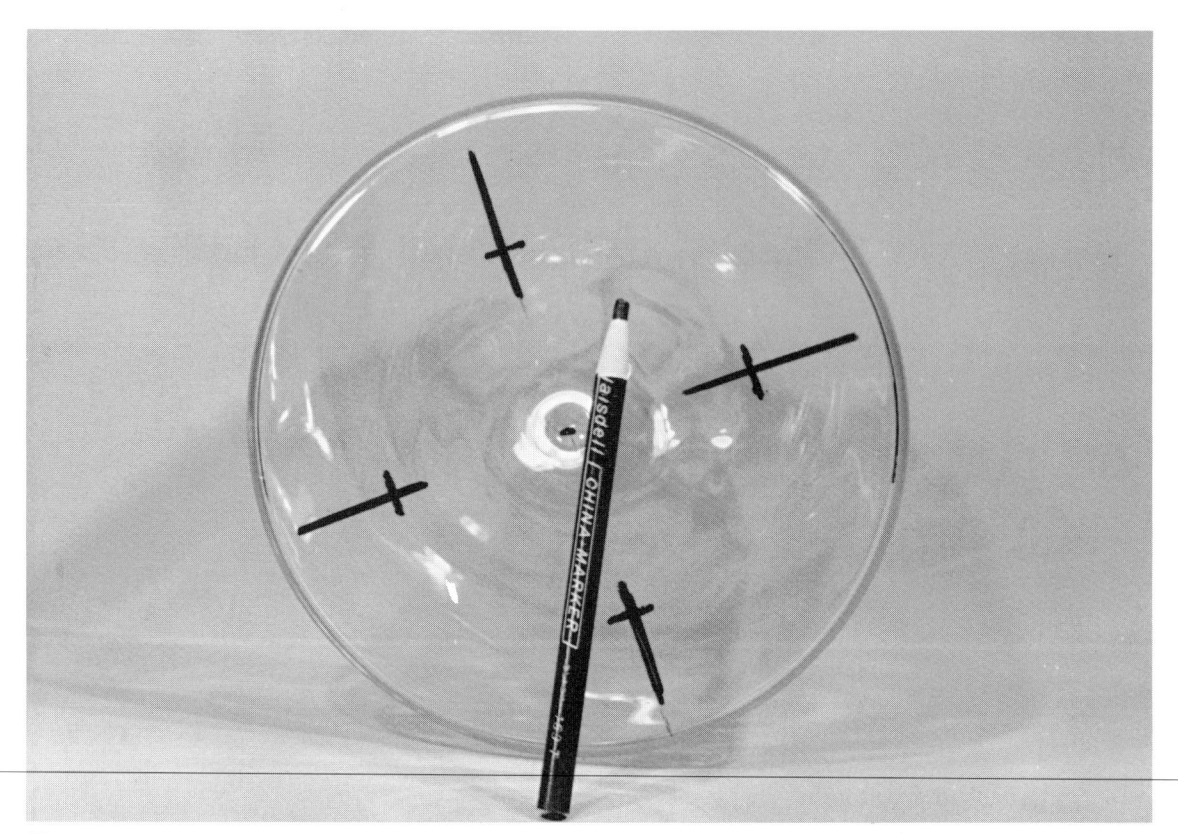

Fig. 6-4. Marks from a grease pencil serve as survey lines on the outside of the bottle's bottom.

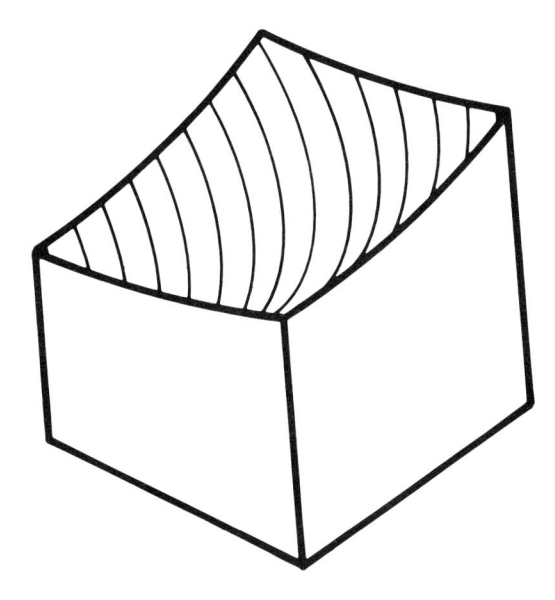

Fig. 6-5. A foundation post, shown here with contour lines defining the concave base, must fit the bottle's inside bottom as neatly as possible.

Cementing the foundation posts into their respective places is the next step in the process. Epoxy cement is applied over each target X using the bent-wire tool. Apply enough cement to create a small pool. The cement should be of a thick enough consistency to avoid running uncontrollably. Next, pierce the top of a foundation block with the needle of the needle-wire tool and insert it into the bottle. Plunge the foundation post into the pool of cement as shown in Fig. 6-6. All four posts installed will appear similar to those seen in Fig. 6-7 and should provide adequate support for securing the entire house structure firmly to the glass.

The earth material is applied to the glass surface around the foundation posts in the next step. Either modeling clay or wood putty must be inserted, spread, and smoothed around the posts. Do so by inserting one manageable-sized lump at a time. If wood putty is used, complete this process without interruptions or delays to avoid excessive cracking. Both materials, however, are applied in the same manner. A lump of the material is wrapped around the bottom of the small-ended bent-wire tool and inserted into the bottle, as shown in Fig. 6-8. When the ground material touches the glass, it is pressed against the glass surface, creating a vacuum. This vacuum makes the material stick. Then, the wire tool is twisted back and forth by rolling its handle between the fingers. The twisting action will help release the tool from the ground material. The released material is spread across the glass surface and smoothed by tamping with the bottom of the bent-wire tool. Tapping and stroking motions will help accomplish this task.

Each lump of ground material is installed and spread in the same manner until the entire bottom of the bottle is filled with a 1/8- to 1/4-inch thick

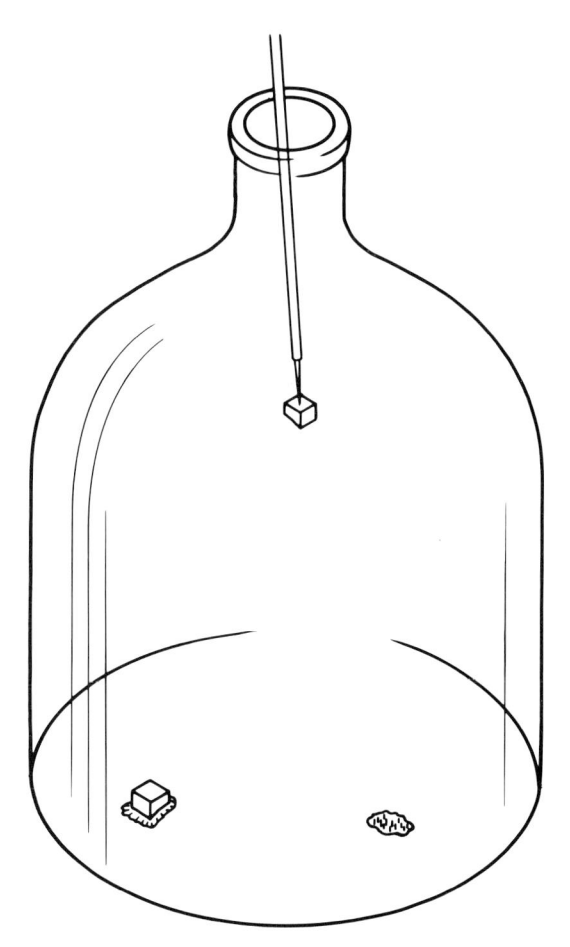

Fig. 6-6. After epoxy cement is applied onto the bottle's inside bottom, each of the four foundation posts is set into the pools of cement and left undisturbed for several days.

Fig. 6-7. All four foundation posts sit quietly while their cement foundations dry.

layer. Avoid covering the tops of the foundation posts. Keep the ground material at a level below the tops of the posts. Depending on your desires, the surface of the ground can be mounded, shaped, and sculptured into a variety of forms.

STRUCTURAL SUPPORTS

Now the real construction of the wood-framed house in a bottle begins. The four foundation posts must be linked, or *tied*, together to provide support for the flooring and walls coming later. Small wooden beams measuring 1/4 inch square are used for this purpose.

First, set a beam on the work surface near the bottle and estimate the size required to link two posts together inside. Allow an extra 1/4 inch in length to cover any "short" estimates. It is far better to cut a beam too long than to waste the whole piece by cutting it too short. Next, the beam is inserted into the bottle using the needle-wire tool and set in its intended location. Note how much more wood must be removed in order to make it fit properly. This trial-and-error process of measuring is repeated until the beam fits satisfactorily. Observe whether the beam appears level. Levelness will be important later, so make adjustments now. Add wood or recipe-card shims to make one end taller, if necessary, or carve away part of the beam to lower the other end. Continue this process until all four foundation posts are linked together, as shown in Figs. 6-9 and 6-10.

At this point in the construction process a square structure has been formed. Only rarely are houses shaped in an exact square. It may be necessary, therefore, to add horizontal beams to the sides of the beams linking the foundation posts to-

shows how these wing support beams are stacked side by side in order to achieve the desired span. Remember, these beams must be installed as level as possible.

FLOORING

A floor separating each level or story of the house is an important feature. Despite the fact that it may not be seen and requires extra effort and materials, the floor structure acts as a barrier, catching any lost parts which may accidentally fall from the

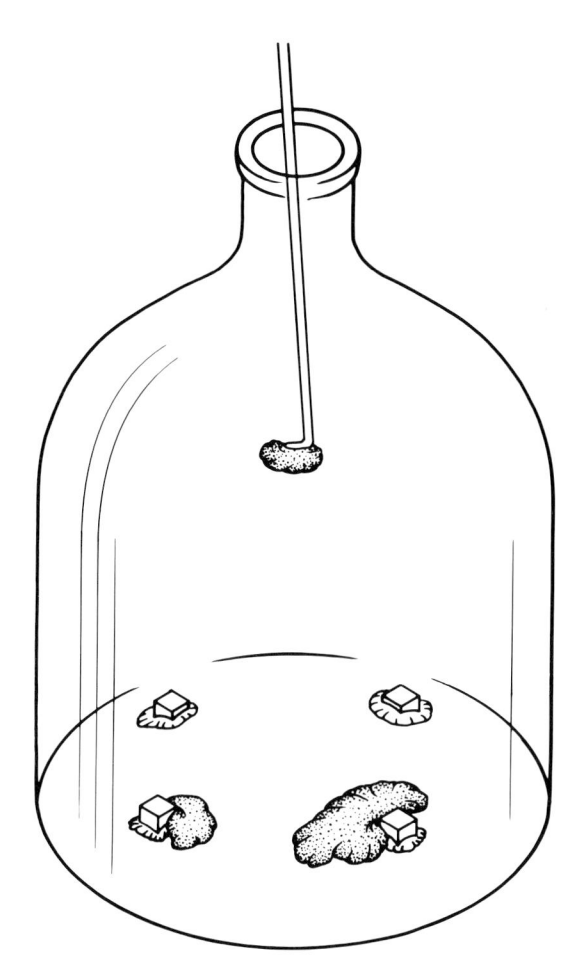

Fig. 6-8. The ground or base material is applied one lump at a time and tamped smooth with the bent-wire tool.

gether. This extra construction will lengthen a room here or expand a porch there. All of this should already have been considered during the design phase.

Turn the bottle on its side, secure it with blocks to keep it from rolling if it is round, and apply glue to the sides of the link beams using the bent-wire tool. Then, using the needle-wire tool, insert the required length of beam into the bottle and set it in the glue. Make any necessary positioning adjustments, and leave the bottle properly secured on its side for a 1/4 hour to allow the glue to set. Repeat this procedure until the wing or expanded room is enlarged to its desired size. Figure 6-11

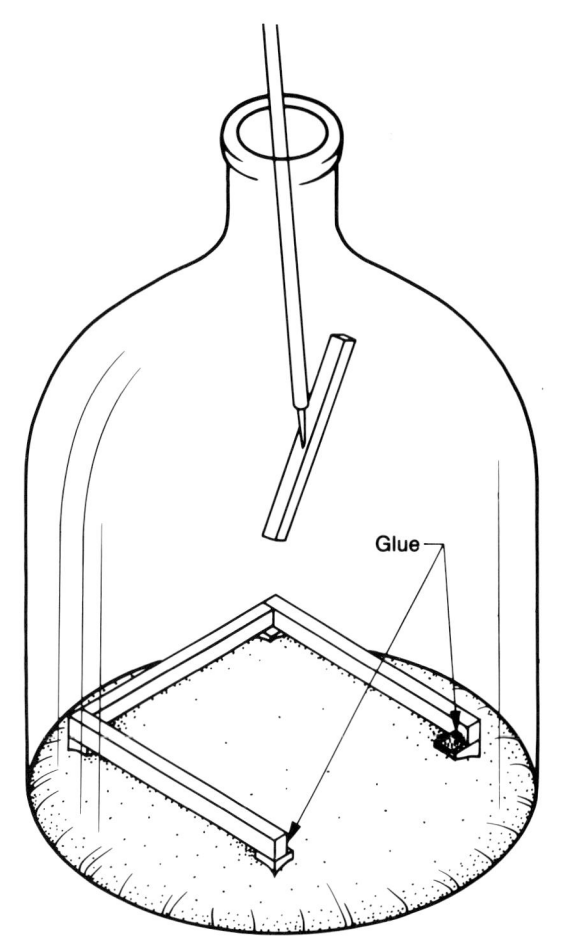

Fig. 6-9. Each of the beams, which will link the foundation posts together, must be inserted through the bottle's neck at a steep, almost vertical angle, and later tapped against a foundation post to adjust the angle to horizontal before setting it into its proper location.

79

Fig. 6-10. A solid support structure is created after all four foundation posts have been linked together with beams.

grasp of one tool or another. Otherwise, imagine the frustration created by dropping a badly needed part from the top of a two- or three-story building and having it wedge itself somewhere near the foundation. Consider, further, the strange view, through a large window on one level, of the windows on another level. That will appear very phony and cheap. A floor on each building level eliminates these problems. Wood measuring 1/16 inch thick and 1/2 inch wide by whatever length you need is a convenient size to use for flooring. Popsicle sticks are ideal for this construction. Estimate the measurements, cut to fit, and glue into place each plank of flooring required to cover the intended floor area. See Fig. 6-11. Remember to stain any planks exposed to view, such as on a porch, balcony, or doorway.

There may be times when round forms or towers will be included in the house design, as seen in Figs. C-2 and C-3. These forms must be constructed in the early stages of building, along with the flooring but prior to wall framing. Corrugated cardboard is cut into disks or rounds of the required diameter. Several disks are needed and are stacked between wood members like a neat stack of coins. They will form a cylindrical support for outside-wall siding, windows, and doors. Each disk is cut in half, like a half moon, and inserted through the bottle neck. One disk half is glued in place, and the other half inserted and assembled to complete the full disk, as shown in Fig. 6-11.

WALL FRAMING

Vertical support members, or *studs* as they are called, are installed next. Select a 1/4-inch-square

the stud. Lick the needle with your tongue to help hold the stud onto the needle just long enough to transport it to and insert it into the bottle without it dropping off prematurely. Next, apply glue to the edge of the floor plank on which the stud is to stand. Use the bent-wire tool to carry the glue and apply it to its proper location. Use just enough glue to help pull the stud from the needle. Once again, gently pierce the end of the stud with the needle-wire tool and insert it into the bottle. Set the stud into the spot of glue and twist to release the stud. If problems in releasing occur, insert another wire tool and

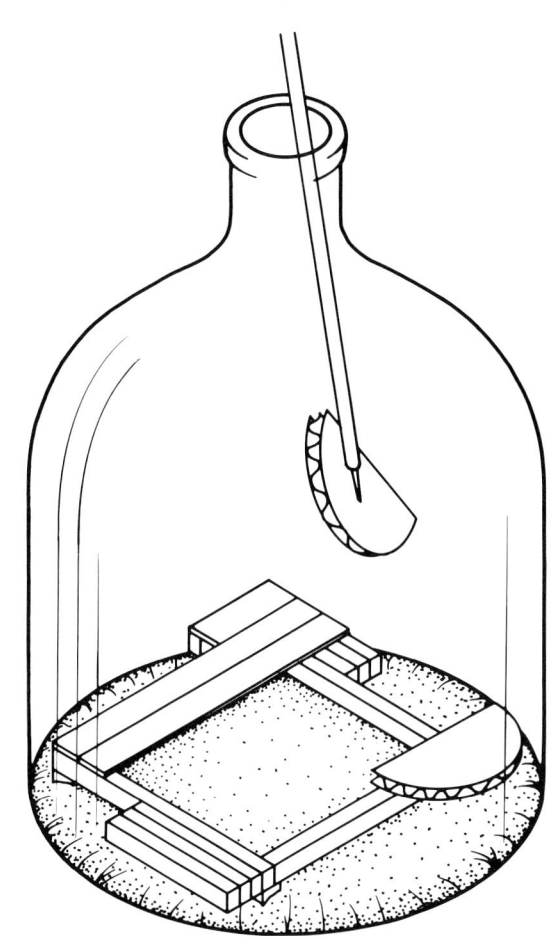

Fig. 6-11. Wing extensions (beams) provide additional support for flooring (planks), while round, cardboard forms provide a cylindrical shape for the eventual tower.

piece of wood and measure the desired length for cutting. Mark this first stud with a brightly colored, felt-tipped marker or a crayon with a symbol or letter to indicate that it is to be used as a master. This particular stud will be used as the consistent and exact stud length for the entire construction project. With it, you save the time required for measuring every time.

Next, cut several more studs and sand the ends to the exact length. Use a black felt-tipped marker to darken any stud whose side may be exposed to view through windows. Using the needle-wire tool, gently pierce one end of the stud, insert it into the bottle, and practice twisting the tool free to release

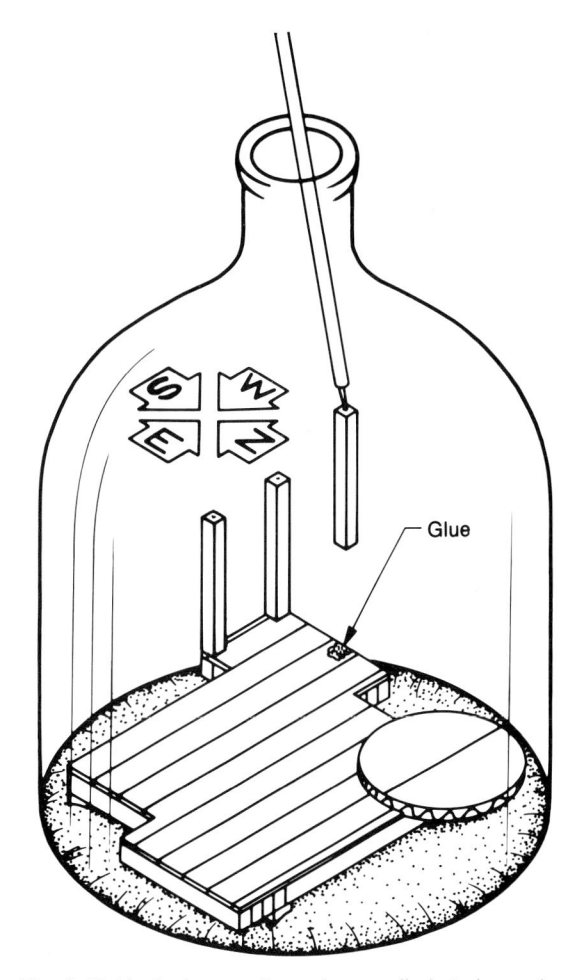

Fig. 6-12. Vertical support members, called *studs*, are installed and then adjusted to stand exactly vertical or perpendicular to the floor. Use the directions of the compass to observe each side of the stud to check these adjustments.

use it to push off the stud from the grasp of the needle.

Adjust the location and vertical angle of the stud by tapping it with the side of the needle. Continue to adjust until the stud is as close to the exact vertical as possible. Use the directions of the compass to check for vertical adjustments. Look North-South and then East-West as shown in Fig. 6-12. As can be expected, the stud may appear vertical when looking North-South but may still lean wrong when looking East-West. Keep adjusting until it appears vertical from all directions. As the glue begins to dry, the stud will become easier to adjust. Place studs on both sides of where windows are planned, on each corner of a wall, and on both sides of doorways. Later, windows will be supported by these studs; so plan accordingly. Doors usually stand between studs, rather than span across them as windows do. Continue installing studs until all have been glued and adjusted (Fig. 6-13).

Carved posts, such as those on the porches of the houses in bottles shown in Figs. C-2 and C-3, require special attention. After the overall sizes have been corrected to the proper dimensions, and the carving is completed, each post must be painted and allowed to dry. This special attention requires a good deal of extra time and effort, but the total impact of these ornamental posts is impressive. Only after each post is completed in every detail may it be inserted into the bottle and installed in its permanent location.

Horizontal beams, called *headers* in real house construction, contribute to the support of the wall frame and are installed next. These beams are attached to the tops of the studs, as shown in Fig. 6-14. They are needed to stabilize the studs and provide support for the roof or second-story structure. They also help indicate the proper vertical location of windows, the installation of which will be discussed later. The ends of the header beams should be notched to mate with its neighbor. Care should be exercised to make sure the header beams are set in a position as level as possible, using the same measures as on the link beams set on top of the foundation posts. You may again need shims to level off each beam. The actual installation of these header beams is the same as for the link beams. (See Fig. 6-14.) Make sure the beams sit squarely on the tops of the studs. Avoid allowing any beam's corners or edges to extend out over the edges of the studs, or you will have problems installing the outside wall siding.

Obviously it is important to build the correct structure at the proper time. For example, it would be unwise to construct the roof support structure and apply shingles before you install the outside wall siding. Common sense should always be considered when thinking about which item should be constructed in which order. It is at this point in construction that the tower should be considered. Another cardboard disk, number two, must be elevated to a height which will support the bottom edge of the tower windows. You must carefully plan for this disk. The second disk will be supported by six short studs, each cut to a length which will elevate the cardboard disk to the proper level. Study Fig. 6-14. Before installation, the tops of the disk halves must be darkened with a black, felt-tipped, marking pen in order to help it disappear from view through the windows. Likewise, the bottom of the third cardboard disk must be darkened for the same reason. A fourth disk must be located at a level flush with the top edge of the surrounding header beams. This completed form provides a consistent support system for windows, siding, and any decorative molding which might be included later.

WINDOWS

Before windows are installed in the next step in the house construction, they must themselves be built. Using various sizes of hobby-shop wood, the windows are constructed according to the requirements of the house design. The separate pieces, which together comprise the window, are cut and sanded prior to gluing together into its final form. After gluing and assembly, the window must be set aside to dry for an hour or two. Paint the window with enamel paint or some other nonwater-based paint. Water-based paints such as tempera or poster

Fig. 6-13. Many studs may be required to support all the walls, windows, and doors.

the open, top window of the tenement building in Fig. C-7.

Installation of the completed window is surprisingly easy. First, lay the bottle on its side with the house wall receiving the window facing up. Brace the bottle with blocks to keep it from rolling. Next, apply glue to the outside face of the studs that are to support the window. Use the bent-wire tool to deliver the glue. Then, pierce the top edge of the window frame with the needle-wire tool and insert it into the bottle, as shown in Fig. 6-15. Set the window onto the supporting studs and remove the needle-wire tool from the frame. Leave the bottle on its side for a few minutes to allow the glue to set. Curved windows, constructed for use on round tower walls, are inserted in the same way as flat ones, but are mounted on the edges of the round cardboard disks mentioned earlier.

DOORS

The installation of doors will present you with a different challenge. Like windows, doors must be constructed as a single unit and later inserted into the bottle using the needle-wire tool. First, the door frame opening must be measured to obtain the correct width and height. Next, build the door according to these measurements. Try a dry run to check for proper fit within the door frame. After checking, paint or stain the door. Allow adequate drying time and add the door knob and window glass, as required. Since the door will slide between two wall studs, two or more retaining blocks must be attached to the back of the completed door. These blocks keep the door from falling forward through the door frame. Study Fig. 6-16 for clarification. Installation involves smearing glue on the contact points of the inside face of the door frame where the door's retaining blocks contact the door frame. Next, insert the door into the bottle and slide it between the door frame posts, as in Fig. 6-16. For variety, some doors may be left standing open, provided careful fitting is exercised. Do not add retaining blocks to any door which is to remain open. A tight fit between the floor and the bottom surface of the header beam over the door frame will

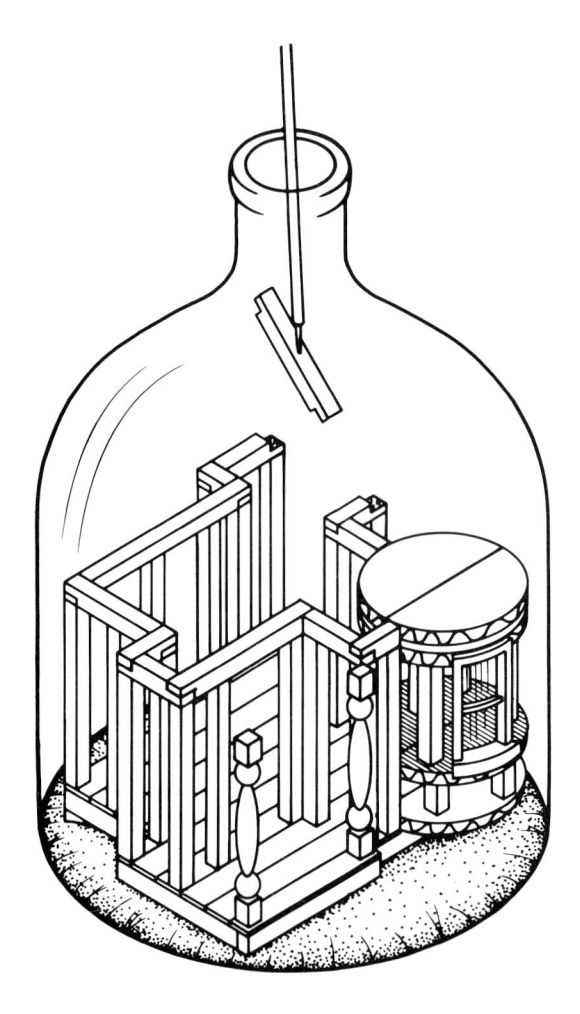

Fig. 6-14. A measured and notched lintel beam is inserted into the bottle, where glue awaits it.

paints are not recommended because they tend to dissolve the glue and crumble the window. After the paint has dried thoroughly, cut and glue plastic sandwich wrap or a similar material to the back of the window frame to act as window glass. Window shades made of paper and curtains made of loosely woven or knitted cloth are glued into place on the back of the plastic window glass. Avoid locating curtans too close to the outer edge of the window frame because they will interfere with the mounting of the window on the studs during installation. For variety, some windows may be left open by adjusting the location of some of the frame parts. Note

84

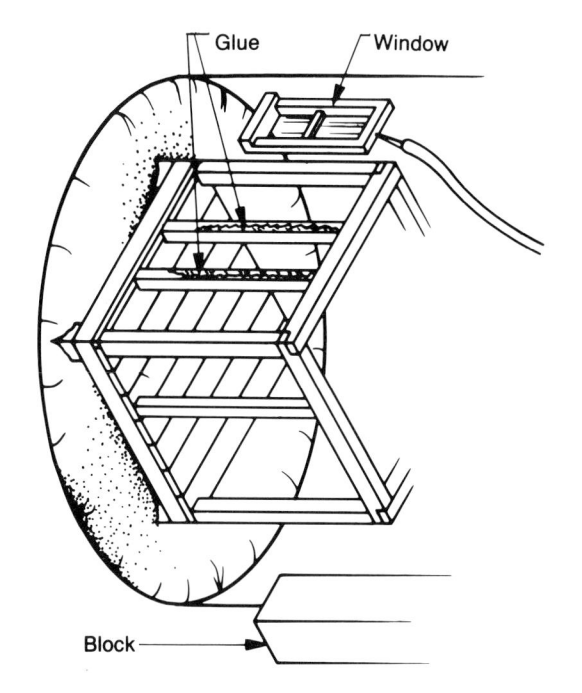

Fig. 6-15. With the bottle resting on its side and securely blocked, a completed window is inserted into the bottle and set into the glue which was previously applied to the outside faces of two, window-support studs.

allow the door to swing open to the desired angle. Apply glue and allow ample drying time before disturbing. All the doors and windows should be installed throughout the entire house (Fig. 6-17) before you start the next step of construction.

WALL COVERING

The application of the outside wall covering is the next step. You must choose from shingles, horizontal lapboards (Fig. C-2) or panels (Fig. C-3) for covering the walls. Brick and stone masonry and plaster or stucco wall construction will be covered in Chapter 8.

A horizontal lapboard is inserted vertically, after measuring and trimming, and then maneuvered into a horizontal position using the bent, needle-wire tool. Next, it is set into the glue previously applied to appropriate locations along the outside faces of the wall studs. This kind of wall covering is the most difficult and tedious to do.

Panels are much easier to install, but they still require great concentration. A panel is composed of a wood veneer sheet 1/2 to 1 inch in width and of varying lengths. Once the width of the panel has been selected, it must remain consistent. Each

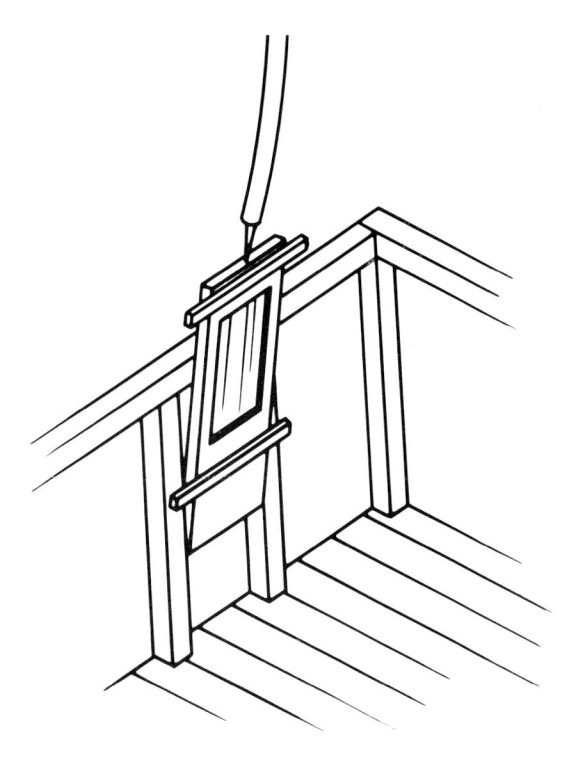

Fig. 6-16. After glue is applied to the appropriate contact points, the door is inserted into the bottle using the needle-wire tool. It is then slid between the door-frame posts.

Fig. 6-17. At this point in construction, all of the doors and windows have been installed.

panel must be measured and trimmed to fit around window frames and other features. The advantage of using panels rather than horizontal lapboards is that the panel is inserted and installed in a vertical position, eliminating the tedious step of turning it 90 degrees.

The first step in installing a panel involves estimating the size required for a proper fit. Lightly mark with a pencil the estimated points at which the panel must be trimmed. Insert the panel into the bottle, as pictured in Fig. 6-18. Make a mental note how close the pencil marks are to the actual required size. Remove the panel, change any marks, and erase the old ones. Insert the panel again to check the new pencil marks. Continue this process until the panel is correctly marked.

Cut the panel on the marks and insert the panel again for a final check prior to gluing. If the panel

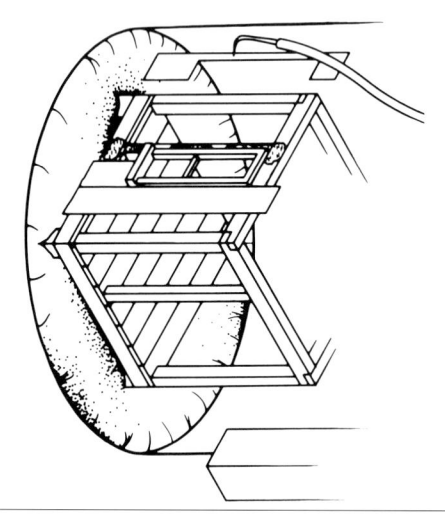

Fig. 6-18. After the glue is applied to appropriate locations with the bent-wire tool, each wall panel is inserted into the bottle and set into position, using the same tool.

fits neatly, remove, and apply glue to the appropriate locations on the studs and beams with the bent-wire tool. Insert the panel for the last time and set it into place. Press down any curled corners to ensure proper adhesion with the glue.

Continue this process with each panel until every wall of the bottom story of the house has been covered. Figure 6-19 shows panels wrapped around the circular form of the tower frame. As you gain experience with this seemingly tough process, the task will become easier and accomplished with greater speed. It should be noted that some panels may be allowed to extend up above the header beam in order to keep all the panel seams from occurring at the same place. Likewise, some panels may be allowed to fall short of the header beam to provide even more variety. In any case, plan carefully to avoid paneling over future window openings or balconies.

FINAL STEPS

Upon arrival at this point in construction, all of the features associated with the first story of the house should be completed and installed before you start to build the second story, as shown in Fig. 6-20. Construction of the second-story floor, which may act as the first-floor ceiling, is installed in exactly the same manner as the first-story floor, but should be delayed until every wall panel, window, and door has been installed. Otherwise, the flooring will block the convenient and often needed access through the top of the first floor. Occasionally, wall panels and windows must be manipulated into position with tools by approaching from the inside of the wall toward the outside, rather than from the outside in. This accessibility can sometimes make the difference between being able to install a window in the proper location or having to leave it out of the intended design. Such valuable flexibility

Fig. 6-19. Panels are wrapped around the circular form of the tower frame.

Fig. 6-20. Complete all the features of the first story, before you begin on the second story.

should be maintained until construction of the entire first story has been completed. Any interior effects such as furniture, wallpaper, floor coverings or even people must be installed prior to applying the second story flooring.

A few other details should be considered for construction and installation while it is still convenient. Porch stairs, moldings, and any other carved porch posts should be completed at this time. As construction progresses into taller areas of the house, the difficulty of installing these pieces will greatly increase. It pays to plan ahead.

The most difficult work is now over. The first story is by far more difficult to build than the remaining levels. The first story requires more effort to construct only because it is further down in the bottle. The second level is more convenient to reach. This point is regarded as a milestone. It often serves as both a reward and an incentive. The reward comes from seeing the completion of a major portion of the total bottled house. This feeling of accomplishment acts as an incentive to maintain the momentum of construction to full completion. Greater rewards lie ahead.

7

Above The First Story

As the chapter title implies, all that exists above the first story, or floor, must be included in the overall plan and arranged into proper order of construction. This may mean more than just a second-story structure of rooms and windows. Planning and construction of successive stories must be considered, as in the four-story bottled house pictured in Fig. 7-1 or the three-story tenement in Fig. C-7. Each story or floor level must not merely be stacked one atop another like simple building blocks, but rather designed and related to one another to form a well-composed whole. Although each story may differ in some respects, they still need to blend together smoothly. An outside staircase or chimney will help tie the different stories together. Beyond this consideration, it should be noted that the third-story level and all successive floors are constructed with the same building materials and techniques as for the second story. The only exception to this would be for the overall roof structure covering the top story. There are a number of other structures which should be considered for construction above the first floor. Any roof areas covering any part of the first story must be framed, subroofed, and shingled. Balconies, chimneys, and bay windows are included among these areas. All of the structures planned for above the first story must be constructed in a logical or convenient building order to avoid conflicts. It can be too difficult, if not impossible, to build one structure if another is in the way. After careful planning, common sense is the best guide in directing which object should be constructed when. Imagine the difficulty in constructing a small roof structure atop the first-story porch after you have completed the second-story walls. Structural beams, subroofing planks, and hundreds of shingles would have to be maneuvered over, around, down, and alongside the second-story walls. It is one thing for a task to be challenging, but still another for it to create severe frustrations! The flooring planks of the second story are installed in the same way as those of the first floor. Any staining or coloring of the planks being used for areas exposed to view, for porch ceilings, or for balcony flooring must be completed prior to installation. It is very important that the planks do not extend beyond the edges or sides of the header beams. Otherwise, there will be conflicts when you install the wall panels or siding. The exceptions are where balcony flooring must extend out beyond the walls, and roof structures extend out over a porch or balcony. Care should be taken to make sure the planks are installed as flat as possible. Avoid using warped wood. **ROOF CONSTRUCTION.** Construction of roof areas covering parts of the first story will be the next challenge. Figure 7-2

Fig. 7-1. A rambling, four-story house, designed from fantasy, had to be carefully planned in order that all the levels relate well with one another.

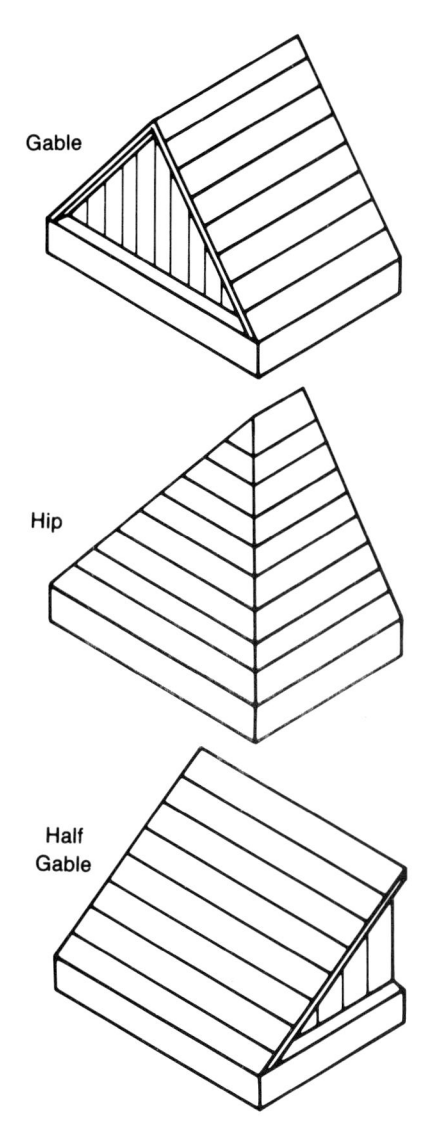

Fig. 7-2. Although other arrangements may work equally as well, these three porch-roof configurations are probably the most popular.

shows three possible roof configurations, but other arrangements may be just as effective. Since there will be so many individual pieces required to complete the roof section, it is wise to complete as much of the construction as possible (Fig. 7-3) before proceeding with the framing of the walls. This is mainly for convenience and ease of construction. Careful planning will help avoid conflicts later.

The appearance of a gable roof adds interest to the composition of the house, and its construction is relatively simple. If the roof section is to cover an open porch, the vertical support posts must be linked together with a horizontal beam or plank (Figs. 7-4 and 6-20). A vertical post, the height of which is determined by the *pitch*, or angle, of the intended roof, is installed atop the center point of this link beam. If a steeply pitched roof is desired, this vertical post must be taller. If a shallow pitch is planned, it is shorter. A second post, usually identical to the first, is located on the other end of the roof area. A horizontal ridge beam is installed atop both posts, linking them together (Fig. 7-5). Diagonal beams called *rafters* are installed and spaced close enough to provide adequate support for the subroofing (Fig. 7-6). Placed horizontally across the rafters, the subroof planks are spaced close enough to provide firm support for the shingles. In most cases, the subroofing planks extend out over the gable end enclosure forming *eaves*, as shown in the gable roof and half gable in Fig. 7-2.

Shingles are installed one at a time, starting with the bottom row. If the shingles are hand-cut from blocks of walnut, they must be tapered into a wedge shape just like real shingles to allow for a neat, flat appearance. Figure C-1 shows a mountain cabin on which hand-cut shingles were applied. A thin, paperbacked walnut veneer works well as shingle material and requires no tapering. You can vary the width and color of the shingles to add interest. The shingles lie side by side, although the exposed ends of the shingles on each row may be staggered for variety. Tiny spaces between shingles can be left to allow each shingle to appear as an individual piece. Otherwise, the shingles may appear to be one wide piece of shingle material, creating a less realistic roof.

Along the ridge, the last shingles to be applied are *cap shingles*. These are two shingles glued together side by side forming an angle, which when installed cap off the shingled roof, making it impervious to the elements, as well as looking more complete. These cap shingles are best installed using a wire tool with modeling clay attached to the end to avoid damaging the piece.

Fig. 7-3. A gable end is installed prior to beginning construction of other structures.

building. It must be planned in advance and integrated into the overall design. A balcony may be an indentation in a wall, or it may extend out beyond the wall, as shown in Fig. 7-7. The purpose of a balcony is to permit an additional exit from an upstairs room. It also provides welcome exposure to the outside, which would not ordinarily be possible without a balcony. Therefore, a door or a least a large window must also be included in order for the balcony to "make sense." A balcony may be sheltered with a roof or remain open to the sky. Balconies always have a retaining rail to keep children and happy party guests from falling over the side. A balcony may appear more complete or "lived-in" if you include potted plants, outdoor furniture, and maybe even an umbrella and table set.

A balcony, including its railing, is not as difficult to construct as it may seem. After the flooring and walls have been completed, the railing and/or roof support posts (if the balcony has a roof above which requires support) are carved, painted, and installed. A railing unit, composed of upper and

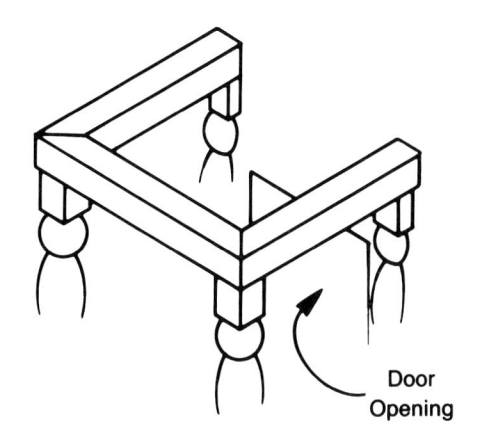

Fig. 7-4. The porch posts must be linked together with beams or planks to provide support for the structural framing of the roof.

BALCONIES

Balconies, like the doorway, provide an exterior house feature which is regarded as accommodating the human form, urging a person to enter. A balcony cannot just sprout from the side of a

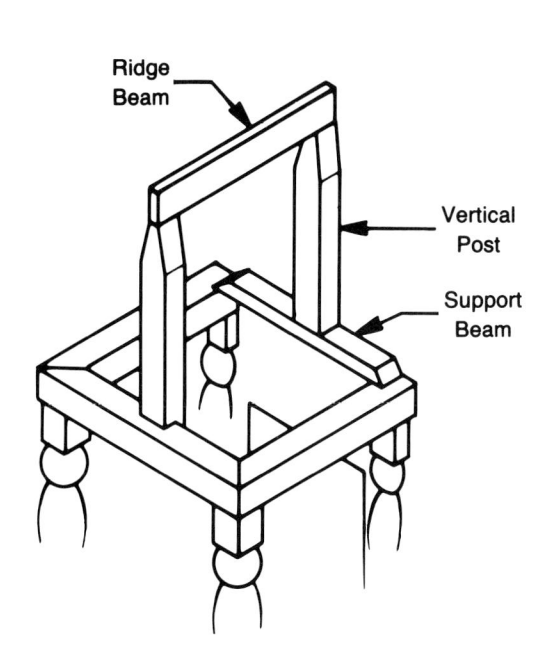

Fig. 7-5. After installing two vertical posts, a thin ridge beam is set atop the tapered post ends.

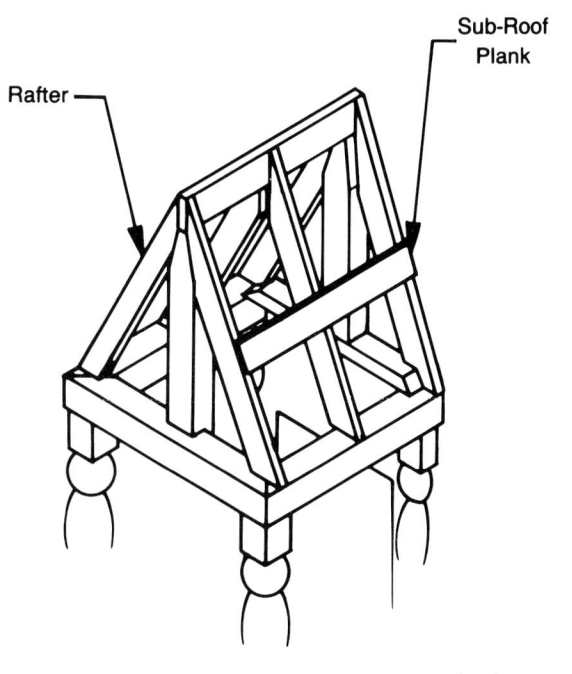

Fig. 7-6. Rafters are set diagonally, linking the ridge beam with the link beams. Subroof planks are installed across the rafters to form a solid, flat surface for the shingles.

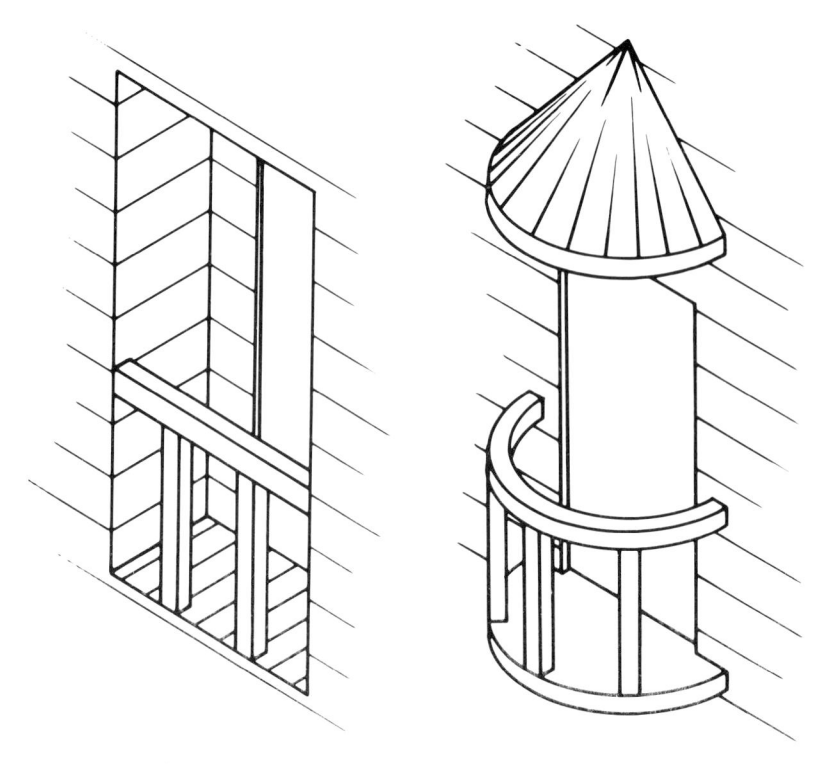

Fig. 7-7. Balconies may be recessed into the outside wall surface or extended out, beyond the wall.

lower horizontal railing members separated by two or more vertical pieces (Fig. 7-8) may be inserted as one unit through the bottle's neck using the modeling clay and wire tool. Retaining blocks on both sides of the two railing posts keep the railing unit from falling through during installation, as well as serving as glue points. Carefully planned and crafted notches would work equally well.

In either case, if the assembly is perhaps ill-fitting, with larger-than-desired gaps or cracks, you can use paint droplets clinging to the bent needle-wire tool to fill most of these problems. Dip the needle point into the paint, allowing just enough paint to hang from the point to safely transport it to its intended location without falling off prematurely. Then, insert the tool into the bottle and smear the paint onto its destination. The paint will run into the crack. Repeat this technique until the crack is filled. This touch-up method works well for many other areas of construction. On the other hand, it can never replace the satisfaction of good craftsmanship.

CHIMNEYS

A fireplace chimney will add great charm and the realism necessary to make any house believable, especially a bottled house. The addition of a chimney helps provide a feature easily recognized by the mind's eye. It helps a structure look like a house. A chimney can be constructed to appear like brick, stone, stucco, or as a metal stove pipe (Fig. C-8). It can be fully exposed on the outside of a house or emerge from the roof as in Fig. C-2.

A chimney for a bottled house may be constructed piece by piece as in Fig. 3-19 (stone by stone) or as a single unit, carved from a block of wood (Fig. 3-12). Individual construction will mean you will need to use many stones or bricks. The bricks may be real ceramic ones purchased in a dollhouse shop or carved, wooden ones painted with appropriate colors. In all honesty, the mortar, if used, is very difficult to manage inside the bottle. On the other hand, a chimney assembled of individual bricks or stones outside the bottle will present few problems while applying mortar. Wiping the stones or bricks and general cleanup will be easy. The only other consideration will be in making sure this type of chimney fits through the neck of the bottle.

Piece-by-piece construction inside the bottle is accomplished by setting each stone or brick in a

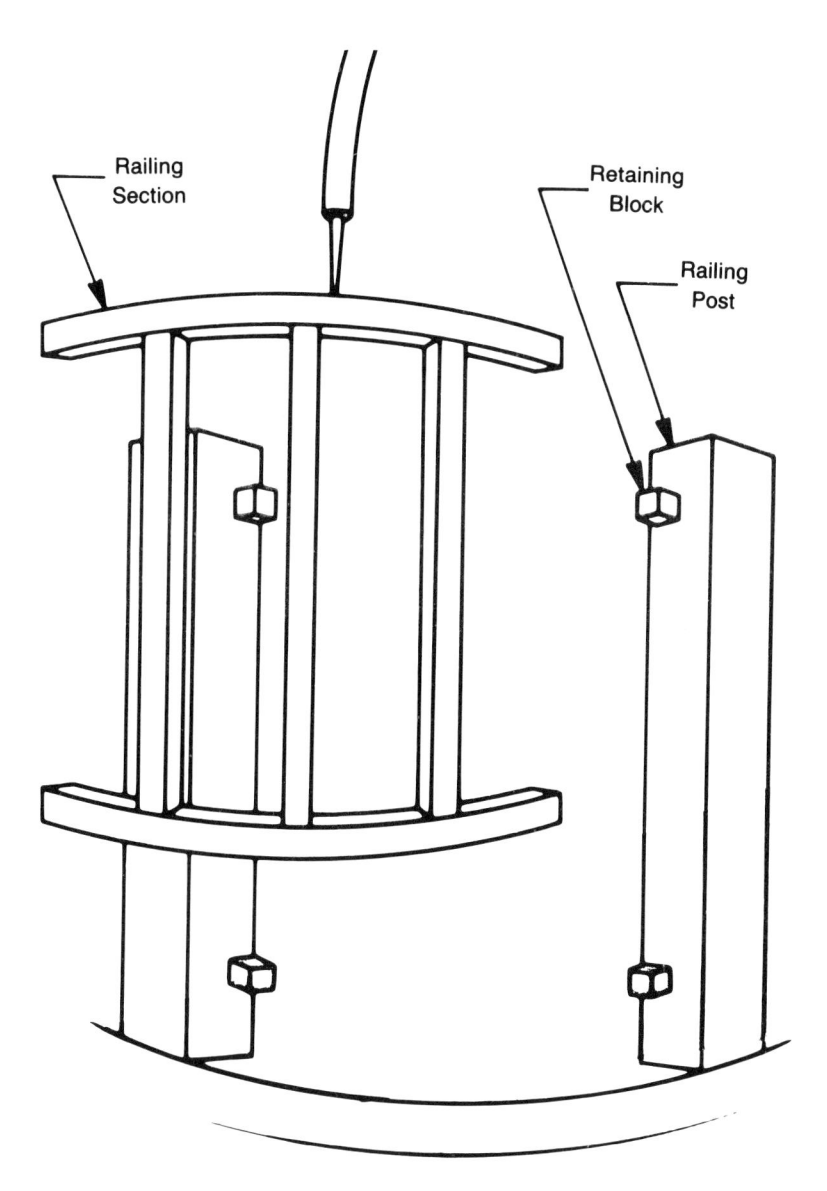

Fig. 7-8. In order to keep the railing section from falling between the railing posts, retaining blocks are attached to the posts prior to installation. Later, the railing section is set over these blocks and glued from the back.

Fig. 7-9. A simulated-stone chimney is first hand-carved from a block of wood, and later carefully painted to resemble mortar and stones.

The other method of chimney construction, made from a single block of wood, is easier to manage. Even a wide chimney too large to pass through the neck of the bottle can be carved, painted, and then split vertically into sections to permit insertion. Carving should include a pattern of grooves representing the mortar between the stones or bricks. Carved stones are rounded in shape, while bricks are squared-off for realism. After the carving has been completed, the flat gray paint of the mortar is mixed and applied to the mortar grooves.

preglued location using the wire and modeling-clay tool. With a little practice, the stone or brick can easily be tapped off after touching its intended location. As each layer or course of stones is set in glue, it is allowed to dry before the next layer is applied. Care should be taken to avoid using too much glue; otherwise, it will run from between stones. If you desire, after all the stones or bricks have dried securely, gray modeling clay can be smeared into the cracks between each stone. Although this is tedious and time consuming, the effects are worthwhile.

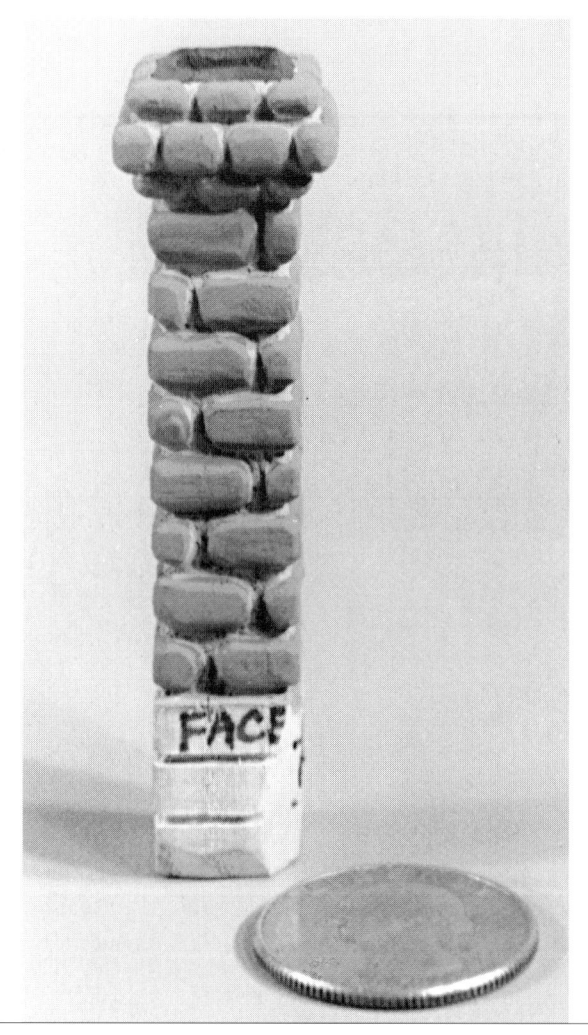

Fig. 7-10. Brick chimneys are constructed in the same way as stone chimneys.

Next, the stone or brick-paint colors are mixed and applied carefully to avoid splashing the mortar areas. These stone and brick colors may differ widely for stones and slightly for bricks for believable variety. Realism may be enhanced by way of a dry-brush painting technique. Flat-finished colors of tan, gray, black, and white are used in this way over a rusty, brick color. This process "dirties" the chimney, making it look used and more realistic. Areas near the top of the chimney may have a darker application of flat black to make it look like soot has settled on the outside of the bricks or stones over the years. A completed, but not yet installed, stone chimney is pictured in Fig. 7-9, while a brick one appears in Fig. 7-10. A space or opening in the subroof allows for a partial chimney in Fig. 7-11. Installation is accomplished easily using the needle-wire tool. Later, shingles are carefully shaped and laid around the chimney for a neat fit.

BAY WINDOWS

A *bay window* is any combination of windows which together extend out beyond the flat plane of the outside wall. It usually requires its own roof unless the bay continues upward into the second story, taking advantage of part of its roof. Although a bay window may extend from the wall of any story or level, it is mentioned here because its roof often extends up onto the second story wall, as in Fig. 7-12. Occasionally, a bay window may emerge from a second-story wall. The first-story bay window, pictured in Fig. 7-13, was constructed merely as part of the floor plan, justifying the use of "skirts" to hide the foundation supports.

Fig. 7-11. An opening is left in the subroofing to accommodate installation of the chimney.

Fig. 7-12. A bay window extends out from the wall and usually requires its own roof.

Fig. 7-13. This "standing" bay window includes extensions of the floor and foundation supports.

Construction of a *hanging* bay window, one which is not supported from below, as in Fig. 7-12, is relatively easy to complete. A large opening is left in the wall after the outside wall panels or siding have been installed. An angular, base plank is installed (Fig. 7-14). Three window units are installed along the exposed edges of this plank to form the basic shape of the bay window. Next, the roof support rafters are installed prior to subroofing and shingling.

There are many other possible configurations for bay windows which can be developed with a little clever planning. Just make sure the design of the bay window is compatible with the architectural style of the house. After all, a Victorian bay window would look grotesque on an adobe-styled house.

SECOND-STORY WALLS

Basically, the construction of the second-story walls requires the same building techniques as with the first story. The individual framing members are the same, as are the techniques of installing windows, doors, and outside wall coverings or siding. The only difference is the order in which everything is constructed. You must plan very carefully. A fireplace and chimney outside the wall must precede the installation or wall panels or siding. Let common sense guide you. Although a first-story porch roof may be started with a gable end, outside wall siding should precede the installation of the porch roof's support beams, rafters, subroofing planks, and shingles. This will all make more sense as construction of these areas actually begins.

THE MAIN ROOF

The main roof covers the major portion of the house or building. It makes little difference whether the roof covers a single-story or a multi-story dwelling, since its visual impact cannot be overrated. The main roof is a massive structure usually dominating the image of the bottled house. Located atop everything, the roof is the first structure a person will see in a bottled house. For these reasons, the roof should be carefully designed and crafted. Depending on the architectural style of the house, and the main roof should be at least interesting in shape, if not sculpturally impressive as in Fig. 3-6.

Almost every house shape has a number of possible roof configurations. The architectural style usually determines the shape or configuration of the roof. For example, although a flat roof is perfect for an adobe-styled dwelling, such a roof shape is unacceptable for a Tudor-styled house. Some study of architectural styles will help you select the correct roof for a a particular style. Many house styles are basic and plain, but have several possible roof

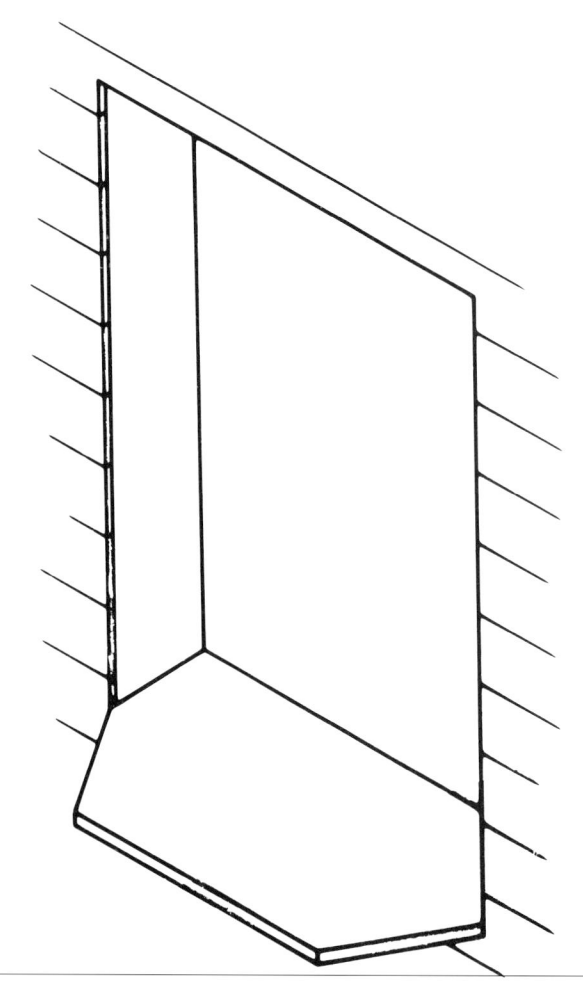

Fig. 7-14. An opening in the wall allows space for the base plank supporting the bay window.

configurations. Figure 7-15 shows how the same basic house shape may be covered by a variety of roof configurations. Diagram "A" shows only the basic shape of the house over which a roof must be located, while diagram "B" shows a simple gable roof with a dormer window. "C" shows a "hip" roof, an adaptation of the gable roof but without the gable "ends." Diagram "D" is a popular combination of both "B" and "C," while "E" is entirely different, using flat, inclined planes to form the roof shape. There are many other main roof configurations which could also be adapted to suit this particular house shape. Figure 7-15 is presented only to encourage your thinking.

Construction of the main roof is similar to that of the porch roof mentioned earlier in this chapter. It just requires a few more pieces and corners. Make sure the attic floor has been installed so you have a smooth "playing field" on which to construct the framework of the roof structure. In the roof configuration in diagram "C" of Fig. 7-15, a single vertical post of appropriate height is installed in the center of one wing of the house an inch or two from the edge of that particular wing. Exact spacing and locations are determined by you, since they can be arbitrary for the most part. Next, complete the same step atop the other wing of the house. A third vertical post is installed, forming an L with the other two posts. Horizontal ridge beams are installed across the tops of the three vertical posts linking them together to complete the L shape.

Diagonal rafter beams are sized, cut, and installed, linking the top end corners of the ridge beams with their respective wall corners (Fig. 7-16). Additional rafters are placed diagonally, connecting the ridge beams with the upper edges of the walls all the way around the dwelling. Maximum spacing of these rafters should be no more than 1 inch in most cases. Subroofing planks are installed across the rafters to provide support for the shingles or tiles (Fig. 7-17). You must keep in mind, however, that an opening in the subroofing must be provided to accommodate a chimney. Any vent pipes included in the plan will also require openings.

A roofing material is selected and applied next. You must select the roofing material which will be

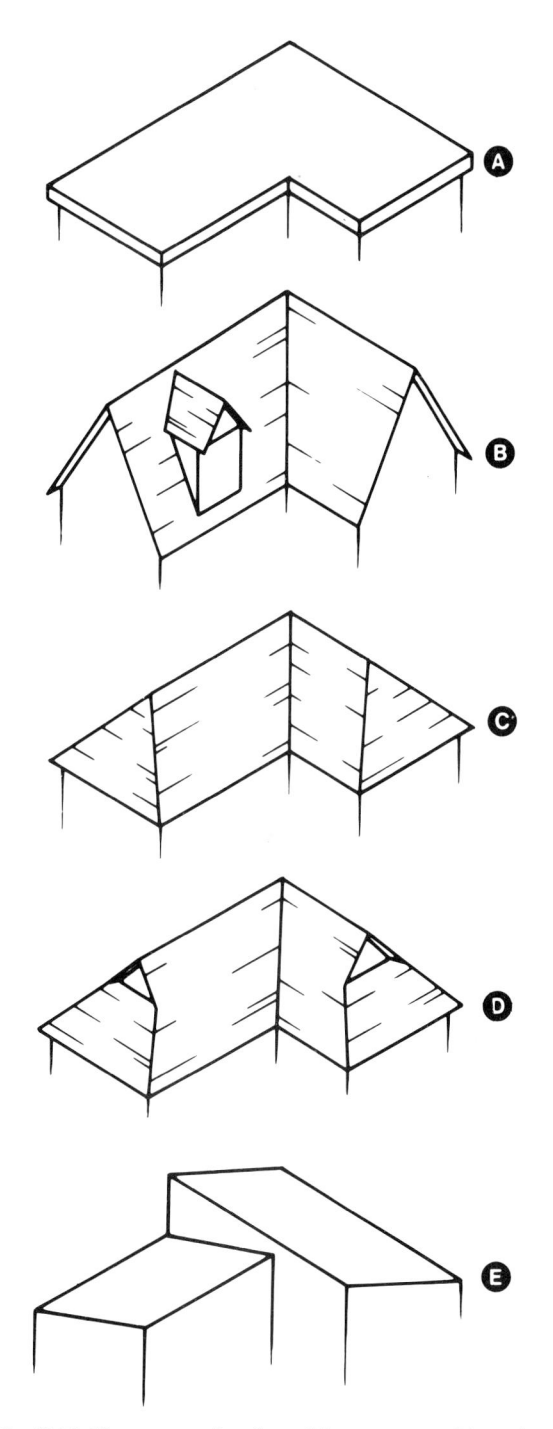

Fig. 7-15. These are only a few of the many possible main roof configurations which can be adapted for almost any floor plan. Style B includes a dormer window in the roof.

A Spanish tile roof such as the one seen in Fig. C-9 is an easy effect to produce. Paper drinking straws (plastic may work as well) are cut to 1/4 inch in length and sliced in half lengthwise. Then, they are painted with a brick-colored, flat-finished paint. Each tile is installed with the modeling-clay and bent-wire tool to avoid damage.

There are many other materials which can be adapted to look like a realistic roofing material. A real favorite is the thatched roof used on the "Hobbit" house in Fig. 2-4. Jagged splinters of oak wood were stacked and glued into place to form this roofing effect. Using your knowledge of materials as well as creativity will produce many other effective roofing materials. As important as the roof appears on a bottled house, it is well worth the effort required to create an impressive roof by using interesting materials and effective design.

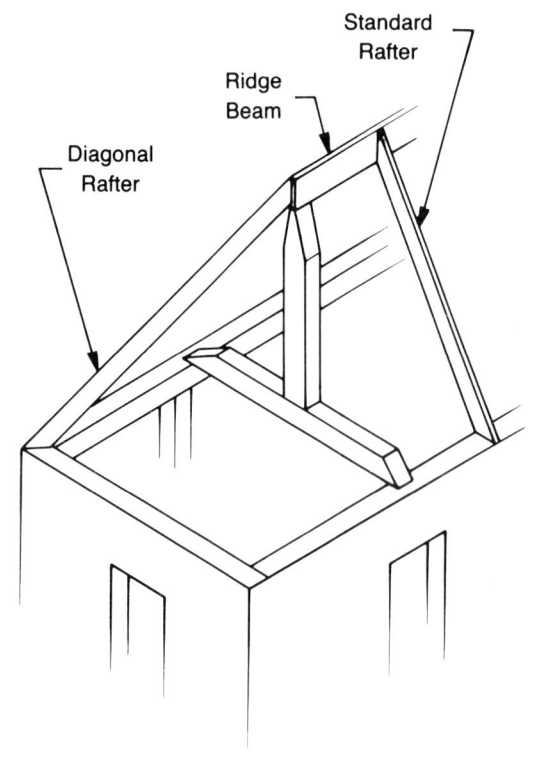

Fig. 7-16. Construction of a hip roof must include setting a diagonal rafter in such a way as to link the top corner of the walls with the end of the ridge beam. Standard rafters are installed in the usual way. Note that the rafters and the diagonal rafters may by design extend over the edge of the walls.

the most appropriate for the architectural style of the house. Some materials will not look right on a specific style of house. For example, decorative rock on tar paper would look disgustingly pitiful on a Victorian mansion. Wood shingles are the easiest to work with, especially if wood veneer tape is used, as mentioned earlier. Walnut veneer shingles were used on the Victorian mansion in Fig. C-2.

Another possible roofing material appears much like "composition" or asphalt shingles. Heavy, fabric-backed, dark-gray sandpaper can be cut into short, narrow strips with an old pair of scissors. Other sandpaper colors are also available in most hardware stores. Appropriately scaled composition shingles were used atop the Dutch Colonial house pictured in Fig. C-4.

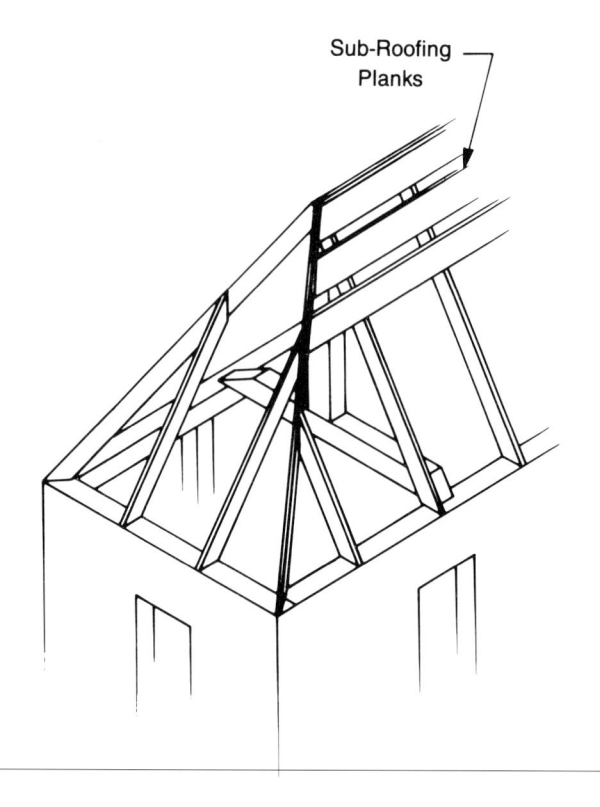

Fig. 7-17. Subroofing planks are installed across the rafters to form a solid, flat surface on which to apply shingles later.

There are many structures developing above the first story. It is easy to see the importance of effectively coordinating the construction of so many features at once. Your excitement can quickly build right along with the construction of a bottled house at this stage of development. Now, the careful planning, fine craftsmanship, and exhaustive attention to detail all seem worthwhile.

8

Building Nonwood Walls

When you consider the tremendous number of houses and other buildings in this world, you will realize that only a few are constructed of wood. Most are made of brick, stone, adobe, stucco, and other materials. Using logical simulations of these popular building materials in bottling houses creates some particular problems, however. Special building techniques, as well as unique tools, must be developed. Tasks requiring special hand-eye coordination present the builder with serious challenges in which only tedious practice and skill development will solve. Some suggestions and guidance may help prepare for these advanced effects. **STONE AND BRICK WALL CONSTRUCTION.** Walls constructed of stone and brick have always been admired for their textured and sculptural beauty, as well as their natural earth-tone colors. Many buildings just would not be as impressive if they were made of other building materials. Independence Hall, for example, might not have survived to this day if it had been constructed solely of wood. These materials are known for their durability, but despite these appealing characteristics, stone and brick construction create some serious difficulties for the bottled-house builder. Obtaining materials of the proper size or scale is a real challenge. Formulating and spreading mortar is another. Trimming the mortar between bricks and stones is an almost impossible difficulty. Most of these problems can be overcome, however, with some practice, patience, and common sense. Obtaining stones which appear of the correct scale is one of the less difficult problems. A small stone must appear large enough when used in or around a miniature house. As mentioned in Chapter 5, stones and pebbles seem to be everywhere. Select a particular size to be used in the wall construction and begin collecting as many as required. Keep in mind that rounded pebbles and stones appear more realistic and "in scale" than those which are jagged. Clean the selected stones with water and allow to dry several days before you attempt to use them. There are three ways of approaching the task of obtaining bricks. One or two sizes of real, but miniature, ceramic bricks are often available at dollhouse shops. They look as convincing as real bricks. Their quality is good, and sizes are consistent. Their disadvantages are substantial, however. Store-bought bricks are usually very expensive. The most serious problem is size availability. Usually, only two sizes are available, 1 inch equals a foot, and 1/2 inch equals a foot. Many builders construct houses at scales other than these two. House walls and chimneys made with bricks of the wrong scale will not look realistic. The builder has an obligation to the admirers of his artwork to construct realistic structures, if realism is the chosen artistic style.

Another possibility for obtaining bricks is to make homemade ceramic bricks. To do so, you will need to develop the proper clay body which will result in realistic-looking bricks. The most serious problem with this method is firing the completed bricks. Clay must be fired to at least 1200 degrees Fahrenheit in order to keep the clay from crumbling. To accomplish this, the clay must be fired in a *kiln*, a furnacelike device. Access to a kiln powered by natural gas or electricity will be a great help in brickmaking, although it is rather extreme to buy such equipment just to make a few bricks.

By far, the most effective way to obtain bricks of the correct color and size is to make wooden ones. An open-grained wood such as mahogany or oak is cut cross grain to create bricks with a linear texture running across the brick's face rather than lengthwise. First, obtain a plank of the selected wood and saw the end off square. Then, saw in almost the same manner an amount representing the desired height of the brick. You will now have one very long brick which is probably too wide or deep. Cut the long brick lengthwise again but along the top to create two very long bricks. Later, the bricks can be cut to the proper length as required for construction. Painting the wood bricks with a flat-finished paint completes the process. The tenement building in Fig. C-7 was constructed with wooden bricks, each of which was made in this way.

An effective mortar must be formulated and mixed next. A combination of 75 percent modeling paste, an acrylic polymer base containing ground marble, and 25 percent white glue makes a realistic mortar which can be tinted to the desired color by mixing with tempera or acrylic paints. Liquitex, a registered brand name, is a modeling paste of good quality, available in most art-supply stores and in some craft and hobby shops. Mix the mortar and store in an airtight container until you are ready to use it.

The actual stone wall construction is a reasonably simple task. The first layer of stones must be secured to the glass with epoxy cement. Using the modeling clay attached to the bent-wire tool or the straight version of this tool, grasp a stone with the tool. Then, dab or smear a generous portion of the mortar along the bottom and sides of the stone. Insert the stone into the bottle and set it on the layer of stones already forming part of the wall inside the bottle. Complete only one layer of stones at a time all the way around the house. Allow each layer to dry sufficiently before you add another layer. The walls of the stone castle in Fig. C-9 were constructed in this manner but without mortar. White glue, which dries clear, was used in place of the tinted mortar. Keep in mind that the mortar is an optional feature which can cause you many problems. It can run uncontrollably, smear onto the bottle glass, or drip onto the ground below.

On the other hand, very effective and attractive stone walls may be constructed without mortar by gluing one stone atop another. With a little care, the glue can be located so as not to be seen. This is especially true when using stones the size of lima beans. Lay them flat like bricks in order to improve stability. The process is not nearly as difficult as it seems. After completing a few layers, install the windows and doors as required and continue to lay the stones between and over them. Make sure the top layer of the wall is laid as level as possible in order to provide a good footing on which to begin the roof structure. If mortar is used, allow it to squeeze out from between stones. In all honesty, attempting to trim away the excess mortar from between stones or bricks, the way most masonry appears, is an almost impossible task. Acceptance of the excess, squeezed-out mortar may be the best solution.

Bricks are even easier to lay. They simply stack one atop another like child's building blocks, although you must remember to lay the middle of each brick over the crack created between the two bricks below. This traditional, brick pattern appears on the tenement building in Fig. C-7. Mortar was used in constructing the walls of this building, and the excess was left exposed and untrimmed.

Construction of a brick wall begins with carving a few bricks to fit the contours of the bottom of the bottle, while keeping the tops flat. These contoured bricks must be secured to the glass with epoxy cement. Make sure that the top of this first layer of bricks is level in preparation for the next layer of bricks (Fig. 8-1). Use the needle-wire tool to insert each brick into the bottle and set it into its proper location. Apply glue to the brick just before inserting into the bottle or apply the glue to its intended location using a wire tool. If mortar is being used, apply in the same way. Tap each brick along its top in order to properly level and set it even with its neighbor. The mortar will squeeze out from between bricks at this time.

If you feel the need to trim away this excess mortar, allow it to dry to the consistency of modeling clay first. Do not allow it to dry completely, or trimming will not be possible. A tool which will effectively trim the mortar is a narrow, wood-carver's gouge attached to a bent-wire tool. Move the gouge along the crack between bricks, cutting away the mortar (Fig. 8-2).

Insert and install a door frame before setting too many layers of bricks. Later, install windows and lay bricks between them (Fig.8-3). Floors within the brick-walled building are constructed by gluing support blocks at the desired levels on the inside of the wall and then installing wood support beams, called *floor joists*, atop these blocks. Later, flooring is glued over these floor joists. Roof support structures are constructed in the same way. Complete the brick masonry with the final layer set as level as possible.

ADOBE AND STUCCO WALL CONSTRUCTION

Adobe and stucco walls have both similarities and contrasts with one another. Actual adobe walls are constructed using unfired clay bricks covered with

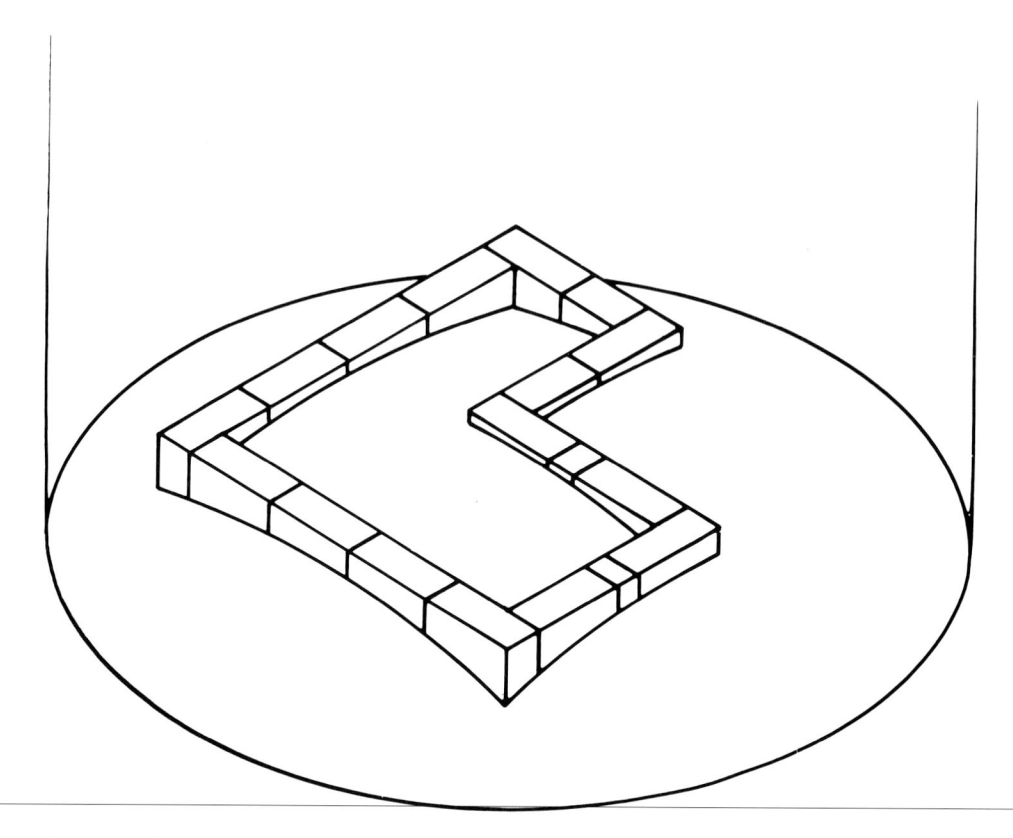

Fig. 8-1. The bricks of the first course must be shaped to accommodate the glass contour of the bottle. This should result in a level first course of bricks.

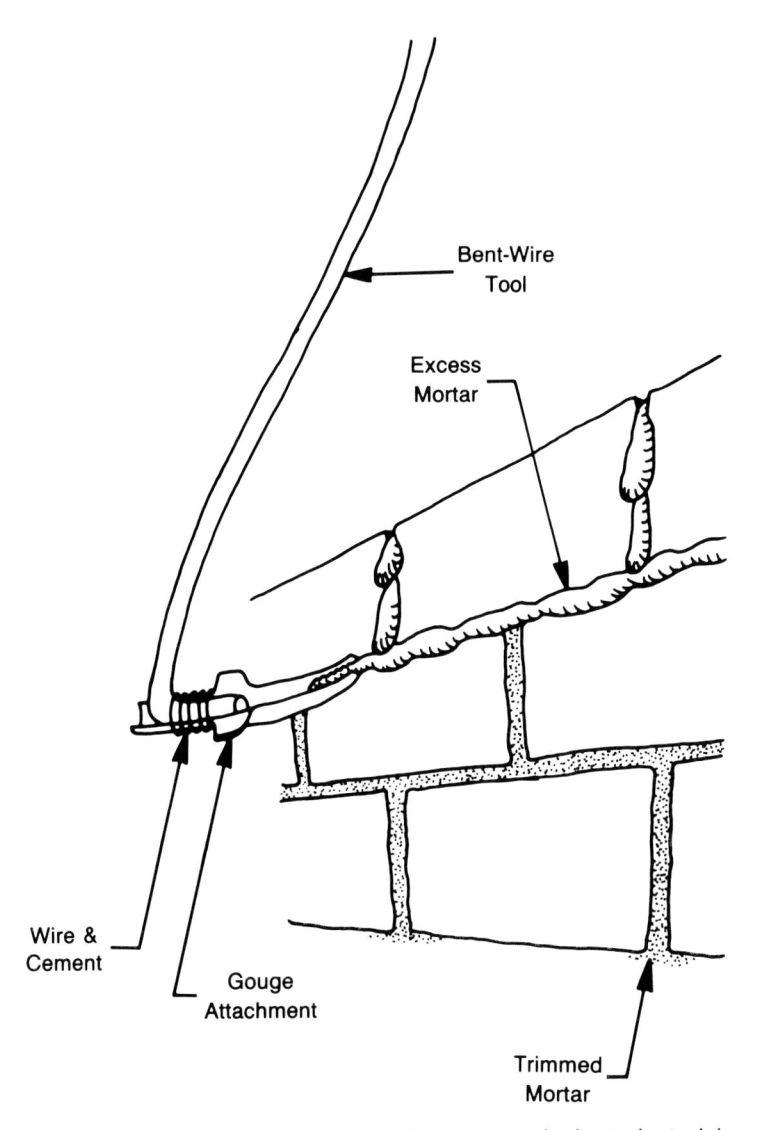

Fig. 8-2. A special homemade tool, composed of a wood-carving gouge and a bent-wire tool, is used to trim away the excess mortar squeezed from between the bricks. You must decide if the final appearance will be worth all the tedious effort.

a layer of clay/mud or plaster to keep the wall from washing away in the rain or crumbling in the winds. Real stucco walls are made by applying a special, sandy concrete mixture to chicken wire stretched over a standard, wood-frame construction or concrete block walls. Adobe wall construction is found in a number of locations throughout the world, but is best known to Americans in the form of pueblos, found in the Southwestern United States (Fig. 3-17). Stucco wall construction, on the other hand, with its characteristic earthquake resistance, appears mostly in the Southwestern United States, but is gaining in popularity in many other regions both foreign and domestic.

Both adobe and stucco walls constructed inside bottles begin with the same basic wall support. Start with constructing a wall of unpainted, wooden bricks without using any mortar. Leave openings

Fig. 8-3. After the doors and windows are installed, the bricks are set neatly between them.

for windows and doors which will be installed after the walls are completed. Build up to one full story only to allow easy access for spreading the adobe or stucco covering. Maintain smooth, exterior, wall surfaces as carefully as possible.

Spreading the exterior covering over the bricks will be the next task in completing adobe walls. Choose from a covering of wood putty, modeling clay, plaster, or any other spreadable medium which experimentation may discover. Plaster is difficult to use, because of its limited working time. Once "cured," it is too hard to spread. Modeling clay, on the other hand, will never harden, but will always have a wet, glossy finish. Wood putty avoids these difficulties, but often has some problems sticking to its intended location at first.

The spreading trowel in Fig. 4-15 is used to deliver the "mud" to the proper wall location and smear it into a smooth surface (Fig. 8-4). Apply the mud to a small area only and smooth completely before applying any additional material. Care should be exercised when applying and smoothing the mud around window and door openings. These should remain completely clear of any overhanging mud to allow windows and door frames to slide easily into their proper location. You may desire to leave some painted bricks exposed, as if the plaster or mud were crumbling away in a few spots. Plan ahead for this effect, however.

After applying mud to the entire first story, continue laying bricks for the second story, if the design calls for one. Admittedly, this mud-spreading task for adobe construction is very tedious and requires great coordination and patience. Practice on some simple walls built in a common, 1-gallon bottle a few times in order to develop the new skills required. It is amazing what incredibly difficult chores can be accomplished when you practice enough and are determined to succeed.

Applying the exterior coating of stucco is similar to applying adobe mud. The stucco effect is achieved by adding fine sand to latex house paint. The sand should be of 60-mesh particle size or smaller and is available in most ceramics supply houses and building suppliers. Start with a mixture of 1 heaping tablespoon of sand to 1 cup of latex house paint of the desired color. Add more sand or more paint to obtain the desired texture. Mix thoroughly in order to avoid pockets of dry sand floating around in the paint. If necessary blend the mixture with your hand, using your fingers to break up any lumps of sand which may resist mixing. Continue to mix or blend until a uniform consistency is achieved. Make sure the latex paint is thick enough so that the sand will not settle to the bottom overnight. The mixture should be the consistency of honey at room temperature in late spring.

Application of this stucco mixture is much the same as with the adobe mud, although the latex should flatten out by itself. Use a bent-capped paintbrush (Fig. 4-6) or the spreading trowel. Turn the bottle on its side and work on only one wall at a time. Complete the wall and allow the stucco to dry while the bottle remains on its side. Then, the next wall may be stuccoed.

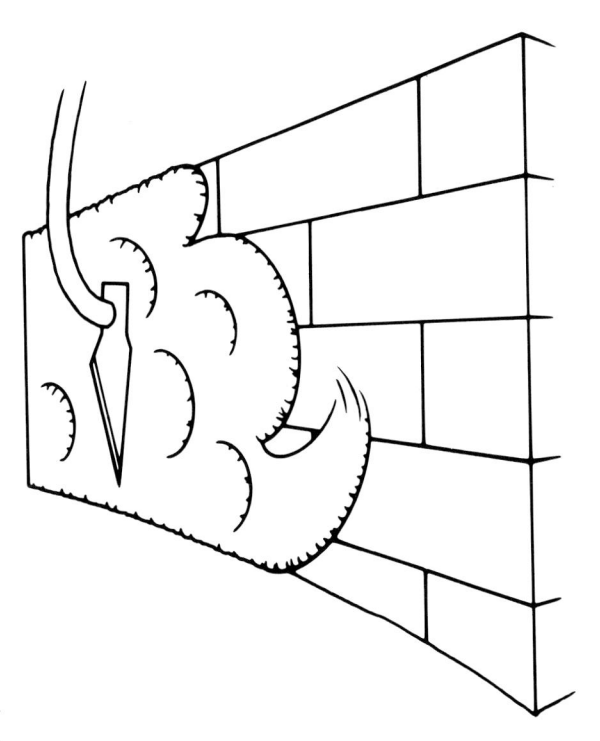

Fig. 8-4. A homemade plastering trowel is used to spread and smooth wood putty so it appears like adobe mud or plaster.

Some practice and experimentation will prove worthwhile in working with stucco. The big problem for most builders will be in keeping the adobe and stucco off the bottle glass. If some material should smear onto the bottle, let it dry completely and simply scrape it off with the spreading trowel. It is not such a terrible disaster if you are a bit clutsy now and then as long as you have the patience to clean up after yourself.

These are not all the effective wall materials with possible applications to houses in bottles. A builder with a clever imagination can easily invent new materials or adapt existing ones. Furthermore, vast improvements on the techniques of building any of the walls in this book are likely. It is a matter of being creative and performing experiments.

9

Landscaping A House

The purpose of landscaping around a house is to artistically enhance the image of the dwelling and soften its strong geometric lines. Trees, rocks, shrubs, flowering plants, and gently rolling lawns all help the house relate to and blend with the land around it. Landscaping should add to the house's appearance, but not hide it. The same is true in bottled housing. The composition created by the relationship between the house and its landscaping is important. It can be as significant to the overall image of the bottled house as the design and craftsmanship of the structure itself. Proper balance between structure and foliage must be determined. Too little plants and trees will look naked and "just planted," while too much landscaping may appear overgrown. Plant variety also contributes to the effectiveness of the composition. A healthy level of variety is achieved by combining vertical shrubs and trees with horizontal bushes and plants. Potted plants can also add to the variety and development of composition. **FOLIAGE MATERIALS.** Materials intended for use as foliage must have realistic characteristics. They must look like real plants at a much smaller scale than the real ones. Naturally, shape plays the most important roll as a characteristic. A realistic shape for a bush might be round or squatty, while a shrub would be more vertical. Ferns, vines, hedges, cacti, and other plants with specific, recognizable shapes must be formed or constructed with materials which best suit their particular needs. Proper color is another important factor used to increase the effects of realism. For example, rather than use a plant material composed of just one color of green, *variegated coloring*, the use of several similar colors on the same area, will help increase realism. New growth is usually recognized by brighter shades of green, sometimes by a yellow-green, while old foliage remains in a deeper green or even in a brown if it is dead or dying. The important rule to remember is to avoid using one color of green for every plant around a bottled house. If you wish to be even more accurate, make sure the trunk and branches of bushes, trees, and shrubs are represented in at least one shade of appropriate brown. Although often difficult to control, texture plays a roll in creating realistic plant effects. New growth should be represented by finely textured groups of material, while older growth is indicated by larger, more-mature-looking textures. Several plant-looking materials are available from a number of sources. One material providing a variety of realistic shapes and excellent textures is that of lichen, a natural-growing mosslike plant pictured in Fig. 9-1. Life-Like Products, Inc. of Baltimore, Maryland, prepares Lychen in dyed colors of green and brown. This material

Fig. 9-1. Materials which may be considered for use as landscaping include (from left to right) plastic aquarium plants, lichen moss (unpainted and painted), and air ferns (untrimmed and reassembled).

is used extensively by architectural model makers, model railroaders, and some floral arrangers. End sections, which contain the newer growth of the plant and the most realistic textures, can be cut or torn into portions appropriately sized and shaped for miniature shrubs, bushes, and trees.

To improve the coloring, each lichen portion can be dyed with light brown or tan leather dye. This process will dye the entire plant one color of brown, but at least the trunk and branches will be of the correct color. The foliage can be painted with several colors of green using enamel paint. Merely brush the paint over the outside foliage areas, allowing the trunk and branches to remain brown. Using a dry-brush technique, apply a goldie-green to the new growth areas of the miniature plant. Use several colors of green. All this transforms the lichen into a miniature bush, shrub, or tree foliage of remarkably realistic quality.

Figure 9-1 shows another useful material called the *air plant*. It is usually found bound in bunches, dyed an unnatural green, and available in some nurseries, plant stores, and gift shops. Each stem appears very fernlike, but the air plant's origins are mysterious. Some accompanying literature claims that the air plant is really an animal, although there has been nothing to substantiate this origin. The air plant can be washed in water to fade the bright green dye color. Standing alone, a stem of the plant appears much like a miniature Norfolk Island Pine. By detaching some of the lower branches and gluing them together at the stem, a very natural-looking fern is created. The tip of a single stem of the air plant can be planted in a miniature planter, later destined for a window sill or porch.

Parts of artificial water plants, made of plastic and intended for fish aquariums, often make an outstanding bladed cactus, as seen in Fig. 9-1. Feathers can also be trimmed and colored to represent plants and trees. The palm tree standing near the Cape Cod house in Fig. C-6 was made partly from a group of feathers. Small ferns can also be made from this useful material.

MAKING TREES

Trunks and branches of trees create particular challenges for the builder. First, make sure there is ample room remaining in the bottle around the house to accommodate a tree. One problem is finding a tree trunk with branches attached which together with added foliage create the illusion of appearing like a miniature tree of realistic quality. Your backyard garden and local nurseries are possible sources. Do not try gathering vegetation, living or dead, in protected areas. The bottled house in Fig. 3-19 contains a tree whose trunk and branches wee once part of a store-bought Manzanita bush.

Another problem is inserting the tree and its branches into the bottle. Although the foliage is inserted and attached to the branches later, there exists a real challenge in installing the trunk and branches without damaging them. Sometimes, they can be bent or folded enough to slip through the bottle neck without breaking. Another approach is to remove the troublesome branches and reattach them later, inside. This technique will allow easier passage of the main body of the tree. Once inside, the tree trunk's base is maneuvered towards its intended location using the bent-wire tools. Glue points may include the trunk's base, as well as spots where the branches make contact with the house. Apply glue to these points using the bent-wire tool and allow overnight drying. Next, the recolored lichen foliage is inserted by hanging it on a bent-wire tool and pushing it through the neck. Once positioned on the end of a branch on which glue has been applied, the tool is disengaged from the foliage and withdrawn from the bottle. Continue this process until the entire tree has been constructed inside the bottle.

PLANTERS

Planters help increase the appealing charm of a bottled house by providing a lived-in look to the outside of the building. A planted flower box here and a ceramic planter there will make a quiet house appear far more than abandoned. A variety of planters will help provide an artistic composition or image, while using the same kind of flowerpot everywhere may appear boring, diminishing the magic created by the overall bottled house. Several kinds of planters are pictured in Fig. 9-2.

Miniature planters can be found in a number

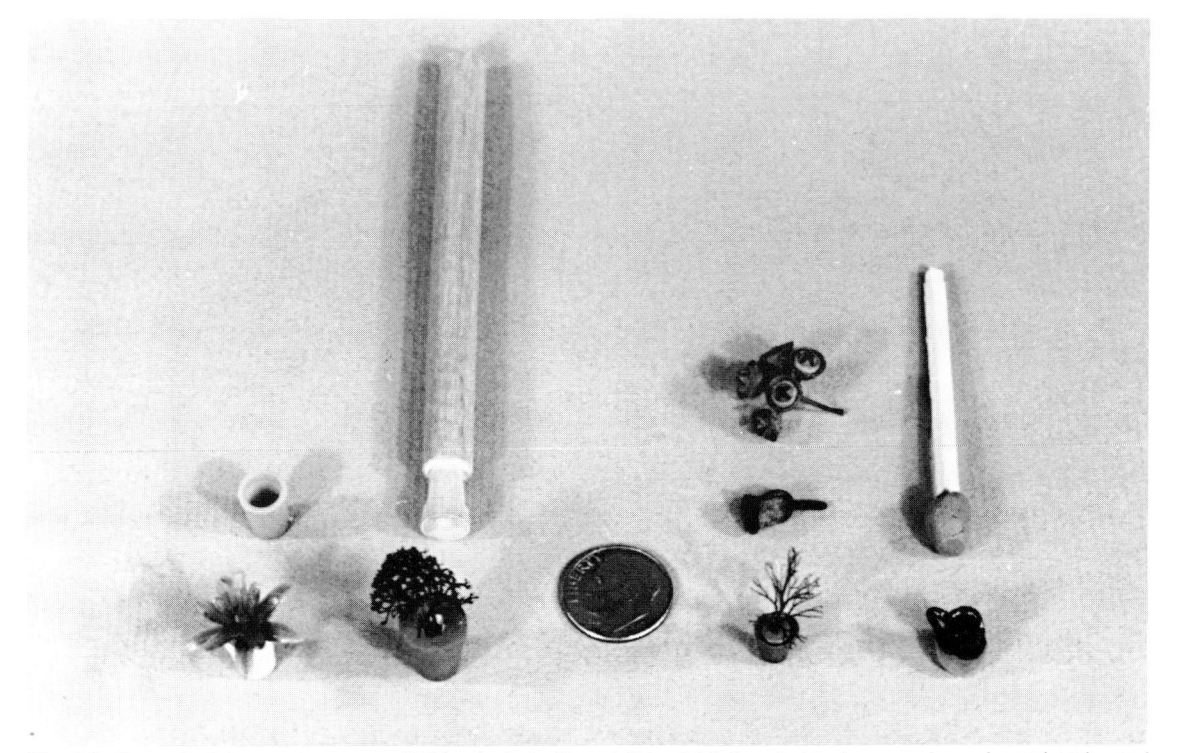

Fig. 9-2. Several miniature planter possibilities include (from left to right) found objects, carved wood, seed pods, and handmade clay vessels.

of places. Some may be purchased in dollhouse and miniatures shops. Others may be fashioned from seed pods and other found objects, as seen in Fig. 9-2. Planters may be made from wood, plastic, or ceramic materials. The only problem with some of these is making them fit the scale of the environment in which they are to appear. For example, buying a flowerpot is easy enough, but it may actually be twice as large as it is intended. This condition will appear awkward and phony. Perhaps the best solution to the planter size problem is for you to make your own pots.

The standard nursery flowerpot (Fig. 9-3) is very simple to construct. A wood dowel is selected, the diameter of which corresponds to the widest diameter of the pot. A cleanly cut end of the dowel becomes the top or rim. Drill a 1/16-inch-diameter hole 1/16 inch deep into this end of the dowel to allow for the plant. The tapered upper section is carved with an X-acto knife first, and the lower tapered body of the planter is shaped last. Then, the planter is parted cleanly from the dowel using a knife or small hobby saw. Refine the pot's surface with sandpaper before painting with a "terra cotta," flat-finished paint. Dirty the paint job with the dry brush technique described earlier using flat-finished gray and tan paints. This should complete a very believable, miniature flowerpot, the size of which will fit the scale of the house. Plant with colored foliage (Fig. 9-2) and install the planter atop a railing or on a porch using the modeling clay attached to the bent-wire tool.

Real ceramic planters create a charm and realism all their own (Fig. 9-2). They are more difficult to make than the wooden ones, but are intriguing nonetheless. If you are fussy about details, you may wish to make your own ceramic planters; however, you should keep in mind the extent of preparation and special equipment required to produce such a small detail. After all, even the most particular of admirers can hardly tell the difference between a good-quality wooden planter and a real ceramic one. Nevertheless, some people find miniature pottery making to be fun. First, try forming a piece of clay the size of a very small pea around the head of a wooden match. Twist the match out of the newly formed clay vessel. Allow the clay pot to dry and fire in a kiln. Apply glaze as desired to the sides, insides, and rim, but not on the bottom. Otherwise, the planter will stick to the kiln shelf during the firing. Next, glaze-fire the pottery to the proper temperature. If you have no experience in pottery making, it is very wise to work with someone who has knowledge of kilns, glazes, firings, temperatures, etc. After proper cooling, remove the pot from the kiln and plant it with some foliage. It is surprising how great these will look.

No doubt, an inventive person will think of many other materials which can be used as foliage and planters. Using your imagination and some common sense, new plant ideas can be created. You must realize, however, that, like the house, the landscaping is expected to last for ages. Materials selected for use as plants should be tested for characteristics of longevity and durability. Foliage materials must be dry, to begin with, and remain

Fig. 9-3. The shape of a typical nursery flower pot is simple and easy to duplicate in a miniature version.

that way. Otherwise, mold and rot may spread throughout the bottle and may even obscure the view. On the other hand, the material should not be so dry and brittle that it will crumble later. All these possible problems should be considered when sorting through prospective foliage materials. Sometimes, half the fun is experimenting and creating.

10

After Completion of the House

Construction of the bottled house has been completed and all the challenges have been met. Now you can enjoy the personal satisfaction of such an extraordinary achievement. The importance of careful planning as well as some clever inventiveness have been recognized, and much has been learned. Hopefully, completion of this first work will inspire thoughts and planning of another. Some important considerations may be how you can improve design, construction techniques, and craftsmanship. Critical evaluation of your most recent bottled masterpiece will generate these improvements. While gaining valuable experience, people learn much from their successes as well as their mistakes. These lessons may result in vast improvements in the next bottled house you attempt. **SOME REMAINING TASKS.** Two additional tasks must be completed before you set the bottled house on the display shelf. The inside of the bottle must be cleaned once more. Use the homemade wire bottle scrubber (Fig. 3-4) to remove the remaining dust and debris clinging to the inside glass surfaces. Work very carefully, scrubbing around the bottle without damaging the house and landscaping. Some areas of the bottle may be inaccessible to the scrubber because of the close proximity of the house to the bottle glass. Try making a smaller scrubbing tool using a single wire and a smaller cloth pad. Modeling clay on the end of a wire tool will be useful in picking up any dust and debris attached to the house. Inspect the neck area of the bottle and remove any excessive dried glue smears. The needle-wire tool can be used to chip away the dried glue. Some observers believe that some dried glue deposits in the bottle neck are acceptable, if not desirable, because the smears help convince disbelievers that the house was indeed constructed inside the bottle. This is an option of the builder. The other required task involves the bottle closure. The cork, stopper, cap, lid, or other device will seal the bottle from the outside atmosphere. A tight-fitting closure will keep dust from entering the bottle. Some builders may feel the need to seal the bottle permanently by applying epoxy cement to the upper neck area prior to sealing with the closure. This will help prevent anyone from tampering with or changing the artwork inside. Closing the bottle in this manner seals in the remaining moisture, creating its own atmosphere surrounding the house. This slightly moist atmosphere, some believe, is useful in keeping the glue and building materials from drying out excessively. Such drying might result in the crumbling of some parts of the building structure and landscaping. Some builders may not wish to seal the bottle permanently with cement. In this case, the closure should fit snugly to avoid falling from the bottle when tipped or turned upside down. Invariably, some admirers will want to see the bottom and how the house is attached to the bottle. Others will want to see if some hidden opening exists on the bottom. Nevertheless, everything including the closure should be secure in anticipation of any such eventuality.

CARE OF YOUR BOTTLED HOUSE

Your bottled house will always be sensitive to extremes. Excessive temperature, light, vibration, and violent shocks will contribute to the deterioration of the bottled house, no matter how well it is constructed. After all, it was designed and built to last for ages. Once completed, a bottled house deserves to be treated with respect. It hardly seems right to diminish its chances for survival through neglect or carelessness.

A bottled house is a fragile piece of artwork that is susceptible to intolerable temperatures. Excessive heat is especially harmful. High temperatures can melt the modeling clay used as the earthen base around the house. It may also weaken glue joints, permitting the structure to crumble. Bottled houses should not be displayed on heaters, fireplace hearths or heat-exposed mantels; in hot, sunlit windows; in automobiles in the summertime, or near any other heat source. Cold temperatures are usually not as harmful as hot ones. The cold will cause moisture to condense on the inside of the bottle. This condensation will disappear, however, soon after the bottled house is returned to average room temperatures. Ideal temperatures for bottled houses range from around 50 to 100 degrees—not that 107-degree summer temperatures will cause any serious problems. Caution should be exercised to avoid causing *thermoshock*, the sudden change from one temperature extreme to another. For example, avoid storing the bottled house in a cold, unheated room and suddenly moving it to some hot location. If there are any flaws in the bottle glass, as many antique bottles have, thermoshock may cause the glass to crack or the bottle to shatter.

Strong light is another harmful element. Almost everyone has witnessed how window drapes fade and later deteriorate from the effects of the sun's light. Similar changes will occur in a bottled house when it is exposed to strong light for long periods of time. Painted surfaces and landscape foliage are especially susceptible to the ravages of excessively strong light. As mentioned earlier, the sun-exposed windowsill should be avoided as a display area for a bottled house. Powerful light sources used in display cases should be used in moderation to avoid these fading problems, as well as the accompanying high temperatures. Flash photography and the temporary use of strong, photographic, flood lamps should not result in any permanent or serious damage, although you should always be concerned with quickly increasing temperatures.

Excessive vibration may result in damage to your newly completed masterpiece. Do not use an electric engraving tool to label or sign the bottle. An engraver operates like a miniature jack hammer, sending strong shock waves through the glass. If there are any flaws in the glass, cracking or shattering may result. Instead of using an engraver, a rotating handheld grinder, like the Dremel Moto-Tool, with a small abrasive bit will complete the labeling job safely and neatly. Similarly, setting the bottled house on vibrating or moving machinery or even on or near a stereo loudspeaker may cause irreparable damage to the bottle. Again, common sense is always a good guide.

As with any fragile object, a bottled house should be handled with care. Violent shocks cause the most serious damage. For example, an aggravated cat knocked over and shattered the bottled house pictured in Fig. C-8. Although the artwork is but a memory now, the cat is still at large. If only the bottle had been tied securely to a small hook near its wall shelf, it might still be in fine shape today, despite the moods of the cat. Another piece of history, pictured in Fig. 10-1, was broken by an overly enthusiastic admirer at an art show. The stones composing the mountaintop inside the bottle created a misleading weight problem. When the art fan lifted the bottled house, he misjudged its real weight. It slipped from his grasp and fell to

Fig. 10-1. The apparent weight of this bottled house was misleading and resulted in it slipping from the grasp of an admirer. Heavy stones composing the mountaintop greatly contributed to its weight.

the concrete floor.

Care should be exercised when setting the bottle on hard surfaces, such as glass tabletops, concrete, marble, stone, and other similar surfaces. Some thin-walled bottles must be set on these surfaces very "softly." If these conditions are realized, disasters can be avoided.

If the bottled house must travel, a few precautions will help it survive. First, try to keep the bottle in an upright position. Otherwise, while being bumped around in transit, the house may become detached from the glass surface and experience extensive damage as it thrashes from side to side in the bottle. The bottled Victorian house in Fig. 2-15 met such a fate while traveling to an exhibition in Japan. Furthermore, pack the bottled house in a strong, crush-resistant carton or box of some kind. A wooden crate or heavy, corrugated-cardboard box will do very well. Next, surround the bottle with sheet-type packing material, rather than the small, individual beads. Sheets of bubbled plastic are especially effective for packing bottled houses. The bottled house in Fig. 7-1 successfully traveled halfway across the United States, while the one in Fig. C-1 arrived safely in New York from California. One traveled by automobile; the other flew with its owner. Someone once said, "An ounce of prevention is worth a pound of cure." It is an accurate observation.

Although some builders strive to better their most recent achievement by starting a new one; others may feel the need to "quit while they are ahead." All who have met their challenge by completing it, however, should be inspired by, and take advantage of their success. Therefore, you should be encouraged to consider your next bottled project. You should take advantage of the newly acquired skills and knowledge developed from this first building experience. Be adventurous in designing and building the next house. Take some chances and experiment with new and different materials. Obviously, you cannot learn and develop without trying something new. Above all, you should always keep in mind that, with only a few exceptions, your artwork will remain for many to see long after you have passed on into history. For this reason especially, your work should exemplify your attempts at achieving excellence.

11 Bottling Ships

For hundreds of years, bottled ships have intrigued mariners and landlubbers alike. Perhaps it is because a ship-in-a-bottle, like macramé, maritime paintings, ship models, scrimshaw, wood carvings, and other artwork of nautical themes is a symbol of passing events, and is like theater and other live performances in that it can only be remembered once it is over. An event is there to enjoy (or to loathe) only for the time at which it occurs, and then it is gone but for its memory. In contrast, a motion picture is an event which can be replayed and enjoyed (or despised) again and again, while it remains exactly the same each time it is relived. Similarly, a photograph of an event can be studied to help recall the foggy details of all that occurred at that particular time. Long before photography and motion pictures, mariners had only shipboard crafts to remind them of their voyages. Bottling ships is such a craft. The actual act of building a ship in a bottle was also a form of recreation for the often idle and bored mariner. During long ocean voyages, these sailors had hours of personal time in which they were not working or carrying out the duties of operating the ship. There were few books (assuming they could even read) and no video games or movies to occupy the free time. Sailors had to find or invent pastimes other than drinking, sleeping and fighting with one another. Their sources of building materials were limited to what was on board the ship or found along their travels. Wood, bone, ivory, sail and clothing cloth, tar or pitch, sail thread, rope, and a few other materials were adapted to compose inventive artwork. When beverage bottles began appearing on board their ships, mariners found a way to make use of them in their crafts. One of the attractive features of the bottles is that they presented the mariner with substantial challenges. If bottles were to be used to contain an object, the artist had to invent clever methods in which to insert the object. It became like a complex puzzle as it evolved into a very time-consuming challenge. **A DESCRIPTION.** It is difficult to determine when the first bottled ship was constructed. Some museum examples seen today date as far back as the middle of the 18th century. As bottlemaking techniques improved the glass quality of the bottles of that time, sailors began to experiment with different methods of bottling their favorite watercrafts. These were constructed both on board ship and on land while in port. Some mariners, yearning to return to the sea, would fill their idle hours by building whole fleets of bottled ships while they waited for another voyage. Sometimes, the completed ships were cast adrift in the ocean in hopes they would wash up on some faraway shore, a novel sailing adventure in itself.

A definition of a bottled ship is offered, like that of the bottled house, to serve as a set of governing rules. These rules preserve the integrity of a genuine ship-in-a-bottle and eliminate imposters which make use of bottle cutting as a way to achieve only a fraudulent effect of a real bottled ship. An authentic *bottled ship* is composed of a handcrafted boat, ship, or other watercraft contained in a glass vessel that has a restricted opening or neck. The watercraft inside must be built up with individual sections, as in the case of the tugboat seen in Fig. C-10, or unfolded inside the bottle, like the one pictured in Fig. C-11, in order to effectively fill the interior space of the bottle.

The resulting image reveals a vessel, which in its completed state, never could have passed through the bottleneck. And, so, the magic of the bottled ship is created. Admirers will wonder how it came to be there, and, perhaps try to imagine what tools and techniques were employed to achieve such an accomplishment. Children especially will be mesmerized by the mystery of the ship-in-a-bottle. Having little or no knowledge of tools or building techniques, they imagine tiny elves who climb into the bottle with tools and wood to perform their secret and creative deeds.

Bottled ships are regarded with great charm and popularity throughout the world. There are several international organizations whose purpose is to actively promote the ship-in-a-bottle as a recognized art form. These organizations are located in Japan—sporting a membership of over 300 craftsmen—several European groups, and at least one chapter in the United States. A builder can join the Ships-In-Bottles Association of America by simply sending annual dues of $10 for North American members to the address in the Appendix. Membership is open to any person in the world regardless of his expertise level in bottling ships. Dues are slightly higher overseas. A very worthwhile publication, *The Bottle Shipwright,* accompanies the membership. Included in the publication are drawings, photographs, and helpful articles about construction tips, exhibitions, and other interesting pieces of information.

SOME CLEVER VARIATIONS

Since bottled ships have been produced for centuries, they are more popular and numerous than bottled houses. An average bottled house usually requires around 400 hours to complete, while the average bottled ship consumes only around 30 hours. Such popularity and relatively short construction time have generated some fantastic variations of bottled ships. These unusual compositions employ images and ideas which far exceed the creativity promoted by the common, traditional bottled ships. Some terrific examples are presented here in order to inspire you to consider building a similar stylized ship-in-a-bottle. After all, creativity is using the human intellect at its best.

The bottled ship appearing in Fig. C-12 is a clever statement capable of amusing most people. Perhaps the builder's theory is that all kinds of creatures have the ability to "put" a ship into a bottle. Consider the difficulty the artist encountered in building the ship in its unusual location in the bottle. How was the monkey attached to the ship? That is the magic of this kind of inventive bottled ship. You can experience real problems trying to figure out the techniques required of a design of this type.

There are days when we all have our "ups and downs," but the poor fellow seen in Fig. C-13 appears to be having more than his fair share of misfortune. It is interesting how the ship acts as the bottle closure, while in the preceding bottled ship, the monkey serves as the closure. Notice how large the figure in the bottle appears. Although the glass helps to magnify the real size, the lucky fellow "living" in the bottle had to be inserted limb by limb and adjusted into a reasonably comfortable position. There seems to be no end to the capabilities of the human imagination.

In Fig. C-14, the enchanting combination of sea gulls, whale, and lighthouse inside the decorative bottle closure contrasts with the main vessel containing a shipbuilder adjusting the mast of the sailing ship sitting in front of him. Planks of wood and several tools lie around the bottled work area. The man had to be inserted in sections, assembled inside, and located at the bottom of the bottle. Later, the sailing ship was inserted into the bottle, also in sections, assembled, and rigged. Notice the macrame "Turk's Head" tied around the neck of the bottle. All of these features make for a very impressive composition worthy of any museum, boat, ship, or home.

A Pinch Scotch bottle (Fig. C-15) holds a *plank-on-frame* sailing ship in the early stages of construction and its builder. Plank-on-frame construction is regarded by most knowledgeable craftsmen as the ultimate in model ship building. The accuracy of the ship's hull construction is phenomenal. It is constructed almost exactly like the real thing. Individual framing members called *ribs* are shaped to the desired contours of the hull and mounted on a miniature keel. Then, planks of wood are attached and bent to conform to the contours of the ribs. For a bottled ship this construction process is further complicated by having to build in sections small enough to be inserted into the bottle. The successful result is an amazing feat of craftsmanship and engineering. This particular bottled ship includes tools, wood shavings, glue pot, and brush. As with the previous bottled person and ship, the figure of the builder was inserted in sections, assembled, and positioned first. The plank-on-frame hull was inserted into the bottle last, section by section. It is a significant piece which fascinates everyone.

Fig. C-16 shows a bottled sailing ship in which tiny people are seen building the plank-on-frame construction. This is another intriguing way of enhancing the magic of the bottled ship. Each individual worker had to be carved from a section of toothpick. The ship, a privateer called *Virginia*, is of an especially graceful design, which forms a very effective and artistic composition within this particular bottle. The closure is likewise interesting as well as functional. The turk's head tied around the bottleneck finishes off the piece. A work of art as great as this is well worth everyone's admiration.

Another extraordinary piece is seen in Fig. C-17. A Pinch Scotch bottle contains the coach scene from the novel, *Great Expectations*. This remarkable composition depicts a coach mired in mud, while four, tired horses strain vigorously to pull their charge free. As passengers squirm impatiently atop the coach, the driver is seen exercising his whip. The attention to detail is astonishing. Even the horses are wearing authentic harnesses. Straps are buckled across the leather-looking baggage. The passengers are all wearing authentic clothing of the era. The closure appears much like a crown, appropriate for this subject. You must consider the order in which each component had to be installed inside the bottle. The material representing soil had to be placed in such a way as to appear like fresh mud. Then, the rear wheels and axle were plunged into the muddy earth. Next, the front wheels and axle were inserted and positioned. Sections of the coach's body were installed, as were portions of each horse. The passengers were inserted in one piece. Although it is neither a house nor a ship, it is an amazing variation, proving that almost anything, even difficult subjects, can be adapted for bottling.

Figure C-18 shows a sinking S.S. *Titanic* immortalized in a liquor decanter. Inside the glass closure stands a lighthouse, a navigational aid the original *Titanic* certainly could have used. The surface of the water is represented by a thin, ridged sheet of plastic, shaped to conform to the inside contours of the bottle. Irregularly shaped blocks of white foam rubber were used to hold the plastic sheet in place. An opening in the sheet accommodates the ocean liner and holds it in the correct position, the same as in which the real *Titanic* sank. The ship model itself is too large to fit through the bottleneck as a single assembly and had to be inserted in sections. The smoke billowing from the liner's stacks is really blackened cotton. This model makes for a very accurate way of honoring a once grand liner.

The harbor dredge appearing in Fig. C-19 is a surprising work of art. Its intriguing attraction is that the dredge itself can actually be operated by manipulating the lines streaming out of the bottleneck. The dredge scoop can be maneuvered to pick up material from the water, rotate back over the vessel, and lower the material onto the dredge. This is a great example of what can result after extensive and careful planning. There are a number of moving parts operating inside the bottle. Careful thought and planning had to precede construction in order to allow so many parts to function smoothly. Remember, too, these are not kits purchased in some local hobby shop. Each of these little marvels were constructed from scratch. Notice the details, including fire ax, searchlights, signal flags, and deck equipment, which help make this an amazing bottled ship.

Years ago Vic Crosby was a fire fighter aboard the Seattle fireboat *Alki*. During his retirement, he constructed a scaled model of the *Alki* in a bottle. The fireboat is shown sailing past the famous landmark, "The Seattle Space Needle" in Fig. C-20. This highly detailed, bottled fireboat is complete with water cannons, life preservers, railings, and deck equipment. A fire fighter aims a water cannon, shown shooting a stream of water, which splashes against the inside of the bottle. This is a novel use of the imagination, which adds to the model's ability to help knowledgeable admirers recall and express events from the past. Even engine exhaust pours out of the boat's stack. A red fire hydrant acts as the bottle's closure, a very clever and amusing statement for this particular work of art. This work is a very special expression of the pride of a man whose past was once a part of the fireboat's history. It is profoundly endearing to others to share some significant, personal experiences.

An Arabian dhow (Fig. C-21) was constructed in a 1-quart liquor bottle. It is a scaled model and required extensive research prior to construction. Ancient and foreign watercraft provide the builder with hundreds of possible subjects not otherwise considered for bottling. This dhow is accurate even to its unique rigging. The vessel's hull was inserted into the bottle in sections and assembled inside the bottle. Later, the masts and rigging were added. The bottle closure is a curious, snakelike chain of wood.

Figure C-22 shows *Hornblower's Flotilla*. Astonishingly, there are six ships sailing in the quart-sized liquor bottle. Each seems to contain the same amount of detail as found in singular ships-in-bottles of high quality. This is no small accomplishment. Appropriately, the artist has constructed a cannon barrel as the bottle's closure, an effect which is both clever and functional.

A Spanish galleon constructed of bone fills a half-gallon bottle in Fig. C-23. Historically, models made of bone were constructed by prisoners in faraway jails. It seems that bones were the only plentiful building material available. This particular bottled ship is very effectively composed. The ship fills the bottle without the bottle appearing too crowded or underfilled. The model itself is extremely accurate for the difficult type of ship it represents. The extensive rigging provided an admirable challenge to the builder. The billowing sails are handsomely constructed as well. The Turk's Head knotted around a cork is very characteristic of the decorative macrame found on the ships of the 17th and 18th centuries. This is one of those museum-quality pieces most everyone would be proud to display in their own homes.

Imagine all the memories a bottled aircraft carrier must hold for a former crew member. The U.S.S. *Constellation* sailing in a bottle is pictured in Fig. C-24, while the actual vessel is shown in Figs. 12-35 and 12-36. Squadrons of jet aircraft are among the incredible details included with the bottled version. Each jet fighter is a highly detailed, miniature work of art in itself. One jet is seen being launched from the bow of the carrier as exhaust smoke streams from the aircraft's tail nozzle. A second fighter is seen landing amidships. The mast atop the carrier's superstructure is cluttered with antennas, weather equipment, radar, and other devices. The authenticity of the many details of this model help make the aircraft carrier believable even to experts. Of course, not every piece of equipment or detail can be represented at such a small scale; however, enough are included to be very convincing. The bottle closure is rather impressive as well. It is in the shape of a massive anchor chain, ending with the anchor itself. The shapes of the chain links and the anchor are easily recognizable. The resulting statement presents a symbol of formidable power and dependable stability.

Figure C-25 reveals a decorative liquor decanter holding the fishing boat, *Sina* as it encounters rough seas. The glass stopper holds a small sailboat also dancing from wave to wave. Since the builder of this bottled fishing boat, Vic Crosby, was once her master, the *Sina* is especially well-detailed and complete. Rigging, deck equipment, wheelhouse, and sail are all represented and clearly recognizable. The angle at which the boat is engaging the large swell quickly draws the attention of passersby. They cannot help but take a second look. The statement made by this bottled memory is appealing to one and all. Clearly, "It's a tough little boat that endures the harsh punishment of an unremitting sea," is a personal appreciation which a sea captain can especially feel toward his favorite vessel. The creation of an ocean swell is extremely effective. This boat is a good example of how you can express important personal feelings through a usually "quiet" art form. The success is evident.

The famed ocean liner, S.S. *United States*, fills a bottle in Fig. C-26. This is a very colorful ship requiring many delicate details. Over 20 individual lifeboats, including their davits, line her upper deck. The ship's patriotically painted smokestacks dominate her image. Cargo cranes, both forward and aft, appear fully rigged. Even tiny deck equipment and ventilators are included in the form of many individually installed parts. Tennis courts adorn the stern and upper decks of the ship. It is interesting to imagine all the pains the builder endured in order to include so many windows for such a complex vessel. Such devotion to detail, however, has made this bottled ship an especially impressive one. An admirer can examine her for hours, trying to discover where the builder had to section the different portions of the ship to allow it passage through the bottleneck. Even the colorful bottle closure—knotted heavy cord—speaks to the pride of such a grand liner. It is easy to recognize that many hours of work have been invested in completing this splendid work of art.

Miniature bottled ships and scenes can be among the most amazing and incredible works seen anywhere today. Inside the tiny bottle in Fig. C-27 is a scene showing a man at his workbench, building a ship in a bottle, while his son and two dogs look on. A ship-in-a-bottle being constructed inside a bottle is an exceptional feat! The artist's attention to detail continues to be his greatest trademark. Behind the tiny man stands a miniature stool. Atop the workbench lie tools and building materials. The little boy is carrying an unbelievably small sailboat. Maybe he is waiting his turn at the workbench in order to bottle his own boat. Tiny liquor bottles like this one are often sold on commercial airlines during flight and in some liquor stores. Such variety among the many bottled ships makes the art form even more intriguing.

Bluenose, a Gloucester schooner, sails in a 500-watt, light bulb (Fig. C-28). This schooner is fully rigged with eight billowing sails. Each sail is lined to make it appear as if ropes had been sewn into the sails for added support, a practice necessary in the days before modern, more durable sailcloth. *Bluenose* is a beautiful ship worthy of its place as a subject for bottling. The composition formed by the arrangement of its sails in relation to its hull is a very appealing one. Adding further to the attraction of this particular work of art are the graceful lines of the light bulb, contrasting with the rustic texture of the cork fishnet float used to support the bulb. The use of the knotted Turk's Head is an effective way of finishing the top edge of the glass. The selection of a large light bulb reveals resourcefulness on the part of the builder as he strives to provide lively variety among his many bottled masterpieces.

In Fig. C-29 a decorative liquor decanter, standing vertically, holds the racing sloop *Intrepid*. The decanter's glass stopper is filled with a whale and a finishing boat. The rigging and sails of the larger vessel are exceptionally accurate and complete. The sails, made of stiff paper, had to be shaped and pressed into a mold in order to hold their authentic, windblown billow. Since the scale of this craft is larger than most, more details are included, and accuracy is greater as well. A human figure is seen relaxing at the helm. Many easily recognizable pieces of deck equipment are seen aboard, including ventilators, winches, pulleys, and cleats. The *Intepid* fills the decanter, effectively creating a pleasing composition, appealing to all admirers.

Mysteries and legends are often the bases for interesting bottled ships. One such piece is the ghost ship *Mary Celeste*, seen bottled in Fig. C-30. The real two-masted, square-rigger was found floating abandoned in 1910. Not a single crew member was ever found. There were no signs of a struggle, and the cargo was still loaded neatly in the ship's hold. Interestingly, this ship is mounted in a bottle which stands vertically rather than on its side as most do. The bottle once contained wine, as evidenced by the vine design pressed into the glass. The ship is constructed with the usual attention to detail and extreme accuracy associated with all the works of Vic Crosby. The completeness of the rigging is at its usual high quality. In contrast with the serious-looking ghost ship is the colorful parrot hanging from the bottom of the bottle closure. An intricately carved, wooden stopper seals the bottle, adding another interesting touch.

Although not a bottled ship, the airplane constructed in a liquor bottle in Fig. 11-1 is worthy of attention. This aircraft is called the B-1, Boeing's first plane. This biplane is composed of incredible details. Lines, which help hold the plane together, run from the front of the fuselage to the rear of the craft. Even tiny ribs in the wings can be seen stretching through the wing skin. A pilot, sitting in the plane's cockpit, awaits permission to take off. To the rear of the plane sits an empty cargo cart and a hangar doorway. This is a very impressive piece of work, which again illustrates how almost any object can be bottled. The builder simply must have some imagination.

Another interesting use of an artist's imagination is seen in Fig. 11-2. A submarine floats, half-submerged, in a solution of glycerine. The glycerine appears like water, but will not promote the breakdown of wood and paint nor permit the growth of algae. It is a novel idea that a ship can actually float around, possibly for many years, inside a bottle. Most bottled ships rely upon artificial water, which must remain stiff and still. Using real liquid adds a touch of spontaneity and realism, which all admirers can appreciate. The model is of the submarine *Nautilus*, launched in 1954 as the world's first nuclear-powered warship. In order to keep the model floating just right, the hull had to be carved and later balanced with weights. This keeps the vessel from tipping or capsizing. After the hull was inserted into the bottle, the conning tower, now often referred to as the *sail*, was added and secured. Later, the glycerine was

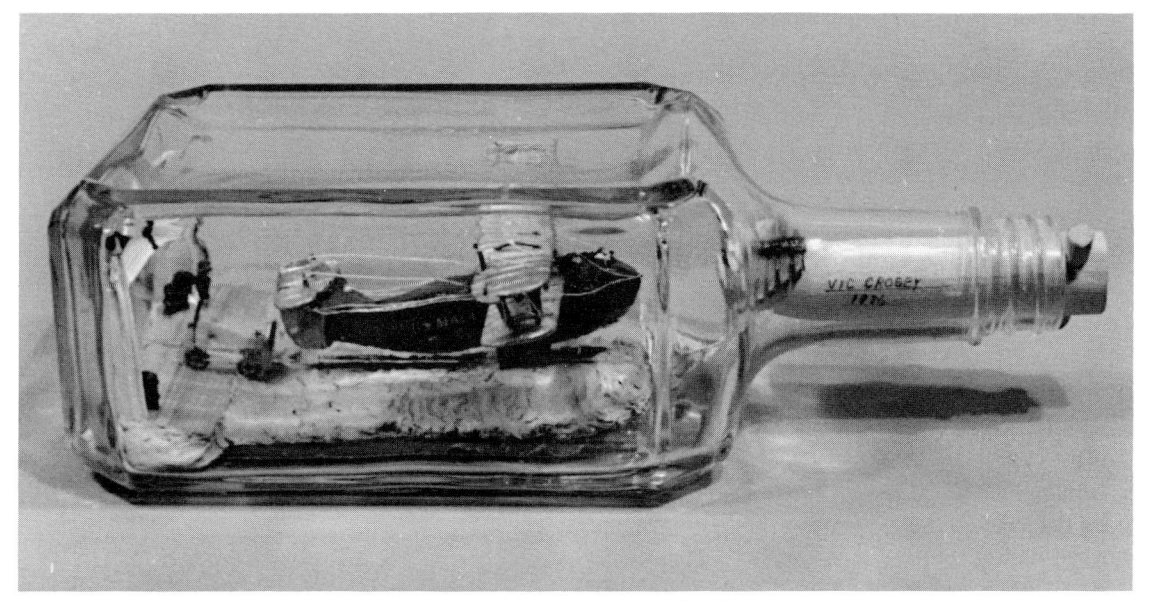

Fig. 11-1. This bottled airplane, the Boeing B-1, was constructed by Vic Crosby.

Fig. 11-2. A bottled submarine, constructed by Vic Crosby, actually floats in a sea of glycerin.

poured into the bottle, allowing the vessel to float. This is a prime example of how your inventiveness can create significant charm and delight for others.

There are many other fine bottled objects of art. Many artists and builders of astonishing skill and craftsmanship only occasionally receive the recognition they deserve. I hope this book will help to develop greater appreciation for these builders and their craft.

There are so many other subjects suitable for this art. You merely have to use your imagination and be observant of your surroundings in order to select a subject worthy of bottling. There are many more objects and ideas besides houses and ships. The continuing study of construction techniques which follows will greatly aid you with whatever is chosen for bottling.

12

A Few Types of Watercraft

Before you can begin construction of a bottled ship, you must select a specific watercraft. Unlike some bottled houses, which can sometimes just evolve spontaneously, a bottled ship must be carefully planned and represented down to the very last minute detail. If not, accuracy and believability are diminished or even lost. Worse still are the assembly disasters, occurring through lack of planning for a specific goal. For most builders of bottled ships, authentic representation and attention to detail are of the utmost importance. Careful planning ensures this authenticity and accurate detail. Only after selecting a particular ship or boat may such planning begin. Otherwise, what may be intended as a dignified vessel could disintegrate into a depressing shipwreck. A ship or boat must be designed and constructed from a single, well-conceived concept. Vessels just cannot be tacked together one part onto another like a rambling ranch house, or they will not be seaworthy. At this point, clarification of some terms is in order. The word *watercraft* is used to include every type of floating vessel, large or small. *Vessel* is its synonym. The word, *boat* is used when referring to small vessels and some German submarines, while large vessels are called *ships*. It might be useful to know at what point a boat becomes a ship. The purpose of this chapter is to provide some possible maritime subjects for bottling. Sometimes, any ideas are worthwhile. After all, some landlocked craftsmen may not have access to much in the way of maritime resources, and a few suggestions could be helpful. This is by no means a complete collection of possible boats and ships, but rather just a handful of interesting vessels worth considering. It is surprising to realize the vast numbers of modern-day watercraft found in use these days. Furthermore, it is more than mildly astonishing to consider how many different kinds of vessels have been constructed since the beginning of recorded history. All together, the numbers of both modern and historical watercraft are staggering. Add to them the variety of foreign vessels, both historical and modern, and such a wide selection may seem bewildering. A novice builder may encounter some difficulty in trying to select a vessel from such a large variety. Choices may be made from a number of watercraft classifications, including but not limited to, passenger, cargo, military, pleasure, ceremonial, and service- (work-) oriented vessels. Most of these types will have historical and foreign counterparts, further complicating the selection process. Keep in mind that bottled art is not limited to houses and ships. The techniques promoted in this book may be adapted very easily to accommodate the bottling of almost any desired subject. Aircraft and automobiles are especially likely candidates. They can be constructed in manageable sections on the outside of the bottle, disassembled, and installed piece by piece through the neck. For example, you would start by installing the wheels of either the automobile or the aircraft, linking them together with an axle, and adding the body and fenders or fuselage and wings later. Almost any favorite subject can be adapted for bottling. It merely requires careful planning and some dry run assemblies outside the bottle prior to final insertion.

WORK VESSELS

Perhaps the largest group of watercraft is composed of those vessels which perform services throughout all the oceans, harbors, and waterways of the world. The kinds of services performed by these work vessels are far-ranging, as the following examples indicate.

Tugboats

A big favorite among many builders is the *tugboat* (Fig. 12-1). No busy harbor that accommodates large commercial ships should be without tugboat services. Tugboats are popular because of their great importance to the smooth, efficient operation of a harbor. Further, their sturdy, upturned design is appealing in itself. Understandably, the tugboat stands as a symbol of the Protestant Work Ethic, promoting hard, uncomplaining work. These traits of the tugboat make it popular.

Although tugboats vary somewhat in size, the basic shape and configuration remain fairly standard throughout the trade. Always present are the bumpers, usually truck and car tires, lining both sides of the tugboat and used to reduce damage and slippage when contacting another vessel. A heavy bumper adorns the end of the bow, providing a prominent identifying characteristic. The wheelhouse, which encloses the helm, is perched atop a main deck cabin, enabling the helmsman to enjoy an ample view of the waterway ahead and along the sides. A large traditional smokestack is usually located just behind the wheelhouse, despite the fact that most tugboats are diesel-powered these days. The boat is slung low in the water concealing a massive, deep-draft hull. Together, these features combine to create a handsome composition worthy of the effort required to bottle it. Figure C-10 shows a bottled tugboat of realistic style which I constructed at age 17. A tugboat of this type would also lend itself well to altering its design into a whimsical style, if the builder so desired.

A new tugboat of revolutionary design is shown in Fig. 12-2. It is propelled through the water using paddles, rather than propellers. It can move backwards as easily as it can forwards, and is often seen running backwards instead of taking the time to turn around to travel with its bow forward. Amazingly, it can even move sideways. Special paddles move the vessel directly to starboard or to port, permitting enormous ease of maneuvering. This new tugboat is a fantastic improvement on an important harbor work horse.

Fishing Boats

Commercial fishing boats are also members of the work boat list. Fishing boats of one type or another are found operating out of most of the harbors of the world. Consequently, there are many kinds of boats whose sole purpose is the gathering of seafood. This group of boats is composed of trawlers, lobster boats, purse seiners, and diving boats for abalone and crab.

The *purse seiner* in Fig. 12-3 has a fishing net shaped much like the configuration of a lady's purse. After a school of fish is sighted, usually from the crow's nest atop the boat's mast, a smaller boat, riding on the stern of the fishing boat, is launched in order to distribute the fishing net out and around the school of fish. Then, the net is drawn up towards the fishing boat, condensing the catch. Individual fish are snagged, brought on board, sorted and packed in ice down in the hold of the boat. Purse seiners come in many sizes, although their general shape and equipment must remain fairly standardized. The large pulley and crane is used to pull in the heavy net laden with fish and water and later the net boat. Almost always present is the highly-perched crow's nest. The stern of the fishing boat usually slopes or tapers down towards the wa-

Fig. 12-1. A typical harbor tug is composed of a very distinctive shape, which has evolved over its many years of specialized use. Every tugboat feature must be made to function with exceptional efficiency.

Fig. 12-2. This revolutionary tugboat is a good example of state-of-the-art technology which controls every aspect of the vessel's overall design. It is the ultimate in maneuverability and efficiency.

129

Fig. 12-3. A large fishing boat, called a *purse seiner*, hurries to its berth after being out to sea for several days or weeks.

ter to allow easy launching and retrieval of the net boat.

Fishing boats of all types represent another classic tradition of the seas and serve as excellent subjects for bottling, like the *Sina*, seen in Fig. C-25.

Carriers

The most extensive group of modern work vessels are those which transport raw materials and finished goods throughout the world. These include freighters, tankers, container carriers, ore carriers, and car carriers. Nations which enjoy access to the oceans and waterways benefit greatly from the relatively low-cost water transportation of goods and materials provided by these vessels.

Common *freighters* are probably the best known of all these ships. Figure 12-4 shows a common freighter characterized by cluttered decks and a forest of cranes used to load and unload cargo from the ship. Massive hatch covers seal the openings of the cargo holds in the hull of the ship. One, and sometimes two, towering superstructures, composed of cabins, the bridge, radio room, and wheelhouse, are spaced along the top surface of the ship's hull. Freighters come in a wide variety of sizes, depending on the space requirements and nature of the intended cargo. So, there is no actual common or typical freighter these days, but rather many design configurations of a single ship classification. A very accurate bottled freighter is seen in Fig. 12-5.

Modern technology has contributed to the development of the *container carrier* as a more efficient transporter of cargo. Container carriers are ships designed to transport the boxlike, truck-trailer

Fig. 12-4. A typical freighter sails out of Los Angeles harbor. Notice the on-board cranes or booms used for moving cargo to and from the ship's hold.

containers filled with goods and products from a variety of countries. After the goods are loaded into the truck-trailer it is driven to the loading docks alongside the container carrier. There, a special container crane is used to lift the trailer box (container) from the detachable truck frame and wheels and deposit it onto the ship. Locking devices secure the containers aboard the ship. Scores of containers are stacked neatly on the container carrier seen in Fig. 12-6. A container ship, carrying stacks of multicolored cargo containers on its decks, would make an easy-to-build, but interesting subject for bottling.

Oil tankers are becoming increasingly visible in today's ports throughout the world. More countries are increasing their dependance on imported petroleum because of developing industrialization and skyrocketing population growth, requiring the use of additional petroleum transport vessels. Although oil-producing nations employ extensive pipeline and railroad systems to transport petroleum products to landlocked importing nations and countries without seaports, they use the cheaper, ocean shipping wherever possible. There are many different tanker sizes and design configurations. Sizes range from small petroleum barges seen in most harbors to massive super tankers stretching several city blocks. A typical oil tanker is seen in Fig. 12-7.

Ore carriers are transports designed for the purpose of carrying vast quantities of loose, usually dry, materials. The ore carrier in Fig. 12-8 often transports coal along the west coast. These ships are especially popular in the Great Lakes region of

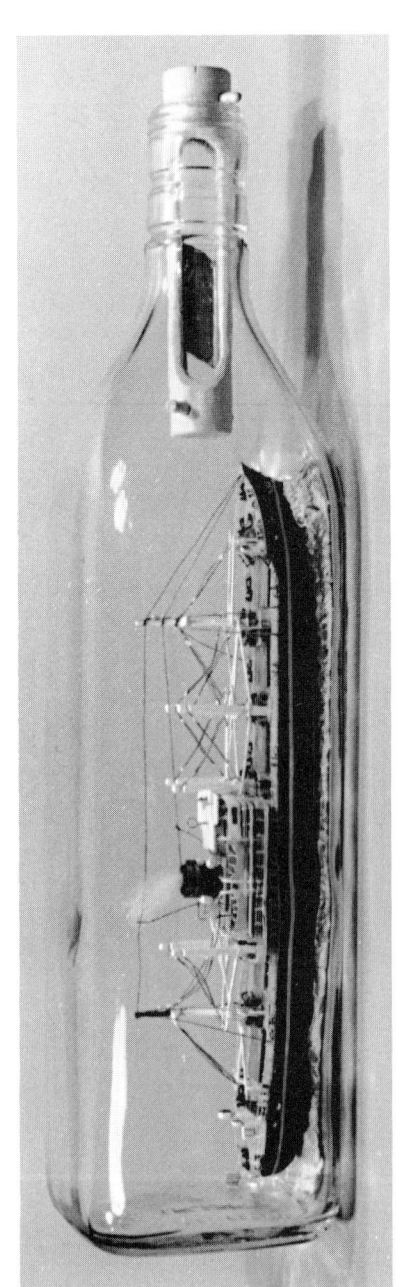

Fig. 12-5. Despite the ship's small scale, Vic Crosby's bottled freighter shows the details of the cargo booms and hatch covers.

Fig. 12-6. A container carrier, its decks loaded with truck-trailer cargo, arrives in port and will be unloaded in a matter of hours rather than days.

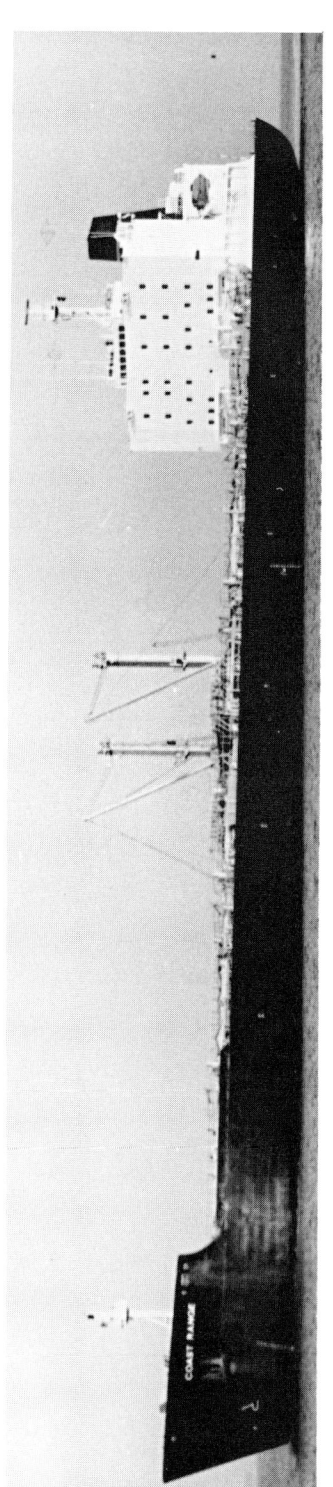

Fig. 12-7. A fully loaded oil tanker, distinguished only by its pipes, valves, and pumps on deck, is guided through a harbor channel by tugboat.

Fig. 12-8. Ore carriers are capable of transporting great quantities and varieties of bulk materials in their specially designed holds.

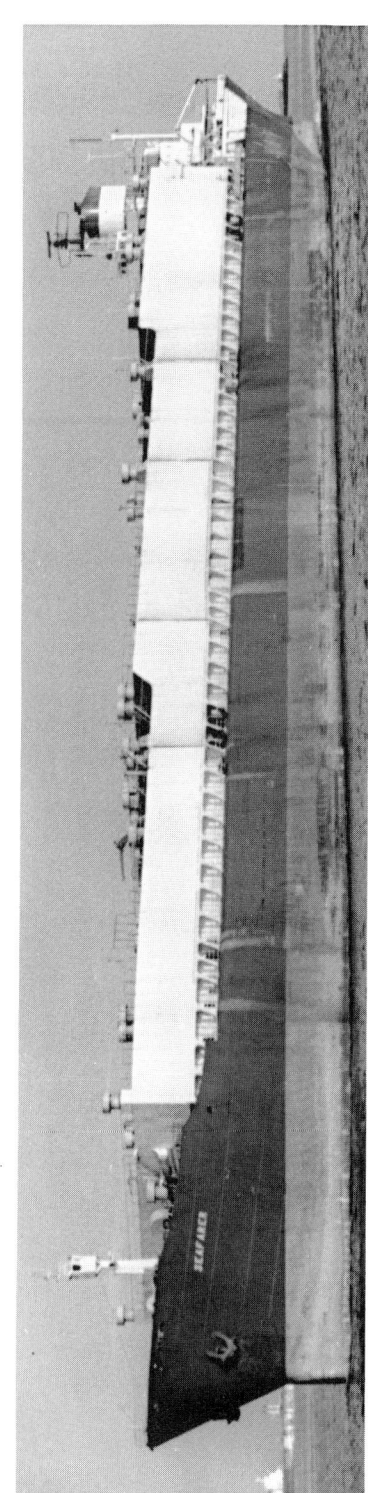

Fig. 12-9. The automobile carrier is another specialized transport vessel whose design has evolved solely for the carrying of cars.

the United States, where the transport of coal and other minerals is in great demand. Ore carriers look much like freighters. They usually have a great superstructure emerging above the ship's stern, while several enlarged cargo openings lie along the main deck and extend through the remaining length of the ship. Some ore carriers are equipped with conveyor devices for loading and unloading the ship. As popular as these ships are in some parts of the world, the ore carrier is an excellent subject for constructing in a bottle.

Probably the strangest looking cargo transport ships are the *automobile carriers*. Nations which export autos to overseas countries must employ these special transports. The shapes of these car carriers were specifically developed to accommodate the loading, careful transport, and unloading of motor vehicles. The transport ship in Fig. 12-9 is an example of an automobile carrier. It is easy to see that the relatively lightweight cars can be carried on each of the many extra decks of these ships, rather than only in the ship's cargo holds in the hull. Some of the car carriers are equipped with large, curved, two-laned, driveways, attached to the ship's stern, allowing two cars to drive onto or off of the ship at the same time. Otherwise, driving ramps are attached along the sides of the ship. This is a very unusual cargo ship which can be counted on to create a real conversation piece, whether bottled or not.

Fireboats

Every harbor should enjoy the security of adequate fire protection. Rarely is land-based fire equipment effective enough for fighting fires on ships out in the harbor or at dockside. The *fireboat* has evolved as a powerful firefighter for use in the water access areas of the harbor. These vessels are capable of shooting extremely strong streams of water onto dockside warehouses and ships, using heavy-duty water cannons mounted on the craft's decks and atop special towers. The fireboat seen in Fig. 12-10 is the oldest such vessel on the West Coast of the United States. Because it is so well equipped and exceptionally effective in fighting harbor fires, no newer models have been considered for replacing it. A smaller, modern version (Fig. 12-11) helps out, but lacks the dignified stateliness of the older fireboat. Fireboats are irresistably appealing as subjects for bottling.

Water Taxis

A problem has always existed for the crewmen of the ships which lie at anchor inside or outside a harbor. The crew must find transportation from their ship to the docks, or they must remain on the ship for days at a time until the ship is moved into the dock area for loading or unloading. Long ago the ship's lifeboats were used to send the men ashore, requiring extra effort and preparations to launch and retrieve these boats. It was only a matter of time until an enterprising businessman began providing badly needed boat rides to and from the anchored ships. The *water taxi* was born. Taxis come in all sorts of shapes and a few limited sizes. Some taxi companies are composed of nothing more than surplus vessels and other bargains. That means some water taxi companies will sail a flotilla of dissimilar boats, while other companies use a fleet of nearly identical vessels. In Fig. 12-12 appears a West Coast water taxi. Although relatively small, a taxi filled with happy crewmen would make an interesting subject in a bottle.

Barges

Barges are usually lrge, boring, platformlike vessels which require a powered vessel to pull or push them around. These platforms are often used to haul a great variety of goods or materials on quiet waterways. Although it may not seem very significant nor the least bit worthy of interest, a barge may be the center of the working world to the seaman who spent a career employed on one. Barges are used to carry railroad tank cars filled with chemicals, petroleum, gases, and wastes. Others are used to carry truck-trailers containing manufactured goods, agricultural products, and mountains of quarry rock, coal, sand, and other bulk materials. These are not seagoing vessels; they sail, instead, on quiet inland waterways and lakes. Some

Fig. 12-10. The many pieces of equipment found on this fireboat are essential to the accuracy required of any fireboat model.

Fig. 12-11. Even smaller fireboats contain distinctive pieces of fire-fighting equipment required on accurate models.

Fig. 12-12. Water taxis are composed of simple but distinctive shapes.

never leave a particular harbor. They usually perform some specific service such as transferring fuel to ships or moving supplies to isolated settlements. Underwater diving operations are often conducted from the decks of specially equipped barges, as shown in Fig. 12-13.

A subject of this nature intended for bottling would require extensive detailing in order for it to be recognized and understood by somebody other than the builder. It is often the multitude of details which help create the magic of a bottled ship. These details might include a tiny diving helmet lying on the barge's deck, tools hanging on a cabin wall, and the products of a recent dive, such as an old ship's cannon and other salvaged artifacts. The clutter of both coiled and tangled ropes, shoes, buckets, pipe valves, and many other logical objects could add greatly to the realism and charm of this model.

Other Work Boats

A similar vessel is the work boat in Fig. 12-14. This type of boat is capable of a variety of tasks, and would be perfect for tending lobster traps, towing small barges or other boats, providing a diving platform, transporting small amounts of cargo, and even being used for a little recreational fishing. The *Walrus* in Fig. 12-14 is composed of one of those irresistably appealing designs which would form the basis for a very effective and charming bottled boat.

Wildly exotic and strange are the shapes of petroleum exploration vessels, which are currently gaining popularity throughout the world. These ships are usually very large in order for increased stability in rough seas. Long counterbalanced arms and towering drilling derricks add to the ship's bizarre appearance. Decks littered with many pieces of important-looking equipment help complete the complicated image. Since these vessels play such an important role in the quest for additional petroleum finds, an exploration ship would make an impressive scene inside a bottle. Considering the large number of individuals now working on such ships, a bottled model might enjoy surprising popularity.

There are many other work-related vessels throughout the world and also passing through history. An entire book could be devoted to all the different kinds. You must determine which type of watercraft will make the most important statement about yourself. Extensive research may be required to reveal enough information about other work vessels, but careful research may contribute to the accuracy required to make a model successful.

Fig. 12-13. Barges come in many shapes and sizes, depending upon their intended function. This one is equipped to facilitate harbor diving jobs.

Fig. 12-14. The *Walrus* is a work boat. Judging from its deck equipment, it is probably used extensively for towing small barges and boats.

137

Fig. 12-15. Although the typical canoe is composed of a very simple and graceful shape, its design affords maximum efficiency.

RECREATIONAL VESSELS

The recreational group of watercraft includes both public as well as private vessels, all of which are used for the purpose of promoting recreation of one form or another. It is also a large classification of vessels ranging from the very small (Fig. 12-15) to the incredibly large (Fig. 12-16). Most people regard these watercraft favorites as particularly appealing because such vessels symbolize fun and relaxation. In contrast, the other types of vessels remind us of hard work or war.

Probably the most popular watercraft of this group are the privately owned *motorboats* and *yachts*. They began gaining prominence during the

Fig. 12-16. The *Queen Mary* is perhaps the greatest and largest passenger liner to ever sail the seas. Its distinctive appearance is easily recognized around the world even to this day.

Fig. 12-17. Even a seemingly simple sailboat requires sophisticated and accurate rigging.

Fig. 12-18. A *yawl* is a popular, recreational, two-masted sailing vessel in which the helm is located in front of the rear mast.

Fig. 12-19. Another popular, recreational, sailing craft is the *ketch*, in which the helm is located behind the rear mast.

1920s, and their numbers have skyrocketed ever since. Both sailboats as well as motorized watercraft are represented in this classification, as are vintage and modern vessels.

Sailboats

Some of the most enjoyable of all the recreational vessels are the sailboats. They come in an enormous assortment of sizes and designs in both one and two masts. Although three- and four-masted sailing vessels used for the enjoyment of private individuals are rare, they do exist, and they contribute greatly to the romanticism of sailing on the seas.

Single-masted sailboats, such as the *sloop* pictured in Fig. 12-17, are more affordable and, therefore, more popular. Although the basic design is more or less standardized, some minor differences do exist. The shape of the hull, for example, may vary somewhat among vessels. The *catamaran,* a vessel formed by the joining of two hulls side by side, and the *trimaran,* a three-hulled vessel, are examples of exotic hull designs employed today. Cabin shapes and their arrangement on the deck also vary. Sails come in basic sailcloth white or in bright colors, and even in multicolored combinations. To the weekend sailboater, no other vessel can hold a candle to his very own favorite. As simple as it may seem, a typical sloop can become an important subject for bottling in the eyes of its owner and perhaps others as well.

Although not as popular as the single-masted sailboat, the two-masted vessel is being seen in increasing numbers in most ports of the world today. There are two basic versions of this craft. One is the *yawl,* a two-masted, fore-and-aft rigged vessel in which the aft mast, or *mizzenmast,* is located behind the steering wheel, or *tiller* (Fig. 12-18). The other vessel is a *ketch,* a two-masted, fore-and-aft rigged craft in which the mizzenmast is located in front of the steering tiller (Fig. 12-19). The significance of the location of a minor mast may not seem great to most people, but it is a big deal to the owner of a yawl or ketch. Both types of sailing vessels would make simple, but interesting, subjects in a bottle, whether you own one or not.

Motorboats

Motorboats and motor yachts compose a large group of private recreational vessels. They have a wealth of sizes, ranging from small, but swift motorboats like the one appearing in Fig. 12-20, to huge, motor yachts (Fig. 12-21). Their shapes or cabin configurations are as varied as their sizes. Some, like the one pictured in Fig. 12-22, are equipped with massive apparatuses for the purpose of private recreational fishing. Although motorboats and yachts are probably a little more difficult to

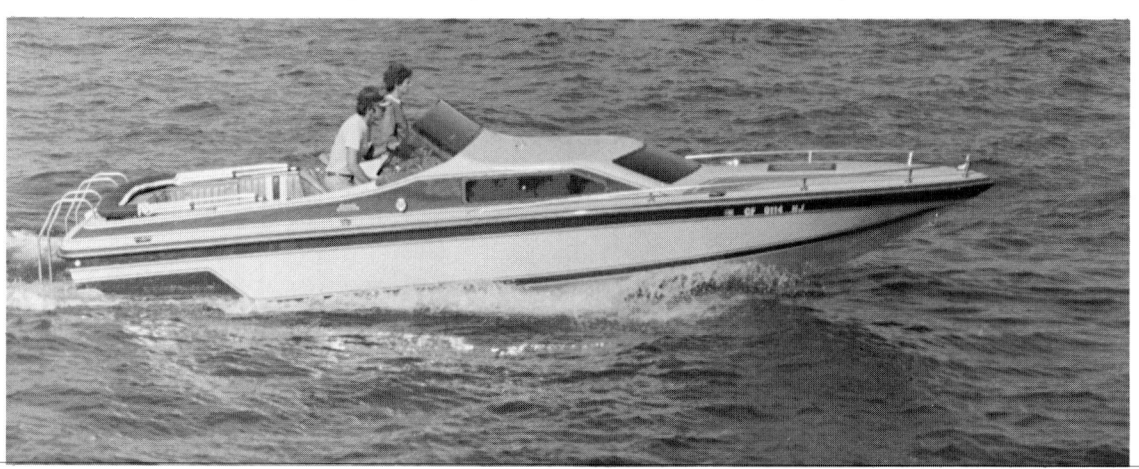

Fig. 12-20. Affordable by many, the popular people's boat, better known as the outboard or inboard/outboard motor boat, is widely seen throughout the world.

Fig. 12-21. Motor yachts come in a variety of shapes and sizes, from big to enormous, and are regarded as special toys reserved for the very wealthy.

Fig. 12-22. Some private yachts are specifically outfitted for sports fishing, allowing their owners to avoid the congestion found on some public, day-fishing boats.

143

build, they can make graceful and stately subjects for filling a bottle—maybe even a bottle which was once emptied aboard such a boat or yacht.

Other Recreational Boats

Other recreational vessels are not confined to private use, but are nonetheless worthy of mention. Without a doubt, one of the most impressive recreational vessels afloat is the *cruise ship*. Once they were called *steamships*, in the days of coal-fired boilers and steam pistons. In their heyday during the middle of the twentieth century, they were referred to as *ocean liners*, and had famous names like *United States, Queen Mary, La France,* and *Andrea Doria.*

Modern ships of this type are mainly used for touring and recreation, rather than as vessels for traveling from one location to another. Some cruise ships merely sail out into the ocean for a few days and later return without ever visiting another port. Nevertheless, the passengers are happy and relaxed as they enjoy shipboard fun and recreation. It is a time when the destination is less important than traveling in style. Today's cruise ships are fast and sleek, almost like streamlined airliners of the sea. The liner *Tropicale*, stands at dockside in Fig. 12-23. A slightly older, but just as gracious cruise liner hurriedly exits Los Angeles Harbor in Fig. 12-24, as it begins its search for fun.

Although they may be more difficult or challenging to build, depending on your point of view, than the average vessel, cruise ships make

Fig. 12-23. The design of a modern cruise ship provides easy classification with its graceful lines and many windows. This one, the *Tropicale*, typically offers almost every conceivable form of sea-going recreation and entertainment for the pleasure of its passengers.

Fig. 12-24. A slightly older (identified by its dated lines), but equally fun-filled, liner sails out of the port of Los Angeles. Although somewhat more complicated to bottle because of the many windows, lifeboats, and other essential details, cruise ships are appealing to most people because they usually symbolize "the good life."

especially appealing subjects for bottling. Their attraction may be based on the fact that a liner stands as a symbol of luxury, relaxation, and the meeting of new friends. What ship classification could offer more?

The *tour boat* is another recreational vessel making significant and increasing appearances in the harbors of the world. Most harbors or ports are intensely interesting to a majority of their visitors. The most effective method by which visitors can explore a port is by some form of tour boat. Unlike automobile and bus transportation, a waterborne tour vessel can maneuver right up into the busiest and most interesting harbor activities. Tour boats are characterized by passenger areas designed to facilitate easy view of all that which is of interest. Seating is located both inside a special cabin, containing large windows, as well as outside on deck, providing enjoyable viewing comfort in all kinds of weather. Standing areas also afford substantial viewing from a number of vantage points. Loudspeakers adorn cabin bulkheads because most tours are accompanied with verbal explanations. A typical harbor tour boat is pictured in Fig. 12-25 and may develop as a clever vessel for touring the inside of a bottle.

One form of recreation enjoyed by many is deep-sea fishing. As most people know, fishing from shore often limits the size and variety of fish. Two alternatives remain: fishing from a boat or from a very long pier. Since long piers are few and far between, a boat seems a likely and appealing choice. Only a small percentage of the population own boats; so the nonowners must settle for pay-ing passage aboard a day-fishing boat (Fig. 12-26). A day boat is designed to accommodate a large number of fishermen, as well as their fishing gear. Day boats are not equipped for using nets, but rather many individual, salt-water rods and reels. On board are tanks for holding live bait, fish-cleaning counters, restrooms, and usually a snack bar. Although it is basically a very simple vessel, a bottled model could sustain fond memories of the good times a fisherman once had.

HISTORIC VESSELS

So many vessels have passed through history that volumes would be required to describe them properly. We are fortunate that thoughtful historians recorded and described many ancient watercraft, actual examples of which have not survived for us to examine today. Although a very few historical vessels will be pictured and described here, source books, some containing descriptions, drawings, and a few photographs of significant vessels of history are available in libraries to aid in the task of research. You should reap great benefit from such books in the form of ideas, accurate designs, minute details, and historical information. (See the Appendix.)

An exceptionally dignified, antique motor yacht appears in Fig. 12-27. Considering its hull shape, this particular vessel was probably constructed prior to 1920. It is rare to find an all-wood watercraft, and the craftsmanship of the woodwork found in this yacht exemplifies the kind of caring that went into vessels built in those days. A very elegant bottle would be required to properly contain and display a model of a vessel of this type.

Old sailing ships have always symbolized the

Fig. 12-25. Tour boats are designed to fulfill only one function—sightseeing.

Fig. 12-26. The design configuration of the day-fishing boat permits a large number of independent fishermen to fish in comfort and safety.

Fig. 12-27. A few antique private motor yachts, like this one, still sail out of some harbors. Their old, but classic lines betray their age.

147

Fig. 12-28. The three-masted sailing bark *Star of India* sails out of San Diego Harbor on a short, rare cruise (Photograph by Ken Clark, 60 Minute Photo, 5482 Complex St., Suite 108, San Diego, CA).

ultimate in the "romance of the sea." There is something very special about a vessel which must relay upon the natural forces of nature to motivate its travel. These are ships on which every task and function was accomplished solely by the strength of the men who sailed them. Every job, from setting sails to hoisting anchor, was performed by the hands and strong backs of the crew. These are the characteristics of the ocean-going ships which sailed prior to the beginning of the twentieth century. Once their masts crowded a harbor's sky like a vast forest. Now it is a real misfortune that so few of these great old sailing ships remain for people to admire.

The *Star of India* (Fig. 12-28) is such a vessel. It has become the pride of the San Diego Maritime Museum, and actually sails on rare occasions. The *Star of India* is a steel-hulled, three-masted, square-rigged *bark*, which was launched in 1863 from the Isle of Man, off the coast of Great Britain. She

Fig. 12-29. The Mexican training ship *Cuajhtemoc* has similar rigging to the *Star of India*, but different hull configuration.

149

remains the oldest merchant ship afloat. This is a classic sailing ship in every sense of the word. The difficulty comes in trying to imitate the complicated rigging system. The most widely perceived image many people have of a classic bottled ship is that of a great, old sailing ship like the *Star of India*.

Some sailing ships are used for the training of naval cadets by a number of countries. The Mexican training ship, *Cuajhtemoc* seen in Fig. 12-29, is such a ship. Over 100 cadets are trained at any one time. Needless to say, the sight of a training ship at sea (Fig. 12-30) is a very impressive one.

Another square-rigged sailing ship is the *Bounty* (Fig. 12-31). This is the second *Bounty*. The first was burned and sank near Pitcairn's Island in the 1840s. This version was used in the filming of both *Mutiny on the Bounty* (1963) and *The Bounty* (1984). A similar ship is the *Buccaneer Queen* (Fig. 12-32). This replica is used for harbor tours and evening dinner cruises, providing an exciting ride under full sail with the engines off. It is another square-rigged sailing ship representing a period of time when pirates often made hit-and-run assaults on merchant ships. Tourists can actually sail on this vessel; it cruises the outer harbor of Los Angeles on a daily basis. Having a real sailing ship to examine and explore while it actually sails is an excellent way to study rigging.

One ship which enjoys a prominent place in world history is the British passenger liner H.M.S. *Queen Mary* (Fig. 12-16). Her off-and-on construction during the early and mid-1930s helped reemploy many workers during the bleak days of the depression. Launched in 1936, the *Queen Mary* made several record-breaking crossings between the United States and Great Britain until she was requisitioned for troop transport during World War II. She carried hundreds of thousands of soldiers and badly needed arms from the United States to Britain. After the war, the *Queen Mary* was returned to private service, ferrying thousands of vacationers around the globe in comforts becoming royalty. As commercial airlines snatched away passengers, who were attracted by low fares and high speed, overseas travel and ocean crossings on all the great passenger liners declined.

Fig. 12-30. The *Cuajhtemoc*, with many of its cadets "standing ready" on the ship's rigging, sailed into port guided by a tugboat.

Fig. 12-31. An exact replica of the H.M.S. *Bounty* sails among a fleet of pleasure craft. It provides an excellent study of rigging and hull design of a ship of its era.

Finally, the Cunard Line was forced to sell off the expensive-to-operate *Queen Mary*. Fortunately, the city of Long Beach, California, out-bid all the other interested parties and refurbished her into a floating museum and hotel/convention center. Now, as a popular tourist attraction, the *Queen Mary* is visited and enjoyed by far more people per year than when she carried only the well-to-do between continents. It is not at all a poor retirement for one of the greatest ships in history, especially when compared with her demise in some depressing scrap yard. Models of every imaginable size of the *Queen Mary* are popular all over the world. Likewise, she provides a very stately subject for bottling.

Figure 12-33 shows the *The Princess Louise* Restaurant, a steamer which once sailed from Vancouver, British Columbia, Canada, to a number of settlements in Alaska, which was a territory of the United States in those days. Even as a floating restaurant, such a vessel provides admirers with a wealth of information. Just walking on her decks can give a builder a greater sense of proportions and design. This is a very attractive and appealing ship, whose graceful lines, proportions, and fine craftsmanship contribute to its air of quiet dignity. A vessel of this outstanding stature, gracing the inside of a suitable bottle, would create a very impressive work of art.

Another vessel representing water travel of an earlier time is the *riverboat* (Fig. 12-34). These were often floating palaces, popular in the last century on the navigable rivers of the midwestern and southern United States. Riverboats were often very luxurious vessels, occasionally containing gambling casinos. Usually the well-to-do were attracted by such traveling comfort. These vessels provided fine food, more-than-comfortable cabins, and enjoyable entertainment. Only a few riverboats are still around today, and some of them are modern replicas. Although they may contain many tiny details, a riverboat presents a very worthwhile challenge for any builder.

NAVAL VESSELS

Naval vessels, or *warships*, make up a particularly large classification, which is composed of historical as well as modern ships. Almost every nation bordered by an ocean or sea has at least one military watercraft to provide protection of ports and shores. Naturally there exists great variety throughout the world as every nation strives to build its own naval armament. Unfortunately, very few antique naval vessels survive today. Wartime attrition and the scrap yards have taken their toll. Each nation must constantly upgrade and modernize its navy as technology improves. This condition results in phasing out older, less-effective warships in favor of more potent and up-to-date vessels. Older, discarded naval vessels are used as target practice or recycled through the scrap yards.

Surprisingly, a few antique warships do survive. One prime example is the three-masted, square-rigged frigate, U.S.S. *Constitution*. Nicknamed *Old Ironsides* during the War of 1812, she remains the oldest, continuously commissioned warship in The United States Navy. Sporting 44 guns, the *Constitution* was a formidable force to reckon with on any sea. She acquired the nickname because British cannonballs would just bounce off her thick, oak wood hull without causing any appreciable damage. *Old Ironsides* was a terrific inspiration to Americans at a time when a young, war-ravaged country badly needed some impressive victories. She remains a very special piece of American history, and, needless to say, has become one of the most popular vessels to reproduce in model form both outside and inside bottles.

Modern naval vessels are somewhat difficult to locate and even harder to photograph. Not every

Fig. 12-32. The *Buccaneer Queen* is a common sight in Los Angeles Harbor as it carries sightseers on tours. Many harbors sport such "fantasy ships" which are only marginally authentic in design.

Fig. 12-33. Rather than fall to the scrap heaps, some old steamers are fortunate enough to be preserved as floating restaurants. The old, classic lines of a steamer are unmistakable, and are of great value to ship modelers.

Fig. 12-34. The typical riverboat carries an unmistakably unique design of strictly American origin. Even this replica is composed of mostly authentic lines.

port has a collection to examine. Those which are around to see are often regarded as sensitive or classified on the basis of national security, which is very understandable. After all, secrets among a nation's weaponry contribute to its national defence and perhaps even to its survival. When touring a naval vessel, a visitor must always obey the instructions of the officer in charge. If photography is not permitted, then photography is simply not permitted, even if he or she seems very polite about telling everybody.

The *aircraft carrier* is probably one of the most impressive naval vessels in any fleet of warships. As the name implies, these ships function as floating air stations for military aircraft. By way of an aircraft carrier, a small but potent force of air power can be deployed on almost any sea on the globe. Characteristic of the carrier is the huge, flat flight deck, used for launching and landing the planes. The carrier appearing in Figs. 12-35 and 12-36 helps illustrate how the flight deck dominates the overall design of the ship. Only the superstructure, housing a control tower, the bridge, and other important observation and control centers, extends above the flight deck. Communications and radar antenna are also mounted on the superstructure. A number of aircraft often sit in formation on the flight deck waiting for a mission. Figure C-24 shows how well an aircraft carrier functions as a subject inside a bottle.

A close relative is the *helicopter assault carrier* in Fig. 12-37. It is almost always smaller than a regular aircraft carrier, since helicopters require much less space for taking off and landing. The basic design of the helicopter assault carrier is similar to that of an aircraft carrier. Helicopters are also seen often sitting in formation on the assault ship's flight deck.

A contrasting naval vessel is the *submarine* (Fig. 12-38). Enough movies have been made about this type of warship that almost everybody knows of its underwater capabilities. Unless it sits in dry dock, there is little to see of a submarine as it lies on the water's surface. Like the superstructure of an aircraft carrier, the submarine's conning tower extends above the main body of the vessel. The conning tower contains the bridge, used during surface travel, priscopes, and antennae for radios and ra-

Fig. 12-35. The aircraft carrier U.S.S. *Constellation* lies at dockside in San Diego Harbor. Its tremendous length allows for the simultaneous landing and launching of aircraft.

Fig. 12-36. A "bow shot" of the U.S.S. *Constellation* reveals the special deck configuration used to launch and retrieve a variety of aircraft.

Fig. 12-37. The helicopter assault ship "Tarawa" is similar in design, but smaller, than an aircraft carrier.

Fig. 12-38. Even when "on the surface," most of a modern, nuclear submarine remains submerged. The adjustable fairweather planes on the conning towers contribute to underwater maneuverability.

dar. A sailplane, mounted on either side of the concning tower, is used to help guide the submarine into or out of a dive as it slips below the water's surface. Although a very simple model compared with most other watercraft, a submarine can be an interesting and fun subject for bottling, as shown in Fig. 11-2.

Another important naval vessel is the *destroyer*, shown in Fig. 12-39. This ship does battle on the water's surface. Besides a few guns, today's destroyers usually carry surface-to-air missiles, rocket-propelled antisubmarine weapons, and torpedos. Its hull is characterized by sleek lines, allowing it to swiftly cut through the water efficiently even in rough seas. A forest of hardware, antenna, and weapons adorn the superstructure and weather decks. Although as many of these detail items as possible should be included on a model of an accurate destroyer in order to maintain believability, some of them may be abbreviated to preserve your mental health. Another way of looking at it is that these tiny details help make a destroyer a stunning model to be constructed piece by piece in a bottle.

One of the most imposing and seemingly invincible of warships included in a nation's navy is the battleship. Also known as *dreadnoughts* and *battle wagons*, these mighty ships of war are also known for their huge guns. Projectiles of these guns may have an effective range of up to 35 miles (around 43 centimeters) and have an effective range of up to 35 miles (around 56 kilometers). The mere silhouette of a battleship reflects tremendous and formidable power, as illustrated in Fig. 12-40. Its terraced gun mounts give an unforgettable impression of undisputed command of any sea through which the battle ship sails. Most battleships are equipped with 16- to 18-inch thick, solid-steel armored plate, covering much of the vulnerable areas of the ship's hull and superstructure. Since these

Fig. 12-39. The U.S.S. *Waddell*, a typical, modern destroyer, is equipped with the very latest armament that modern technology can provide.

Fig. 12-40. The mere shape of the battleship U.S.S. *New Jersey* creates a feeling of formidable firepower. Tier after tier of enormous guns contribute to its awesome silhouette.

Fig. 12-41. A guided missle frigate sits high and dry while modifications are completed. Such occasions for studying hull configurations are relatively rare.

enormous floating fortresses are so extremely costly to operate and maintain, few are still around, and fewer still are commissioned as part of national defence. The last of the battleships were constructed during World War II. The United States is at this time, the only nation which continues to make intermittent use of such expensive ships. Although the U.S.S. *New Jersey* (Fig. 12-40) was launched in 1944, it has been modified, updated, and retrofitted repeatedly to accommodate the most modern of high-tech weaponry. Now, surface-to-air and surface-to-surface missiles, as well as huge guns, make the *New Jersey* an incredibly ominous warship. Models of such fantastic vessels must be regarded as the absolute "ultimate" in model building. Just imagine one sailing in a bottle!

An unidentified *frigate* stands high and dry in Fig. 12-41. Often warships, like other vessels, must be overhauled or modified to keep them up to date with new technology or for periodic maintenance. Hauling a vessel out of the water is the most effective method of accomplishing these tasks. A sight like this is valuable to model builders because many more important contours composing the hull are revealed.

The United States Coast Guard sails some rather interesting vessels, too. The ship shown in Fig. 12-42 is a *buoy tender*. Its function is to locate, retrieve, service, and redeploy buoys on a regular schedule. Some buoys are composed of elaborate warning horns or bells and flashing lights, all of which require regular maintenance. The Coast Guard's buoy tenders are designed to accommodate these tasks. Each tender is equipped with a buoy crane. The low-level mid-deck is designed to allow a buoy to be hauled aboard the tender. Much of the servicing of the buoys may take place aboard the tender itself. Occationally, however, when a large tanker or freighter has run over a buoy, the tender must retrieve "the remains" and take it back to the

Fig. 12-42. The functional design of a Coast Guard buoy tender provides great efficiency in retrieving, servicing, and launching navigational buoys.

overhaul shops on land for major repairs. Some buoys stand 12 to 15 feet tall on dry land; so this is no small undertaking. A Coast Guard vessel is characterized by its distinctive red stripe and insignia running diagonally across the side to the bow portion of the hull. This, together with the tender's unusual shape, would make for a very interesting bottled model.

The numbers of additional watercraft choices could fill many books. The prospective builder must recognize that there are many more possible vessels from which to choose for eventual bottling. A builder can do extensive research in order to discover the perfect historical, modern, or foreign vessel. An alternative would be to design an all new watercraft. The style of the vessel can be realistic, whimsical, wrecked, or burned. You have seemingly endless choices to make. Considering the great investment of time and effort required in bottling a ship, careful thought should be given to them all.

13

Bottles and Materials

A suitable bottle and quality building materials are as important for bottling ships as they are for houses. Design and craftsmanship cannot be expected to carry the entire load for success. The right bottle and building materials contribute substantially to the success of a bottled ship. You should search exhaustively for these key elements before attempting any construction. As with so many other projects, the extra efforts of preparation will help the actual tasks progress more smoothly. The bottle itself is a profoundly important component of a ship-in-a-bottle. It not only contains the ship, but often helps convey the artist's intended statement concerning the ship. It becomes the display case of the ship mode. The bottle can present an attitude of common existence or one of classy elegance. It is for these reasons that you should put forth much effort in searching for and selecting a proper bottle. Most of the considerations regarding shape and glass quality discussed with bottling houses apply to bottling ships as well. Bottle selection is a significant part of the preconstruction preparation. Therefore, the study of some special concerns regarding particular features of the bottle is worthy of attention. **BOTTLE SHAPE** The shape of the bottle is of particular interest to you, the builder. The bottle should relate somewhat to the shape of the watercraft constructed inside. Unlike houses, which can be composed of a variety of shapes and proportions both vertically and horizontally, ships and boats are more restricted to their possible shapes and proportions. Naturally, the bottle should reflect these restrictions. Since there are so many kinds of bottles in this world, you must recognize the tremendous number of possible bottle shapes. Some shapes are unacceptable for containing ships or boats, while others seem to be made especially for them. For example, a short, flat vessel should not occupy a bottle which would be better suited to contain a tall-masted, sailing ship. There must be a close relationship between the shape of the bottle and that of the ship. A ship should occupy at least 2/3 of the interior space of the bottle. Filling less than this proportion would make the ship seem lost. Such an unfortunate misjudgment will always appear as an aggravating mistake, which can never be corrected. If your name is somehow attached to an awkwardly proportioned bottled ship, the continued association may last a lifetime. It should be of further consideration that, unlike bottled houses, most bottled ships are composed in a horizontal position. This means that if the bottle is of a round shape, it will roll around uncontrollably unless a stand or cradle is provided. One way to avoid this problem is to select bottles which are in the form of a square or rectangle, like the one pictured in Fig. 13-1 or the three-sided bottle seen in Fig. C-17. These are very stable bottles standing on their original bottoms or lying on their sides. They are simple in that they require no additional pieces or distractions such as a stand or cradle. Simplicity is an element of art which can be very effective in drawing attention directly to the artist's intended statement. On the other hand, an artistically designed cradle can also enhance or complement the artist's work. A well-crafted cradle can function to stabilize the bottle, as well as help intensify the importance of the work being presented inside. After all, presentation is a significant part of any showing. A simple bottle stand is shown in comparison with a more elaborate one in Fig. 13-2. Both stands perform their intended functions well; however, some people may find greater interest and value with the one which is carved to resemble dolphins straining under their burden of supporting the bottle.

These are all important considerations of bottle shapes. The stability of the bottled ship as well as the aesthetic relationship between the bottle and its contents are both affected by the shape of the selected bottle. The builder should select wisely.

GLASS QUALITY

Glass quality remains a central concern to the builder of bottled objects. Every effort should be employed to reduce the effects of eyestrain. Selecting a bottle which has little or no glass distortion and color tint will help limit eyestrain.

An important factor affecting glass quality is the cleanliness of the bottle. Previously used beverage and antique bottles are susceptible

Fig. 13-1. A 1-gallon square bottle like this one is ideal for a great variety of vessels, from tall sailing ships to larger-scaled, motor-driven boats and ships.

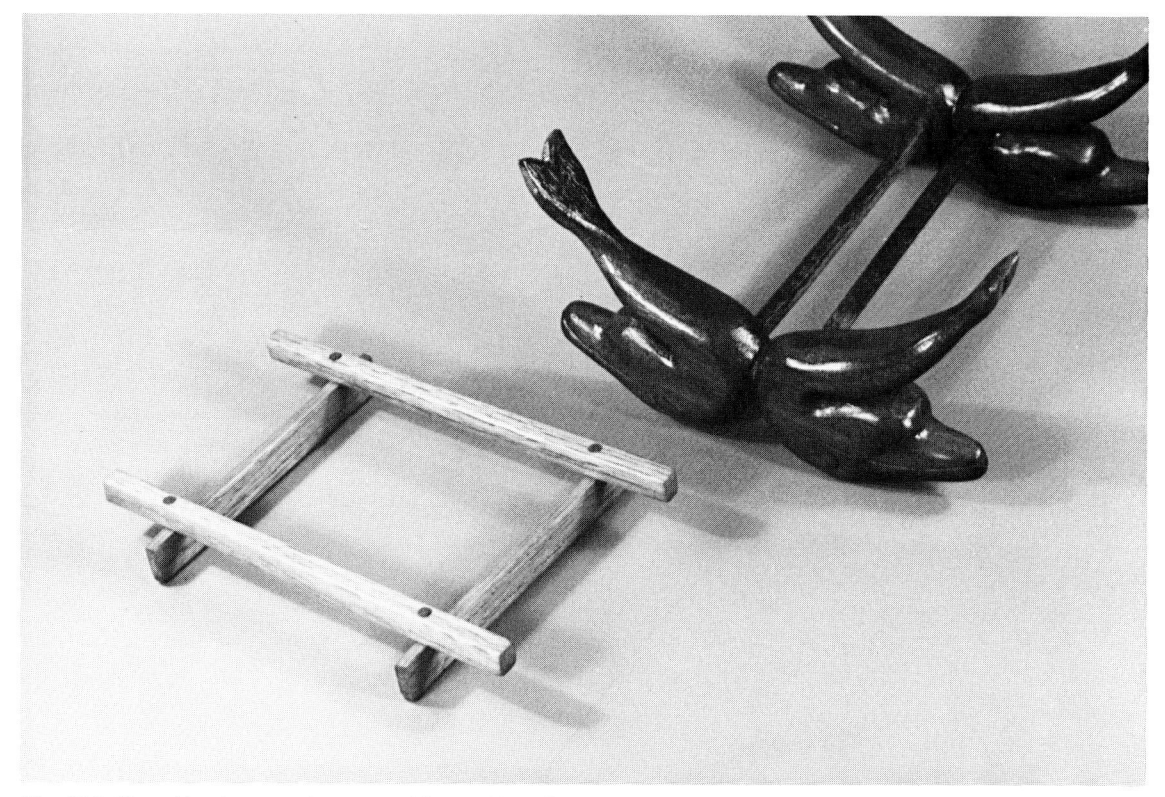

Fig. 13-2. Round bottles must be secured from rolling. Cradles may range from very simple to exceptionally elaborate.

to these conditions. The bottle-cleaning techniques covered in Chapter 2 were developed through personal experience and have been found to be very effective.

TYPES OF BOTTLES

Unlike bottled houses, in which the house shape is almost always altered or stretched in order to conform to the interior space of the bottle, traditional bottled ships portray the watercraft in close to true shape or proportions. This condition requires the use of bottles whose shapes are most nearly related to the proportions of the ship. Liquor bottles seem to conform to these proportions more often than other types. A tall sailing ship, for example, would effectively fill the liquor bottle pictured in Fig. 13-3. This bottle not only accommodates the basic shape of a tall ship, but it also has the capability of standing on its side without any other support. It is a perfect bottle.

There exists a tremendous variety of shapes and sizes of liquor bottles. No matter what kind of watercraft is to be constructed there is bound to be a liquor bottle whose shape is perfectly suited for it. Bottle sizes range from a few ounces (Fig. C-27) to a full gallon (Fig. 13-4), although liquor-store display bottles are even larger (Fig. 2-9). Naturally, liquor stores are the best sources of these bottles. It is only a matter of finding an effective way of emptying them after purchase. Occasionally, old liquor bottles can be found in antique stores, flea markets, garage sales, junk stores, and swap meets. Refer to Chapter 2 for more comprehensive details.

Juice bottles are another source of suitable containers. In Fig. C-11, the square-rigger *Columbia* sails in a 1-gallon, apple juice bottle. The bottle's proportions relate reasonably well to those of the sailing ship. As mentioned and pictured in Chapter 2, additional examples of juice bottles can be studied (Figs. 2-21 through 2-23). If a particular juice bottle is found to relate well to the shape of the ship intended for building, its use is justified; however, you should never select such a bottle merely because it is so easily obtainable. Select a juice bottle only if it appears to be right for the particular ship to be constructed in that bottle. Otherwise, the search for a suitable bottle should continue until the best one is found.

Large light bulbs can be surprisingly useful for containing ships. Whether standing on its top or lying on its side, a light bulb can create an interesting effect surrounding a ship. An effective ship-in-a-light-bulb appears in Fig. C-28, and an unaltered bulb is pictured in Fig. 2-32. Although the glass is very thin and extremely fragile, there is little or no distortion of the image inside. One disadvantage is that a light bulb almost always requires the use of a stand or cradle to keep it from rolling around. Naturally, sizes range widely. The most useful size is the 1500-watt bulb. Such large sizes may be difficult to find, but industrial-type, electrical shops and supply houses may be helpful in locating them. Light bulbs of this size are used to light factories, older stadiums and race tracks, and some theatrical stages. Chapter 2 contains the techniques for dismantling the filament and preparing the bulb for construction. The use of a light bulb to contain a ship can add even more fascination to an already intriguing art form.

Many other bottle and container possibilities exist. Often selection is based upon the personal preference of the builder. As evidenced by the large number of bottles described in detail throughout Chapter 2, however, such a selection may be very difficult to deal with for the novice builder. If the relationship between the intended ship model and the bottle can be recognized, those difficulties will be minimized.

THE CLOSURE

The bottle closures for bottled ships differ greatly from those of bottled houses. There exists a much greater variety of closure styles and types. Bottled ship closures are often much more expressive and artistic than those found on bottled houses. They can make a statement of the artist's attitude which may complement or contrast with that made inside the bottle. With a little imagination, a bottle closure can be remarkably expressive.

A clever closure can be created by most anybody. A few extraordinary examples are presented here for the purpose of inspiration. A closure may express a special relationship, as exemplified by the fire hydrant used to seal the bottle containing a fireboat in Fig. C-20. It may convey humor, as with the monkey closure seen in Fig. C-12 and the ship closure appearing in Fig. C-13. A closure may be a simple, added attraction like the one shown in Fig. C-14. Expressions of tradition and pride may be the statement of the closure, like the one shown in Fig. C-15. Mechanical intrigue may be the idea, as promoted in Figs. C-16, and C-21. A very traditional cork and Turk's Head knot form the closure used on the bottled ship in Fig. C-23. An anchor and its chain act as a closure for the bottled aircraft carrier in Fig. C-24. These examples show how using your imagination can create exceptional ideas for closures. Who would have ever thought that a closure could be elevated to such a high level of importance!

Of course, a closure is not required to make or complete a statement. It can achieve just as much dignity by existing in a simple form and doing its job well. A common cork graces the bottle containing a sailing ship shown in Fig. C-11. Glass stoppers and original bottle caps and lids may also be used to adequately seal a bottled ship. We all must admit, however, that the creative bottle closures add a great deal more charm and amazement than those which simply seal.

It is obvious that a wide variety of objects and creations can be used to perform the function of sealing a bottled ship. It is merely a matter of using your creativity. You must analyze the ship's situation to determine what other or continuing statement may be expressed. It does not necessarily have to involve the ship. A closure may even contain another boat or ship not at all related to the main bottled ship, as in the glass stopper pictured in Fig. C-14. It is almost like having two bottled scenes in one work of art. So, there seems to be

Fig. 13-3. This gin bottle is especially excellent for tall sailing ships. A bonus is the fact that this bottle can lie on its narrow side without the aid of a stand or cradle.

Fig. 13-4. A 1-gallon whiskey bottle was used to contain two sailing vessels and an extensive village. It requires the use of a cradle for support.

no end to the innovative approaches to the function of sealing a bottle.

BUILDING MATERIALS

As expected, the building materials required for building a ship in a bottle will be different than those composing a bottled house. Typically, a house has little need for sail cloth and rope; however, ships and other forms of watercraft require these and several other materials. Since some bottled ships must often perform mechanically as part of their construction process (i.e. the fold-up method of construction), materials should be of the best possible quality. Material failure occurring at a critical point in construction could be disastrous and irreparable. The novice builder will benefit greatly from a few sage recommendations concerning quality building materials. Every builder must know what materials are useful and where to obtain them. Without such valuable information, you might search for months trying to locate the best materials or have to resort to blundering from one kind of material to another through painful trial and error. I hope that the following sections will help avoid these misfortunes.

Wood and Paper

Probably the material used most often in the building of a bottled ship is wood. It is the most suitable of all materials for a number of specific parts or components of the ship. A number of parts of the ship model, including the hull, masts, cabins, smokestacks, and many other important parts, must be constructed of wood. More often than not wood is used to form the bottle closure. This material is easy to shape and carve, enabling extraordinary creations. It accepts paint well in most cases. It can be used to form mechanical parts. Some woods are durable, lasting for many years, even when unprotected. It is the perfect material for building most parts of a bottled ship.

Blocks of wood, from which the ship's hull and cabins or superstructure must be made, are available in hobby shops or lumberyards. Numerous species of wood are available and acceptable for this craft. Pine, Douglas fir, spruce, bass wood, and balsa are softwood species which are used most often. Hardwoods such as maple, birch, mahogany, and oak are too expensive and difficult to work with, especially for beginners.

Caution should be exercised when using balsa wood. Balsa will simply crush as knife-blade pressure is applied during the cutting process. The knife blade must be kept very sharp when attempting to cut this kind of wood. Moving the blade in a gentle "sawing" motion will often help make a clean cut. Balsa wood is an open-grained wood, characterized by small, elongated holes, or pits, along the grain figure of the wood. These holes must be filled with wood putty if a smooth, painting surface is to be achieved. Some hardwoods such as oak, mahogany, and walnut are also open-grained and must be filled as well.

You may find it convenient to stock up on a few blocks of your favorite carving wood in a variety of sizes and shapes, as shown in Fig. 13-5. From these blocks the different model parts can be conveniently shaped or carved.

Thin sheets, called *veneer*, is another useful wood form. It is used to make thin, exposed walls (*bulkheads* in proper nautical terms) or for any structure which must be represented by thin, sheetlike wood. Wood veneers are sold in some hardware stores, most lumberyards, and in many woodcarving supply shops. Although usually found in the form of hardwoods, some veneers of spruce, pine, and fir are available as well. Sometimes, wood veneers come in the form of paperbacked tape (Fig. 13-5) 1 to 2 inches wide and around 80 inches long. This is a very convenient product in that a relatively small amount of veneer can be purchased inexpensively. Wood parts made from these veneers are easily bent or carved to provide additional shapes and building material flexibility (substituting for other more expensive or hard-to-find materials). Considering the low cost of wood veneers and their versatility, their contribution to the craft is significant.

Wooden dowel rods of very small diameters are a definite essential. They are used to form spars, specifically masts, yards, booms, and gaffs, of sail-

Fig. 13-5. Sheets of veneer, wood blocks, and a variety of dowels are the basic materials composing the model portion of a bottled ship.

ing ships and smaller sailboats. The most useful dowels to the builder of bottled ships range in size from an incredibly small .025 inch up to .125 (1/8) inch in diameter (Fig. 13-5). Most lumberyards sell the 1/8-inch dowels, while some dollhouse shops stock the remaining small sizes. A reputable mail-order business, Many Goode's, sells 4-inch and 12-inch lengths of dowels from .025 to .093 inch in diameter. (See the Appendix). Another source of useful doweling may be found in the handles of some cotton swabs (Fig. 13-6). These dowel handles usually measure around .062 inch in diameter and are made of a hardwood, probably birch. They provide very inexpensive and easily obtainable material for spars.

Bottle stands, or cradles, used to keep the bottle from rolling around, are also made from blocks or strips of wood and doweling. Sizes of wood materials are determined by the shape and size of the stand required for a particular bottle.

Paper products are another useful building material. Paper is easily obtainable, often seen everywhere. Sometimes sails can be made from carefully shaped pieces of paper. They hold their shape exceptionally well and may even be made to billow as if filled with wind. These paper sails may be made of medium-thick stationery, off-white in color, with some, very slight, embossed texture. Some stationery stores sell this kind of writing paper by the pound, a very inexpensive way to purchase large or small quantities.

Parchment paper is also often used to represent sails. Parchment holds its shape very well and can be formed to appear like wind-swollen sails. It is available in most art supply stores. Its golden color and rich texture makes sails appear well aged.

File cards are also very useful. They are thinner than the wood veneer and are handy for bending a lip around a curve or irregularly shaped part. Flat sections may be used for canopies or cabin roofs. Recipe file cards are available in 3 × 5 inches or 4 × 6 inches and are sold in supermarkets, drugstores, stationery shops, and some department stores. If thicker material is required, laminate two cards together with paper paste or white glue or buy a manila folder from a stationery shop. It is amazing how often paper can be used to substitute for other, more-expensive materials or those which are more difficult to form.

Adhesives

Without proper adhesives, bottled ship construction would not be possible. The separate pieces comprising the ship model itself must be held together in some way. These parts cannot be expected to stay together with only pins, tacks, and spit. The use of an adhesive is the most effective way of holding a number of pieces together neatly.

One easy-to-use adhesive—white glue—works very well and is relatively inexpensive. This glue, classified as a polyvinyl, is available almost everywhere. It is very effective for gluing wood, paper, cloth, and porous rock together and to each other. White glue is not so successful, however, for holding glass, plastics, metals, and other nonporous materials together or to each other. Plastics should be secured with any of a number of plastic cements which dissolve the plastic surface slightly to create a welded bond. Glass and metals must be held together with still another adhesive.

Epoxy cement is especially useful to the builder of bottled ships. It works effectively to bond wood and metal to glass. Epoxy is made from a resin and a catalyst, purchased together in separate tubes, and mixed just prior to being used. Shortly after equal portions are combined, the thick, viscous substance hardens into a consistency much like that of hard plastic. Then, it seems to grip most every nonflexible material extremely well.

Although the adhesives just mentioned have

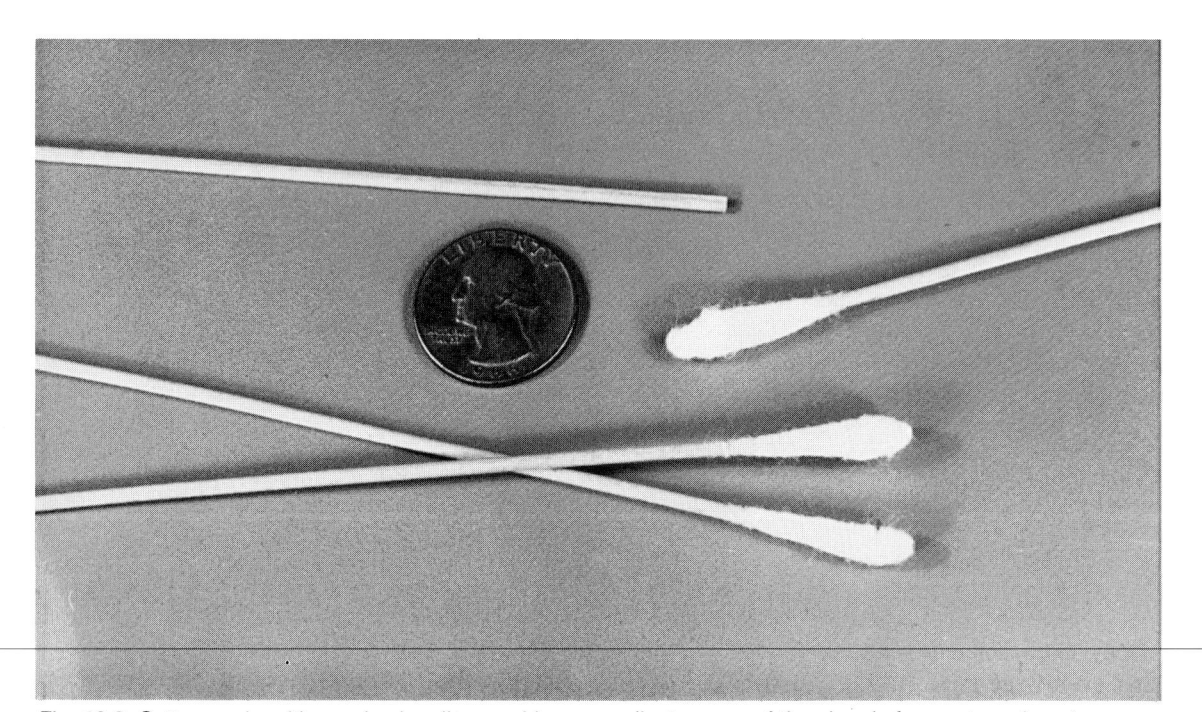

Fig. 13-6. Cotton swabs with wooden handles provide an excellent source of tiny dowels for masts and yards.

proven to be reliable for use in bottled houses and ships, they are by no means the only ones available. Many other types of adhesives are available to the craftsman; however, these other types are unproven as to reliability. They require experimentation if they are to substitute for the proven ones. Make sure a particular adhesive will not dry out or break down in time, allowing an assembly to crumble.

Paint

Paint serves a number of essential functions, the most important of which is to provide the accurate color required to affect increased realism. Stripes, trademarks, metallic colors, and colors representing recognizable pieces of equipment contribute to making a ship model appear realistic and authentic. Paint also acts as a protective coating, promoting durability despite harsh conditions around it. This is not so important inside a bottle, but worth mentioning nonetheless. Paint helps blend rough textures remaining on the surface of wood, plastic, and metal parts. Joints and seams are softened or disappear under a good coat of paint. An effective paint job helps unify an object composed of several parts into a single, harmonious entity. Painting the assembly in one base color and adding bands of other colors meet this function well.

Among all the many kinds of paint available, only a few are acceptable for bottling ships. Water-based tempera paints are usable, but their texture is not variable. A flat finish is all that is possible. The same is true of latex paints, which are also water-based. Enamel paints, on the other hand, provide both glossy and flat finishes in a great variety of colors. Unlike the tempera, enamels do not smear when handled with perspiring fingers or splatters of water. The only disadvantage with enamel paint is that clean up requires a solvent. Small bottles of paint thinner are sold, conveniently located alongside the bottles of paint. Often referred to as *hobby* or *model paints*, enamels are usually sold in hobby shops, some drugstores, department stores, and even large supermarkets. Bottles of enamel paint, each containing 1/4 or more ounce of paint, are usually labeled with color name, stock number, and texture type. Brushes and other painting supplies are sold in the same location.

Cloth and Thread

Cloth and thread are two more materials often required in the construction of bottled ships. They are used to represent sails and assorted rigging on sailing ships and the smaller sailboats. Cloth and thread are almost always used together, since sails cannot be used without some kind of support rigging. Occasionally, however, sailing ships may be seen standing in port with rigging supporting the masts without sails. Sailing ships always require some form of rigging whether they are equipped with sails at that particular time or not. The greatest challenge at this point is finding sail and rigging materials which characteristically appear to be in proper scale with the rest of the vessel you are constructing.

Cloth used as sails for small-scale ship models must be basically white or off-white and finely woven with very thin thread. The cloth should not be so thin that it is transparent. Cloth made of large thread loosely woven will appear out of scale with the rest of the ship model. The cloth should be of a weave which can endure cutting with scissors without excessive fraying, but maintain a smooth texture.

A textured cloth would also betray the scale of the ship model. The color selected may be at your option. A stark white sailcloth may appear too "new" to properly represent realistic sails. A light beige or ivory color may prove more appropriate. Every possible measure should be employed to enhance realism. It is an easy enough task to purchase cloth of a texture, weave, weight, and color capable of appearing, when cut into authentic shapes, like tiny sails.

Several types of modern-day cloth are adequate to excellent for representing miniature sails and are available from several sources. A variety of names identify these particular types of cloth. These names are necessary for locating and acquiring these cloths from local merchants. Stores which

169

specialize in many kinds of cloth are usually referred to as fabric shops n the telephone directory. Other sources of cloth may include drapery shops and tailors. If you are seeking information on where to buy the proper cloth do not be reluctant to ask any of the employees of these sources. If they do not sell the required cloth, they will probably know where you can find it.

One type of fabric is called *broadcloth*. Typical bed sheets are an example of a use of this type of cloth. Although miniature sails made of this material may appear a little too thick for its scale, they will be adequate in most cases. Sometimes you must accept the characteristics of a building material considered "second best," when other more appropriate materials have limited availability. One advantage of using broadcloth is that it is so plentiful and easy to obtain. Most people have access to old bed sheets, and a plain white or ivory-colored sheet should be relatively easy to locate. It can be cut easily with scissors, and will not fray as readily as some other types of cloth.

Cotton batiste is another possible sailcloth. It is thin enough to relate well to its intended small scale without appearing transparent. It is available in a variety of colors, allowing for the white and ivory tints required for realistic sails. One particularly advantage of batiste is that it contains a warp or grain running in one direction through the cloth. This grain appears as streaks, which should run vertically when the cloth is hung as sails on a "square-rigger" to enhance realism. Batiste, like broadcloth, can be cut easily with scissors without excessive fraying.

Sails may also be made of *Irish linen*. Fine handkerchiefs are often made of this refined cloth. Its advantage is with its thin composition. For ship models of very small scales, Irish linen sails are thin enough to appear appropriately to scale. There is one disadvantage with using sails of Irish linen. The cloth is so thin that it is excessively transparent sometimes. With small-scaled sails, the problem is not a serious one. In the case of larger scales, however, the transparent effect is noticeable and somewhat undesirable. Take care to avoid using Irish linen that is composed of decorative textures. These designs, woven into the cloth, will also be unrealistic. If handkerchiefs are being cut up for use as sails, only the areas free of unwanted textures should be used.

Other types of cloth could be used for sails, too. Certainly there are many more knowledgeable persons who can suggest other equally effective fabrics. Employees of fabric shops may be willing to help you find these additional types of cloth.

Most ships and boats require the use of lines and ropes for a variety of reasons. They must be represented in a miniaturized form on the bottled ship. Some lines are used to secure masts and operate sails. Others support antennae and equipment masts which elevate a number of pieces of electronic devices found aboard some ships. Some cables operate booms and cranes used for loading and unloading cargo. All of these ropes, lines, and cables play an important role in the efficient operation of various boats and ships. Therefore, their significance should not be diminished during miniaturization. Wherever lines, ropes, and cables occur on a ship, they should be properly depicted with miniature ones. Naturally, you must be reasonable in representing the rigging of a complex sailing ship. Not every line can be included at such a tiny scale. The challenge remains to find some kind of line which fits the scale of the watercraft being bottled.

Sewing threads are often used to imitate these ropes. Although cotton thread is becoming a rarity in fabric shops and the notions sections of department stores, it is an acceptable material for use on bottled ships. Tiny *hairs* are, however, an undesirable characteristic of cotton thread. These hairs extend out from the line, making it look fuzzy. This condition betrays the scale of the line. A great number of colors are available with cotton thread, but black is used most often with boats and ships. To add a little variety, white, tan, and gray thread may also be used.

Polyester is the modern substitute for cotton thread. It appears just like the cotton, although it is a little "hairier." Rubbign the thread with candle wax or beeswax will help eliminate this problem, but this requires an additional step and more time and effort. Color variety is as great as with cotton thread. Polyester thread is found wherever sewing supplies are sold, including some supermarkets, drugstores, and dime stores. This type of thread is the easiest of all the thread materials to use and obtain.

Nylon fishing line is another interesting possibility. It is a transparent thread known for its reliable strength. A real plus is that nylon has no little hairs attached. There are, however, some disadvantages to using it. Since transparent lines, ropes, and cables are unacceptable on a realistic ship, nylon line must be colored with a black, felt-tipped marker, an extra step. A second problem involves securing the nylon line. It seems to have a mind of its own. It resists attempts to tie knots in it. Nylon line seems to come untied unless extra knots are added to the first one. A tiny drop of white glue applied to the knot will also keep it from coming untied, but it is another extra step.

Perhaps the very best miniature line you can use is the most difficult to obtain. A braided surgical thread, known as *nonabsorbable, surgical suture*, works very effectively as rigging lines on all types of ships. It is a thin, black thread with hardly any little hairs attached. Since it is braided, it will not unravel, and it handles and knots well. It is manufactured by Ethicon, Inc. of Somerville, N.J. and is available through local medical supply houses throughout the United States and Canada. A size and material designation of "60-0 silk" seems well suited for ships of most scales. One advantage of using this suture thread is that it appears like miniature rope or rigging line. A disadvantage is that it is expensive compared with other threads or lines. It runs around $13 per 100-yard spool. Nevertheless, it appears to be the best solution to the problem of selecting a minature rigging line, if you are willing to locate it.

Modeling Clay and Putty

One problem peculiar to bottled ships is that of representing water in a realistic fashion. You must select a material in which the watercraft will appear to be sailing. Waves must be sculpted in this material after it is installed into the bottle. It must have the ability to grip the inside of the glass bottle even after it dries. The material must be of a smooth texture, free of lumps. It cannot appear grainy when it dries or hardens with the passage of time. A preferred characteristic is that the material appears wet for eternity. All of this is asking a great deal of a building material, but there are some materials which can effectively fill these requirements.

Modeling clay is one such material. This substance never dries out, therefore it never loses its ability to always look wet and grasp the glass walls of the bottle. Modeling clay comes in a number of colors, enabling you to create more interesting and realistic water. For basic water, you should select blue, green, and yellow. For muddy, river water, a shade or two of brown or tan should be included. Colors are mixed together in the hand by kneading lumps of the individual colors into one uniform blend. Later, it is easily inserted into the bottle, one lump at a time, and mashed into place with a simple, aluminum wire tool. After the modeling clay has been installed in the bottle, a few carefully placed brush strokes of white paint are applied to represent wind-whipped whitecaps. They will add to the water's realism. Modeling clay is available in craft and hobby shops, dime stores, and even in some drugstores. It is perhaps the most highly recommended material for representing water around a watercraft in a bottle. It is almost perfect.

Window-sash putty may also be adapted to effectively represent water. Sash putty usually comes in a can and is sold in hardware stores and some lumberyards. Straight from the can it is gray colored and therefore must be tinted with common enamel model paints. Tinting is accomplished by removing a generous portion of putty (more than the estimated amount required) with a putty knife, spatula, or butter knife. Apply the putty on a sheet of glass, acrylic plastic, or some other nonporous sheet material durable enough for vigorous mixing. Add some blue enamel paint, the amounts and color of which must be determined by experimentation. Mix this combination by stirring with the knife until the entire mass is the same color. Add other paint colors if necessary and mix until the desired color is achieved. Before installation into the bottle, apply a coat of white glue to the interior, glass-wall location intended for the putty. After the glue is completely dry, begin installing the colored putty, a lump at a time. Attach it to the bent-wire tool, insert it into the bottle, drag it off the tool, and mash it into place. Continue this operation until the desired "pool" of water is assembled. The surface of the pool can be textured with the bent-wire tool to form waves. Later, the tops of the waves can be brushed with a few smudges of white paint to create the illusion of whitecaps on a windy day. When the ship is installed later, the hull is mashed into the putty, which grips the ship securely for eternity. This gripping action is especially important while rigging the ship, a shaky and wiggly process.

Wire and Pins

Wire makes a surprisingly significant contribution to the construction of bottled ships. Metal hinges, used to allow the folding of masts and gaffs prior to insertion into the bottle, are made of thin wire loops. Usually it is easier and faster to construct railings using lengths of thin wire. Antennae and other modern electronic apparatuses may also be constructed with wire. A special eyelet, located on the end of the bowsprit of bottled sailing ships and used to guide control lines for folded sails and masts, is fashioned with thin wire as well. Almost any kind of wire will work well for these purposes, although wire which springs back into its original shape is unacceptable for obvious reasons.

Copper, brass, and steel are the most likely metals found in the form of wire available in hardware stores. Whichever kind of wire is used should be easily bent, hold its new shape, and not be easily broken. The wire sizes may vary. Hinge wire may be up to around .035 inch in diameter, while railings and eyelets should be around .015 inch in diameter or even slightly less. A small paper clip measuring .035 inch in diameter may be cut and bent to form a U-shaped hinge, provided the diameter of the wooden mast or gaff is large enough to accommodate the proper-sized hole drilled across its length. This process will be more fully explained in Chapter 15. The size of the wire used for railings and electronic apparatuses is arbitrary. You can decide which size to use based on aesthetics and wire availability. In the case of small-scaled ships, the classic, air-scooping ventiltor seen

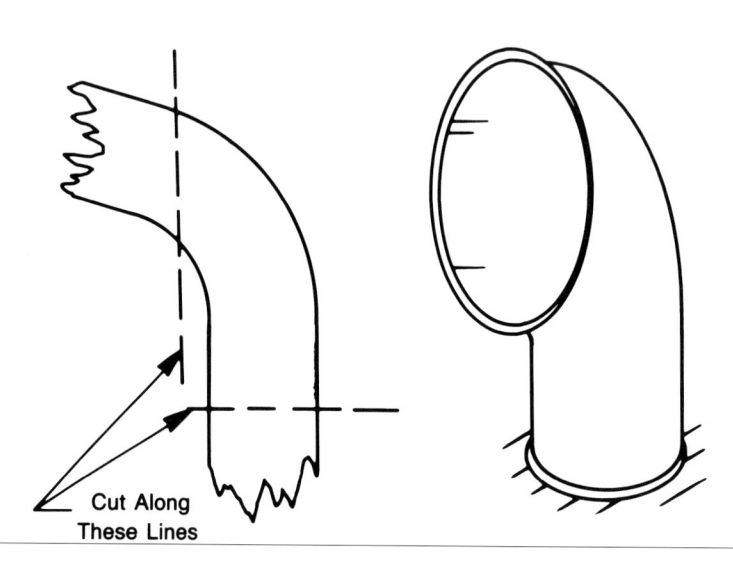

Fig. 13-7. The diagram on the left shows how a carefully bent and cut coat hanger can resemble the classic ship's ventilator, shown in the right-hand diagram.

standing on the upper decks may be constructed using coat-hanger wire, bent and cut as in Fig. 13-7. Sometimes it is amazing how helpful a little wire can be.

Small straight pins are also part of the construction scene. Standard sewing pins are often used to hold an object securely while gluing or painting. Similarly, pins may be used to hold an object flat while it dries in order to avoid curling. These pins are usually around 1 inch in length. Smaller pins, only a 1/2 inch long, have a smaller-diameter shaft compared with the longer sizes. These short pins may be used to secure some of the rigging lines to the sides of the hull of the boat or ship. Usually these small pins are cut in half and pushed into the soft pine, fir, or spruce wood used to form the vessel's hull. Such small pins are often available in hobby shops selling supplies used in constructing wooden sailing ship models. Otherwise, they may be a little difficult to locate. In that case, the standard sewing pins may be substituted by cutting their length down to a manageable size. There are, of course, other building materials not mentioned here. Some materials are so new on the market, they are new to the "experts." Others are discovered only by more adventurous and resourceful craftsmen. The important thing to remember is that through observation and careful experimentation, other useful building materials may be found to contribute far more than some mentioned in this book. It always pays to keep an open mind!

14

Tools

Bottling ships is a prime example of a craft requiring the use of both special and common tools, without which the construction process would be impossible. While some tools are store-bought and easily obtained from a number of sources, others must be homemade. Still other tools are store-bought and later altered to accommodate special and unusual construction tasks. There are no known special tools being manufactured and sold which are specifically designed to aid the builder of bottled ships. You must construct these tools or adapt others yourself. **STORE-BOUGHT TOOLS**. The store-bought tools used to construct bottled houses are also applicable for bottled ships. In order to avoid unnecessary repetition, these tools are mentioned again only as they apply to the specific construction processes required to complete a bottled ship. It is important that you recognize how the use of the proper tools will help complete these construction tasks more quickly, with greater ease, and with neater craftsmanship. Although an expensive tool to purchase, the Dremel Moto-Tool, (Fig. 4-1) is a real time and work saver. It can be used to quickly and neatly carve the hull of a ship or boat, as well as drill the many holes required for completion. Its greatest advantages, however, are found in its lathe-turning capabilities. By clamping a wooden, cotton-swab handle in the Moto-Tool's chuck, short spars and masts can be shaped to their required taper by using files to grind away the excess wood. Other small wood turnings, such as capstans and other deck equipment, of up to 1/8 inch in diameter may also be shaped in the same manner. Naturally, a protective face shield should always be worn during such machining. The Dremel Moto-Tool as well as other electric, handheld grinders are often available in hobby shops, hardware stores, and tool catalogs. Carving tools are probably used more than any other tool for bottling ships. X-acto brand knives and cutters (Fig. 4-2) are of good quality and reasonable prices. These knives are capable of carving and trimming wood, shaping spars and masts, and cutting paper sails and thread. A number of blades and handles are available. The number 11 blade is an effective cutting tool with an exceptionally sharp point. This point is perfect for cutting paper sails to exact shape and lining grooves in the decks of boats and ships. While clamped in its convenient holder/handle, this blade also works well for carving hulls, cabins, and some deck equipment. X-acto knives are sold in hardware stores, hobby shops, and some large drugstores. It is perhaps the one tool the builder cannot do without. The most effective tool for fast, rough cutting of wood, some metals, and plastics is a saw. The problem is in selecting the proper saw for a particular material. Figure 4-3 shows a variety of saws. The most useful to the ship bottler are the coping saw, X-acto #35 box saw, and jeweler's saw. The coping saw is perfect for cutting off a portion of a block or plank of wood and roughing it out to its approximate shape. The X-acto #35 box saw is composed of an extremely thin but strong blade, which is capable of very clean and straight cutting of woods and some plastics. This saw can provide final shape cutting and trimming of wood blocks used as boat and ship hulls. It can also cut to length any strip material, such as dowel rod, used for masts and spars.

The jeweler's saw is used for very delicate and intricate cutting of soft metals, most woods, and some plastics. Its blade is very fragile; so all sawing is done with extra care. The jeweler's saw is handy for cutting windows in sheet materials. Simply mark pencil lines for the window's edges and drill a hole in the center of the window. Next, disconnect one saw blade end from the saw frame, and thread the blade through the drill hole. Then, saw along the pencil lines until the entire window is cut out. Remove the saw blade. It seems like a lot to do, but it is so easy. Furthermore, the jeweler's saw can cut complex filigree or scroll designs.

Of great importance is a suitable work area. Personal comfort, steadiness of work surface, and effective working light are features of a work center in which many hours of relaxing construction will take place. Inadequacies in any one of these conditions can be responsible for causing work-related pain, as well as frustration, not to mention possible friction with a spouse or roommate resulting from damage to table or counter tops during construction.

Most people work more efficiently while seated. A padded chair or stool which seats the body at the correct, working height, will minimize back strain and buttock fatigue. This height is relative to body proportions and work-surface height. More simply, it is the height at which a person can sit comfortably and work for long periods of time.

The work table or bench is another important consideration. It should be heavy-duty and steady enough to avoid wiggling during work activities. A television tray or stand is an example of a work surface considered very inadequate. It is never steady enough. A table or bench with thick, well-braced legs is more acceptable.

Next, a durable cutting surface is required to protect the table or bench from the cutting, chopping, and slicing actions required during construction. A kitchen cutting board, such as the plastic one in Fig. 4-4, is especially effective. A board of this type will withstand those abusive actions, including drilling and punching of holes without excessive dulling of the cutting blades, while protecting the surface of the work table or bench.

Lastly, adequate light in the work area is essential to preserve the health of your eyesight. Perhaps nothing else causes as much painful eyestrain as working in poor light. Basic room light is not enough. A high-intensity lamp or drafting light are possible solutions to the lighting problem. Both provide you with the convenience of being adjustable. This feature is important as construction proceeds from task to task, resulting in changes in lighting requirements.

Clamps are very helpful in constructing bottled ships. Figure 4-5 shows a variety of clamps which you may consider using. Clamps are used to hold parts together while glue dries. This is especially valuable when gluing the skin or siding along the outside frame contours of a watercraft's hull. Such skin or siding materials never conform to the hull contours on their own. A clamping device must be used. Clamps are also used to hold sewing pins on which a soon-to-be-painted part has been impaled. This clever arrangement avoids painted fingers. After paint has been applied to the part, the whole clamp assembly is set aside to dry.

Paintbrushes can be a terrific help in applying paint to ship and boat hulls and deck cabins. Of course, cotton swabs, scraps of cloth, and even fingers can substitute for store-bought brushes. Brushes, however, are especially designed to apply paint efficiently without creating messes. Figure 4-6 shows a variety of paintbrushes, the smaller of which are the most appropriate for applying enamel paint to small parts.

No wood craftsman should work without proper files and sandpaper. These marvelous inventions are designed to provide the final shaping and finishing touches to a variety of materials. It should be noted that files (Fig. 4-7) and sandpaper are designed to work with certain materials and not with others. Basically, they are classified into two groups: those which can work with metals and those which can work with wood and plastics. Metal working files can work with almost all materials, but the wood and plastic files cannot be used on hard materials like metal. Check with the salesperson in your local hardware store. He should be knowledgeable enough to direct you to the proper files and/or sandpaper for the correct material. Sandpapers really become complicated, considering all the many types: garnet paper, aluminum oxide paper, wet or dry paper, emery cloth, and others.

All prudent craftsmen put forth the effort and take the time to carefully plan their prospective endeavors prior to beginning construction. The right tools can be a great help in accomplishing this planning. Pictured in Fig. 4-9 are several drawing tools which may prove beneficial in completing the drawings required to develop and finalize these plans. The compass is a mechanical drawing instrument used to draw perfect circles and arcs. This tool could come in handy when drawing cross sections of a bottle in order to study the relationships between the interior space contained within the bottle and the watercraft intended for that space. Such a study may lead to redesigning the arrangement of the model to create an improved composition. Another drawing aid is the 45-45-90-degree triangle. This tool works as a straightedge with set angles. Often equally useful is the 30-60-90-degree triangle. A protractor is used to determine the number of degrees in an angle. This handy instrument is available in both 180- and 360-degree versions and is useful for setting the angles of gaffs on masts of fore-and-aft-rigged schooners. The carpenter's square is an *L*-shaped tool used for marking 90-degree angles on planks and beams of wood. This square is a must for any craftsman who desires precision-squaring of lumber.

As can be expected, it is likely that a number of other store-bought tools will be helpful in tackling some of the tsks involved in bottling ships. It is important that you keep an open mind and remain alert to the debuts of new tools, as well as the improvisation of standard tools currently available. Knowledgeable tool salespeople can suggest the use of some tools which have not yet been considered for a particular ship-bottling construction task. Imaginative and inventive builders will have few problems discovering additional tools to aid them in their tasks.

HOMEMADE TOOLS

Some construction tasks require the development and fabrication of special tools not already available in stores. After all, store-bought tools cannot be expected to perform every function essential for the creation of new as well as some traditional art forms. Homemade tools fill these needs. It should be apparent that without these homemade tools, bottling ships would be impossible. Yet they are simple enough to be exceptionally easy to use with only moderate hand-eye coordination. These homemade tools are so simple in design that almost anybody is capable of constructing them. The materials required to make these simple tools are readily available from a number of sources, which will be mentioned later.

The tool used most often for inserting small objects into a bottle and then positioning them in their proper location is the needle-wire tool (Fig. 4-10). It is based on an embarrassingly simple tool idea. It operates by sticking or impaling a wooden object onto the needle, which is permanently attached to a long, stiff wire, and tapping or twisting the object in order to release it from the needle once inserted into the bottle. After checking the fit of the part in its proper position, it is shaken out of the bottle. Next, the part is again impaled on the needle-wire tool. Glue is smeared onto the appropriate surface of the part. Then, the part is inserted into the bottle and positioned into its intended location. (The tool can also be used to nudge the part into proper alignment.) The needle-wire tool is constructed by drilling a hole in one end of a 3/16-to 1/4-inch-diameter aluminum wire, extending to around 18 inches in length. A 1-inch-long, point-end portion of a thick needle or hat pin is cemented into the hole.

Two needle-wire tool variations can be especially helpful to the bottler of boats and ships. The bent needle-wire tools shown in Fig. 4-11 are often handy for reaching those hard-to-get-at places in and around masts, cabin structures, and deck equipment, found on many bottled ships. These crooked needles can reach behind many shipboard objects, allowing you access to spots and areas previously untouchable. They are especially effective in adjusting the alignment of newly glued deck equipment. The short version of the bent needle-wire tool can also be used to rip out a mistakenly located object, even after its glue is dry. After placing the needle's point in the crack between the object and the surface from which it is to be removed, the gentle action of pulling or prying up usually pops the object off its glued location. Best of all, these bent needle-wire tools are made much like the basic needle-wire tool. Only the type and shape of the needle is different.

Figure 4-14 shows several aluminum bent-wire tools, which are used to adjust the position of individual parts that have been inserted, with or without glue, into the bottle. The bent-wire tool with the small crooked end is great for shaping waves along the top surface of artificial water after it has been installed in the bottle. These are, obviously, the easiest of all the homemade tools to construct. Simply bend the wire with a pair of pliers.

The tool used as a plastering trowel on bottled houses, (Fig. 4-15) can be adapted for use with bottled ships. After adjusting the wire "neck" nearest the X-acto blade, a totally new function is provided. The cutting edge of the blade can be used to cut unwanted rigging lines off sailing ships and boats. One especially valuable trick enables this tool to cut short threads which cannot be pulled taut during cutting. Simply smear a thin coat of white glue around the thread nearest the point at which it is to be severed. Allow the glue to dry and cut cleanly using a gentle sawing motion.

Sandpaper boards (Fig. 4-16) are excellent for sanding those irregularly shaped parts required for bottled ships and boats. Shapes for these abrasive boards are as varied as your imagination. The sandpaper, usually 200-grit, is applied to wood or plastic blocks with contact cement, although white glue will work almost as well.

Another important homemade tool is the "boat press," (Fig. 14-1). It is used to exert heavy pressure upon the hull of a boat or ship when it is being embedded into the material used as artificial water. While some ship's hulls may be cemented directly to the glass surface and artificial water smeared around it, others may be plunged into an already prepared sea. The boat press is composed of a metal rod, 3/16 to 1/4 inch in diameter, which will provide a generous amount of leverage when needed. A wooden or padded handle gives comfort to the hand operating this tool. Depending upon hull-mounting method used, this tool can be very handy. really very simple. If the dimensions are known in either feet or meters, anything can be scaled down with surprising accuracy. Often scaled plans or drawings are available for many ships, especially the old, sailing variety such as *Old Ironsides, Cutty Sark,* and *The Bounty.* These may already be dimensioned in feet or meters. If the plans are dimensioned only in the size for which the finished model ship is intended (usually in inches or centimeters), then those measurements must be adapted to another size to fit the selected bottle. Normally, these drawings are copies of the original shipwright's plans and will be dimensioned in feet or meters. If the dimensions are in feet, you must

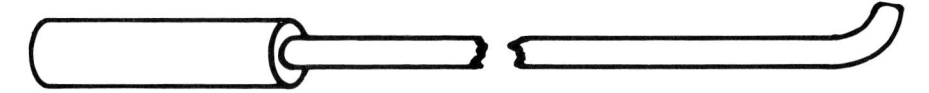

Fig. 14-1. The homemade boat press is made by bending a length of 1/4-inch diameter or larger steel or brass rod to the angle indicated. Great pressure may be brought to bear through this tool, if the angle is correct.

How do you apply paint to an object inside the bottle? By altering the shape of a paintbrush and attaching it to a bent-wire tool, perfect control of paint can be the rule rather than the exception. First, purchase a hobby-type paintbrush, the kind with a metal cap, used with enamel paint. Using pliers, bend the cap, holding the bristles, to a 45-degree angle. Attach the brush handle to a spare, bent-wire tool—one with a straight end rather than a bent one. Use duct tape, heavy twine, or some other strong fastener to provide durability. Although little stress is created within this tool during use, it should still be constructed in such a way as to maximize its dependability. This tool is especially useful for painting whitecaps on the tops of the waves or along the top surface of the sash putty used to simulate water.

Certainly any inventive artist can very well create homemade tools not already mentioned here. It only requires a person to recognize a need and then invent a way to achieve success with it. Most anybody can think up these homemade tools. Experience in constructing bottled ships will help the novice builder perceive those tasks requiring additional tools for completion. Likewise, there may be some, more effective, homemade tools which could substitute for the tools outlined in this chapter. Just because I use a particular method of construction and its required tools to complete a task, does not necessarily mean that is the only way of accomplishing that task. Keep an open mind.

15

The Fold-Up Method of Construction

Bottled ships have been constructed by mariners and other craftsmen for well over 100 years. This great passage of time has been extremely beneficial for the craft. Not only has its popularity increased as an art form, but ingenious construction techniques have been developed and refined. The result is greater authenticity and improved craftsmanship of the bottled ship models. The speed with which a bottled ship is completed has also been increased. Naturally, novice as well as advanced craftsmen are the real beneficiaries of this artistic evolution. We have the privilege of learning and using the products of the many years of painstaking experimentation tried by all the nameless, bottled-ship builders who have gone before us. The fold-up method of constructing a bottled ship is one of those still evolving products of someone else's hard work. The basic idea behind the fold-up method is really very simple. A model of a sailing ship or boat is constructed in such a way as to allow the vessel to be folded up prior to being inserted through the narrow neck of a bottle. Once inside, the model is secured to the glass with a strong adhesive and unfolded by pulling strings to raise the masts. Obviously, only ships and boats with masts can be bottled using this method. Another method, described in the next chapter, must be employed for other types of watercraft. When using the fold-up method, the hull or main body of the sailing vessel usually remains as solid piece, and so must be small enough to slip through the bottleneck together with the folded masts, sails, and rigging. Later, a material representing water, complete with waves, is laid around the ship's hull. Cabins and deck equipment are set in place after the masts are raised and the rigging is adjusted. It is a fast and relatively easy construction method, requiring little inside-the-bottle manipulation. Most builders should manage the fold-up method without much difficulty. **PREPARATIONS.** Some preconstruction preparations are required. Assuming a suitable bottle has been acquired and cleaned, and an appropriate watercraft has been selected, some careful planning must take place. For example, the inside dimensions of the bottle must be measured accurately. This information will aid in scaling down the size of the vessel so that it fills the bottle effectively. Measure the bottle. Start by measuring the inside of the bottleneck. Locate the narrow most passage and cut a small piece of wood which will just manage to squeeze through. Next, using coat-hanger wire, form a hoop or circle representing the bottleneck. Check the hoop's measurements by passing the wood piece through it as if it were the bottleneck. The inside dimension of the wire hoop should be equal to the inside dimension of the narrowmost portion of the bottleneck. This wire hoop is just used as a convenient check for the final assembly of the folded model to pass through.

If the bottle is in the form of a rectangular solid, much like a brick or a square, three measurements will be required. Cut wooden sticks to approximate these dimensions and insert one at a time into the bottle to check the actual size, using the needle-wire tool. Start with the largest (tallest) measurement. Manipulate the stick into a horizontal position and cut or add until the wooden stick reflects the accurate size required. Mark this stick with a colored pen or a bright color of paint so it can be easily recognized as the maximum height that the ship model can stand. Repeat this procedure for the inside bottle width. The measuring process will remain the same. Then, using a longer stick, determine the length of the bottle's interior space. Merely insert a stick lengthwise into the bottle and remove, mark, check again, and cut until accurate. The actual effective length will include a good portion of the bottle's shoulder but will not extend into the neck area. The dotted line in Fig. 15-1 represents the actual effective length or usable length available for the model. When measuring is completed, the height, width, and length of the bottle's interior space should be recorded on paper and carefully labeled for future reference. For a round bottle, you will have only the length and width (diameter) with which to deal.

The next step is to scale down the size of the vessel you intend to bottle. There are two ways of accomplishing this process. One method is merely guessing and "eye balling it," while the other is very precise and scientific. The first method requires that a person's mind be capable of careful proportioning and some practical experience. The second method requires a mind capable of using some simple mathematics. It is

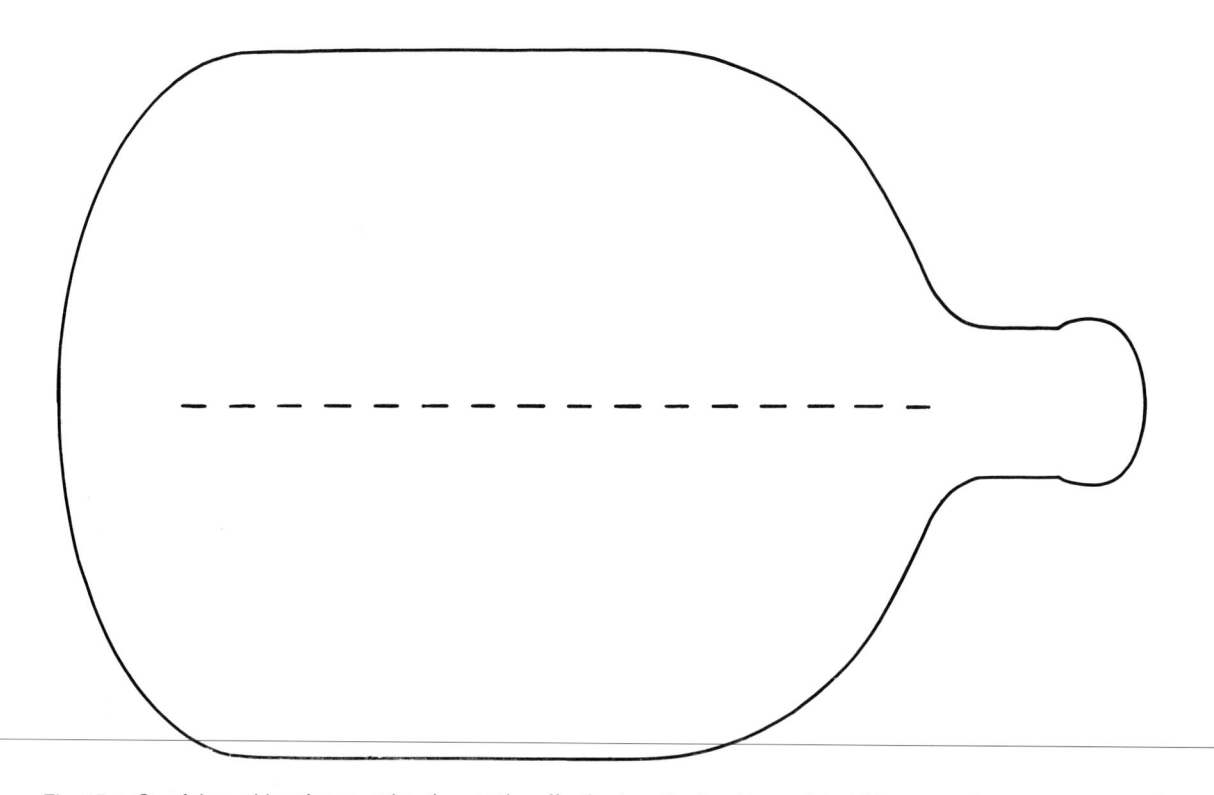

Fig. 15-1. Careful consideration must be given to the effective length of a ship model which can realistically be expected to fit in a particular bottle. Space must be allowed for folded masts.

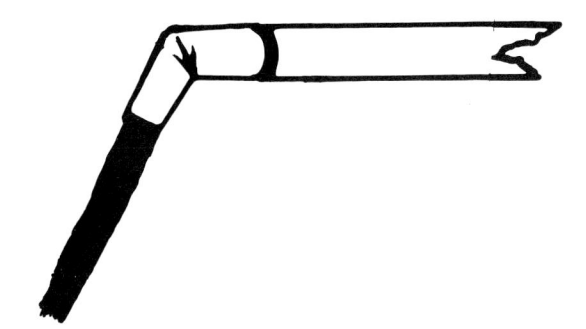

Fig. 14-2. An in-the-bottle paintbrush is made by bending the cap of the brush to a 45-degree angle and lashing it to a wire tool with twine or tape.

multiply those measurements by 12 to produce the number of inches of each object. Then the maximum height allowable in the bottle must be factored in. If the selected bottle will permit only a 3-inch-tall model inside, divide the number of inches representing the real height of the actual ship to determine the rate of scale to be used for that particular bottle. For example, if the sailing ship is 90 feet tall, then 90 multiplied by 12 will equal 1080. In other words, the ship is actually 1080 inches tall. Since the bottle will only permit the ship to stand 3 inches tall once inside, you must divide 1080 by 3 to determine a rat eof scale of 360. This means that the bottled ship will be 1/360 the size of the real ship. So, every measurement in feet must first be converted into inches and then divided by 360 to produce a scaled down size that can fit in the bottle. Continuing, if the actual, overall length of the ship is 240 feet long, it is also 2880 inches long. At a scale of 1/360, the bottled-ship model will be only 8 inches long. This measurement is achieved by dividing the 2880 inches by 3760. Furthermore, if the real ship's deck cabin is 27 feet long, then as a model, the cabin will be only 0.9 inch long in the bottle. Repeating, this is achieved by multiplying the cabin's actual length (27 feet) by 12 to convert to inches (324) and dividing that by the scale (360) to end with a result of 0.9 inch.

If the plans are in meters, the conversions are just as easy. First, measure the interior spaces of the bottle and record the dimensions in centimeters (1 centimeter equals .3937 inches). Then, refer to the plans and convert the meters to centimeters by multiplying the number of meters by 100 because 100 centimeters equal one meter. An example might proceed like this: the bottle height is 9 centimeters by 28 centimeters long and 5 centimeters wide when the bottle is lying on its side. If the sailing ship's actual height is 30 meters, then it is also 3000 centimeters tall. When 3000 is divided by 9 centimeters, a scale of 333 is produced. If the actual length of the ship is 75 meters, the model's total length must be only 22.52 centimeters. This is achieved by first converting the 75 meters to 7500 centimeters. Next, divide the 7500 by the scale (333) to produce a length of 22.52 centimeters for the bottled model.

There is only one major problem which may interfere with this scaling down process. The bottleneck may be too small to accommodate a ship model of these proportions. If this is the case, the prerogative of artistic license is practiced by altering the proportions of the vessel in order to allow passage through the neck. Simply change some dimensions so the ship will fit. Otherwise, the hull of the ship and several other parts must be inserted into the bottle in sections, creating a whole new set of problems to entertain you.

CONSTRUCTION

The hull of the ship model is the first component to be constructed. Since the scale has already been determined, measurements for this main body of the vessel should be readily at hand. Select a block of wood such as fir, pine, spruce, birch, maple, or cherry. Cut out the general shape of the hull using a band saw or jigsaw, if machine tools are handy, or use a coping saw, if only hand tools are available. Next, use an X-acto knife to carve and refine the shape or contours of the hull. End by smoothing with sandpaper.

A flat-bottomed hull will eventually be cemented directly to the bottle glass itself. A round-bottomed hull is embedded into the blue putty representing water surrounding the ship. Either of these two techniques are acceptable, but you must decide which method to follow when the hull is being shaped. The correct hull bottom is appropriate only with the proper mounting techniques. The advantage of using the flat-bottomed, mounting method is that the ship model is slightly more secure. The model rarely comes loose from the glass surface using this method. The disadvantage is the appearance. The cemented mounting point, surrounded by water material, is somewhat unsightly showing through the glass bottom. However, it shows only when the bottled ship is picked up and the mounting point examined. In contrast, the advantage of the second mounting method is that the appearance of the mounting point is so much neater. After the blue modeling clay or putty has been spread inside the bottle, the ship is mashed or embedded into this material, eliminating the ugly glue points along the bottom of the hull. The only real disadvantage is that on rare occasions the ship model may come loose from the grip of the putty or modeling clay. it is a decision which only you can make.

The hull is not yet ready to be installed into the bottle. Rather, it is painted and set aside while construction continues on other components of the model. A clean-edged, contrasting-colored, water line should be painted along the lower third of the hull. The top surface of the deck can also be painted, using varnish or other clear finish.

Square-Riggers

The masts are the next components to be constructed. Obtain a cotton-swab handle, or any wooden dowel measuring 1/16 inch in diameter, and shape one end to a long, gentle taper using sandpaper. Selecting a drill bit 1/32 inch in diameter or smaller, bore a hole across the shaft of the mast around 1/8 inch from the bottom end, as illustrated

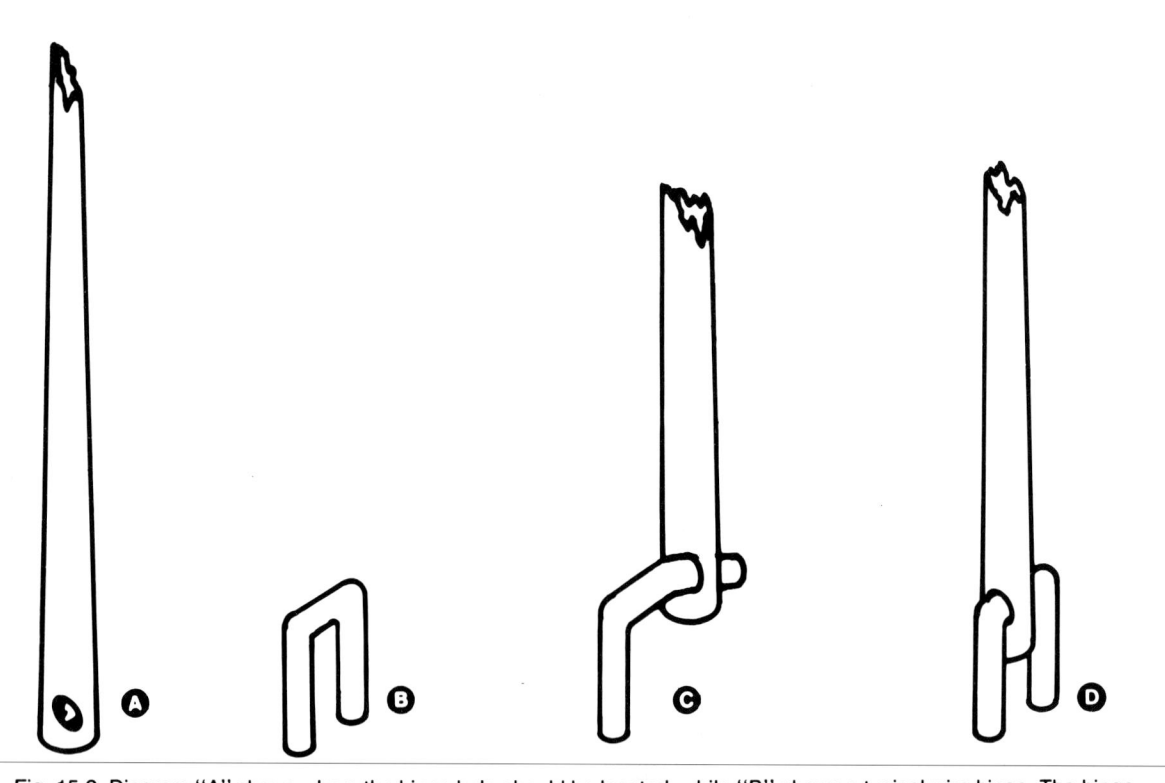

Fig. 15-2. Diagram "A" shows where the hinge hole should be located, while "B" shows a typical wire hinge. The hinge is bent open to allow the mast to be threaded onto the hinge in diagram "C." "D" shows the hinge leg bent back to its proper position after assembly.

Assemble all the mast parts by lashing them together with waxed thread, surgical suture, or thin copper or brass wire, as shown in Fig. 15-3. In cases where mast parts must remain adjustable, especially when squeezing through the bottleneck, the lashing should be tied loosely to allow for easy movement. Later, paper or cloth sails are sewn or glued in place on the masts.

The mast hinge may be constructed from wire or bent a straight pin. Straight pins are especially well adapted as mast hinges, because they are both thin-shafted and strong. First, cut off the pin's head with wire cutters. Then, bend a right angle at a point 1/4 inch from the cut end using pliers. Next, using needle-nose pliers bend another right angle 1/16 inch from the first. Cut off the pin's point. This should form a squared-off, horseshoe shape, as pictured in Fig. 15-2, diagram "B. When it is time to connect the hinge to the mast, straighten one right angle bend in order to slip the hinge through the hole in the base of the mast, as shown in Fig. 15-2, diagram "C." Then, bend the hinge arm back to form a horseshoe again. Once attached to the mast, the hinge should pivot back and forth easily (Fig. 15-2, diagram "D").

Some sailing ships and boats require a bowsprit to complete its rigging. A bowsprit is a spar extending beyond the bow of the vessel. A hole must be drilled into the bow of the hull running lengthwise, as shown in Fig. 15-4. First, cut a notch in the very end or point of the bow to allow a secure start for the drill bit. Select a drill bit size which will accommodate the shaft of the bowsprit plus a little extra room for the glue. Complete the drilling, being careful to maintain the correct angle at which the bowsprit must eventually extend. An electric drill works best for this task. Bore about 1/2 inch deep. Next, cut and taper the bowsprit by gluing together with white glue. Finish by applying a coat of varnish to the bowsprite.

A tiny eyelet must be made and installed at the point of the bowsprit. Obtain a single strand of very thin copper or brass wire. Wind the strand one time around the shaft of a thin sewing pin. A small paper clip will do. After you wind the wire around the pin to form a loop, twist the wire around itself many

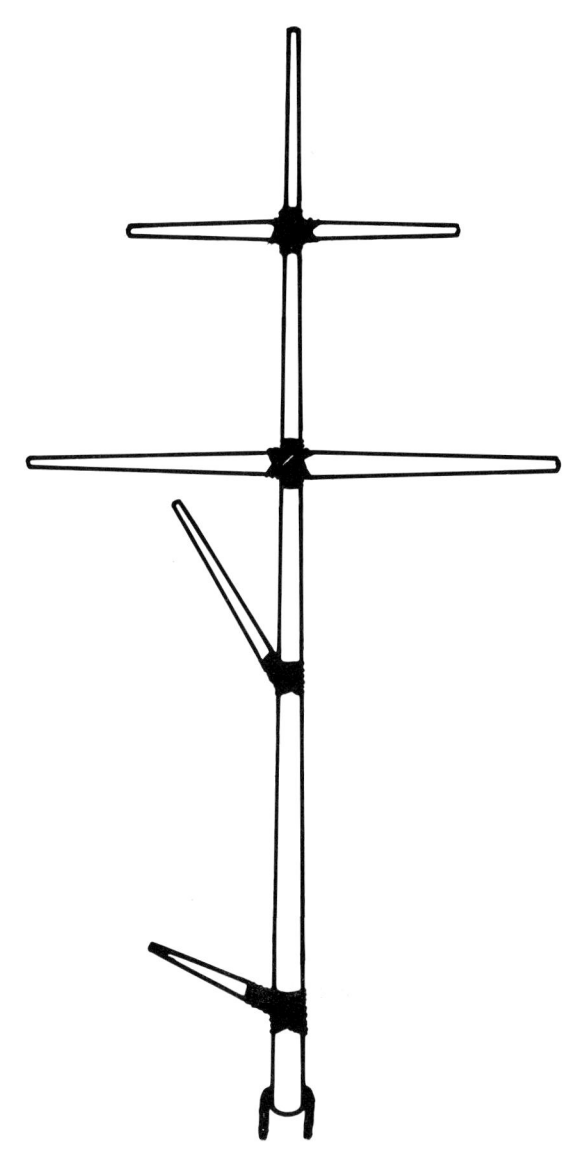

Fig. 15-3. Waxed thread or surgical suture may be used to lash together the other parts of the mast assembly (yards, booms, and gaffs). Some lashings may be loose to allow some movement.

in Fig. 15-2, diagram "A." This hole will hold the mast hinge. Continue this process until all the required masts are shaped with a taper and the hinge holes bored. Cut and taper any other spars, gaffs, yards, or booms needed for the vessel's rigging design. Apply varnish or similar finish if desired.

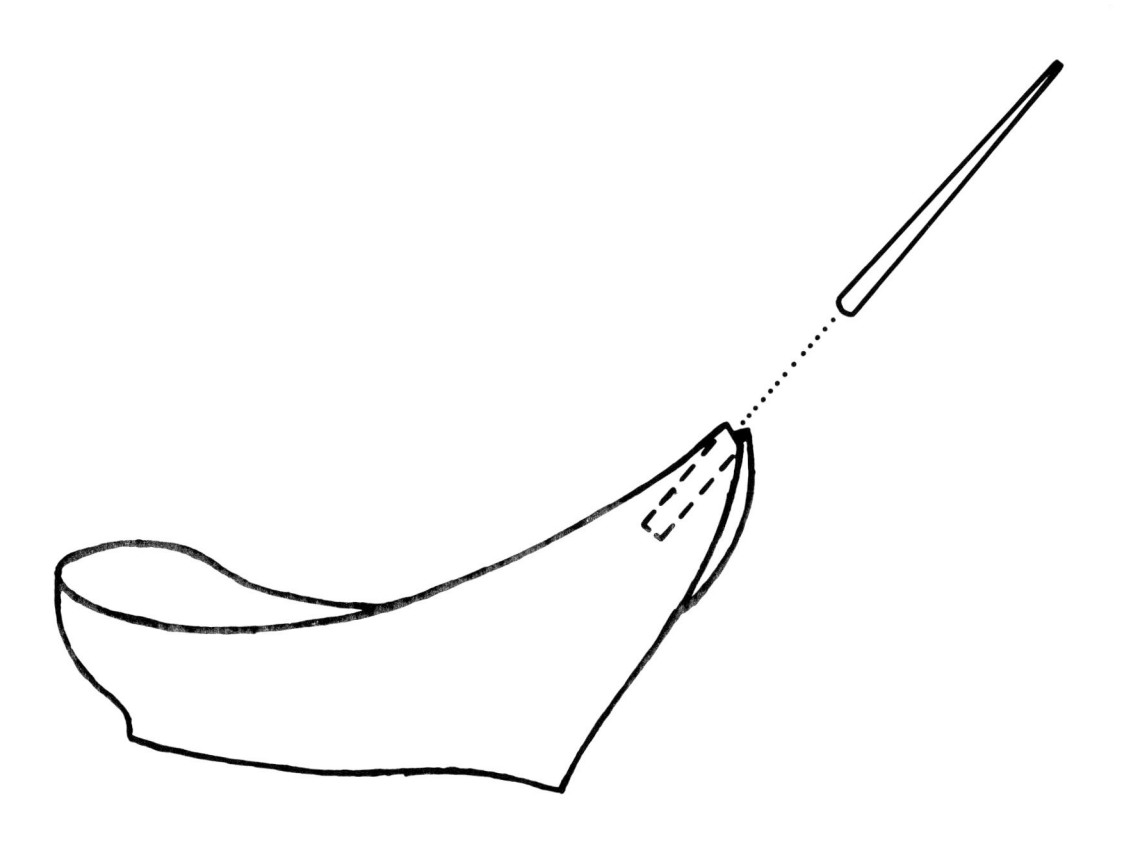

Fig. 15-4. In order to attach the bowsprit to the hull, a hole must be drilled into the hull point as shown, and the bowsprit inserted with glue.

times for a length of 1/4 inch, as shown in Fig. 15-5. The excess wire remains attached to the eyelet and is used to secure it to the end of the bowsprit end. The loop should extend just beyond the wood point. Wrap or wind the excess wire around the bowsprit several times and apply a small amount of glue to secure the assembly permanently.

At this point in the construction process, some assembly should be completed. The masts, together with their sails, are attached to the hull. First, however, holes must be drilled into the deck of the hull to accommodate the mast hinges. After drilling, apply glue to the holes and insert the hinge posts, as shown in Fig. 15-6. Test each mast to determine if it will lie flat. When working properly, the masts should swing on their hinges, from lying flat to standing straight up and back again with a smooth, steady movement. Insert the model partway into the neck of the bottle to check for proper clearance. The ship assembly should slip back and forth easily.

A retaining line is required to control the masts. First, a thin, waxed thread or surgical suture must be attached to the stern of the ship. Use either a small, 1/2-inch-long, straight sewing pin embedded in the wooden hull to secure the retaining line, or drill a tiny hole in the same location. Then, stuff the line into the hole along with a small amount of glue. Tie the other end of this line to a point 2/3 of the way up the aft (rear) mast, as shown in Fig. 15-7. Be sure, however, that the mast is standing upright or only leaning slightly aft before you secure the line to it. Use the excess line from the knot to secure the next mast, tieing it just below its top. Be sure the second mast is standing at the same angle as the aft mast. If the bottled ship is composed of a third mast, it too must be secured

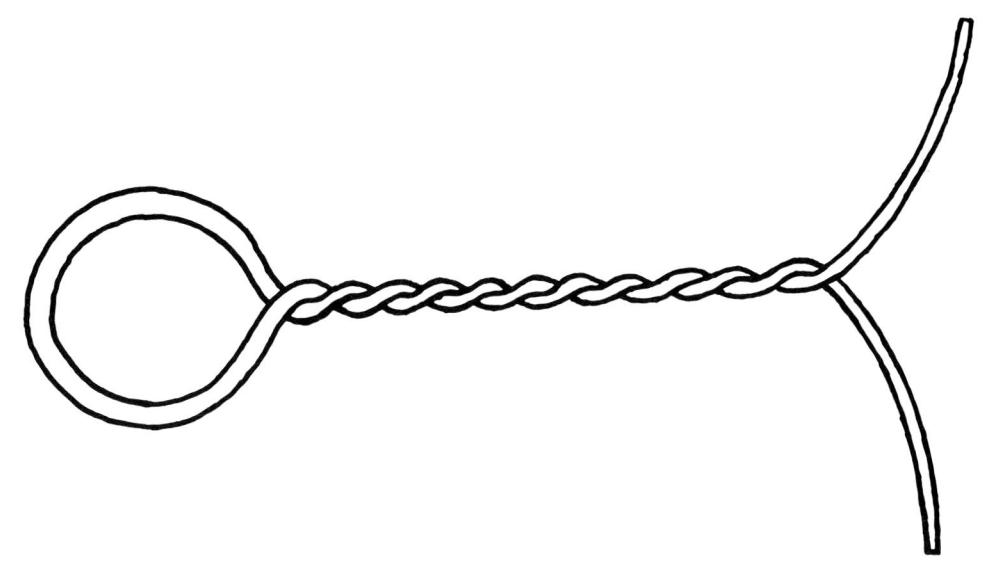

Fig. 15-5. The bowsprit eyelet is made by forming a loop around a small straight pin with very thin copper wire. Twist the wire around itself for a length of 1/4 inch, but leave the wire ends free for 1/8 inch, as shown.

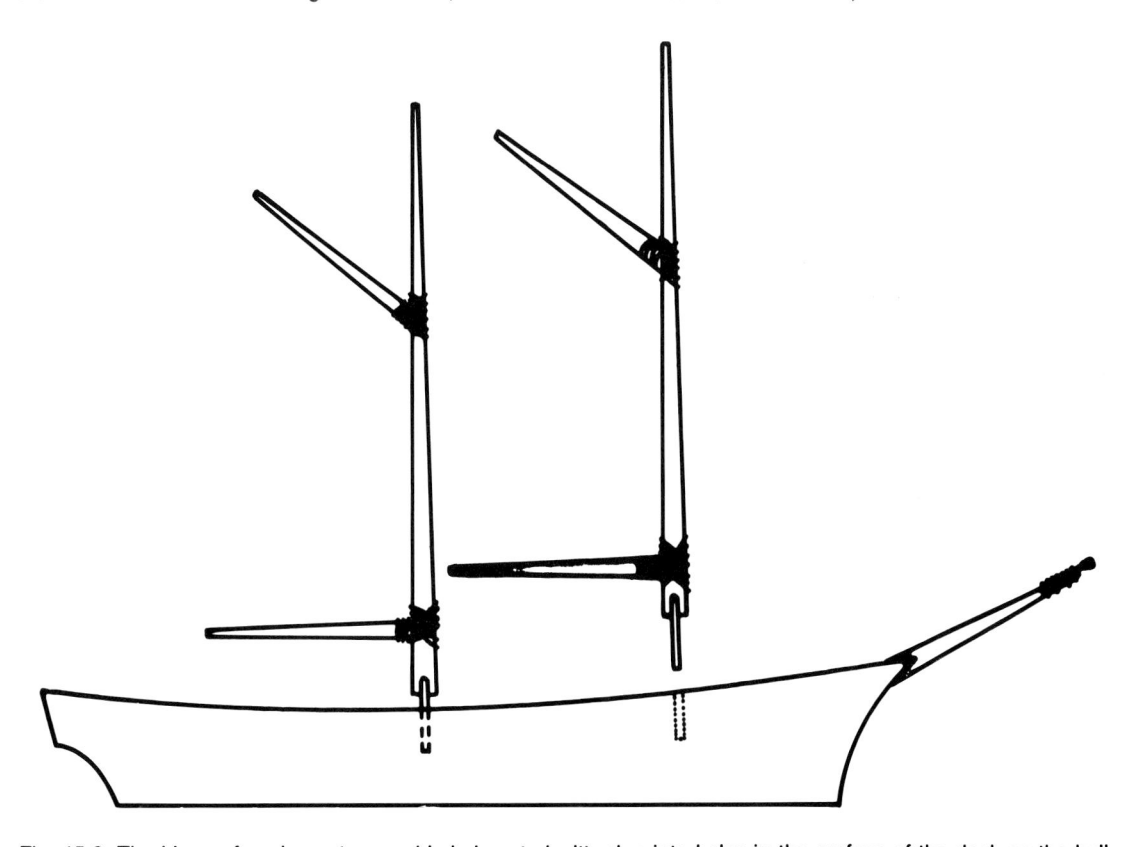

Fig. 15-6. The hinge of each mast assembly is inserted with glue into holes in the surface of the deck on the hull.

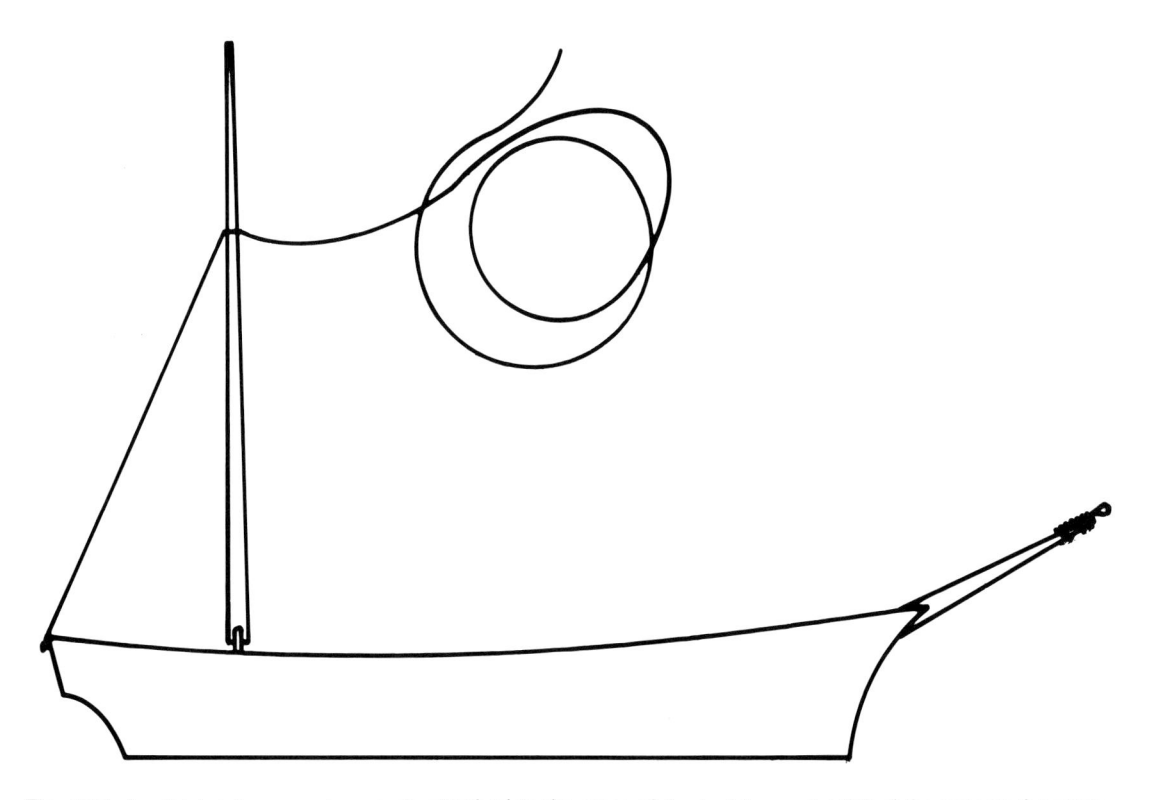

Fig. 15-7. A retaining line runs from a pin attached to the stern of the hull to a point 2/3 of the way up the mast.

with a retaining line tied near its top. Add a 2-foot section of retaining line, attached to the fore (front) mast, and run it down through the eyelet on the tip of the bowsprit, as illustrated in Fig. 15-8. Wrap the line around the eyelet several times just to hold everything in place for a while. Do not cut away any excess retaining line, since it will be used later to pull the masts to an upright position once the ship is inside the bottle.

Shrouds and ratlines are attached to the hull and threaded through holes drilled into the masts or tiny wire eyelets attached on either side of each mast, as shown in Fig. 15-9. Release the retaining line, allowing the masts to fall flat, in order to test the ease of raising and lowering the masts despite the addition of the shrouds.

If the ship is a square-rigger, lines must be attached to the free corners of the sails, and other lines must be connected to the ends of the yards. The lines from the sails extend down to the sides of the hull. The lines on the yard ends also run down to the hull sides. Additional lines run from the yard tips back up to the masts. Keep in mind that the lower, wider yards must be able to pivot diagonally for easy passage through the bottleneck. Again, release the retaining line and lower the masts as a test.

If jib sails are to be included among the rigging, lines must extend from selected points along the bowsprit and run through predrilled holes in the foremast (or through eyelets secured to the mast). The line is circled back down, joining the first retaining line, as it passes through the bowsprit eyelet. It is from the first portion of these lines that the jib sail is hung, glued, or sewn. The remaining corner of the jib (the lower corner) is secured with a line running down to the hull of the vessel. A careful study of Fig. 15-10 will clarify this procedure. Add other jiblike stay sails as required. Release the retaining lines (two now, maybe more) and

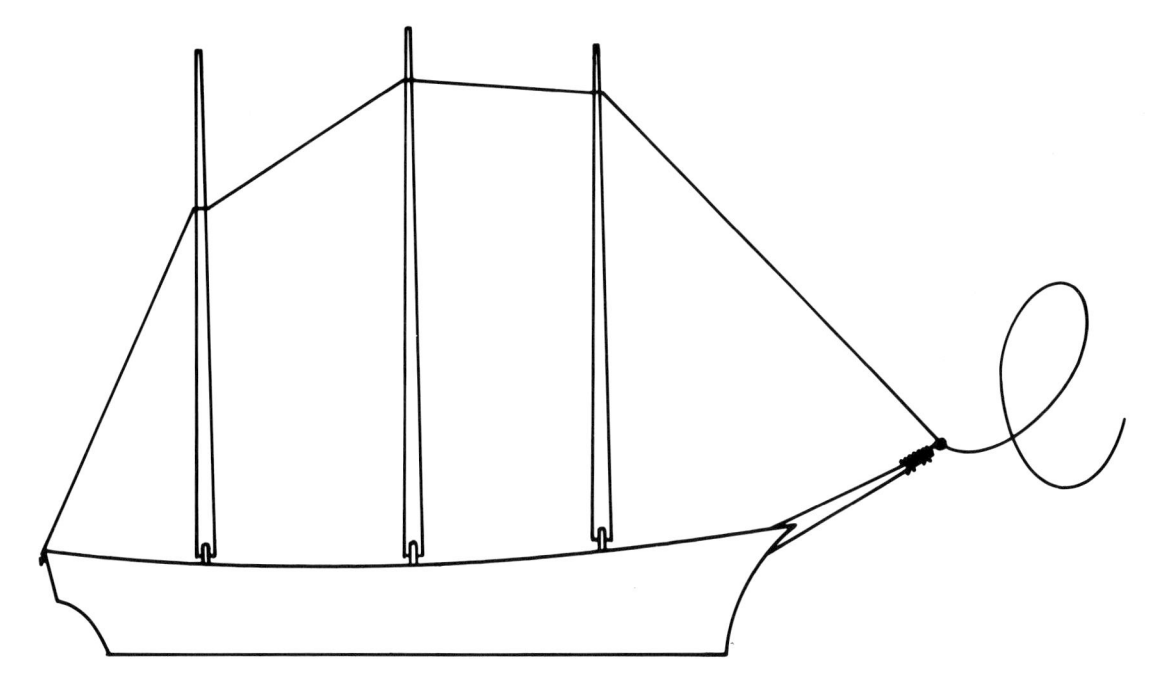

Fig. 15-8. The retaining line continues on to link together the other masts, with knots tied to each one, and then extends down, passing through the eyelet, as shown.

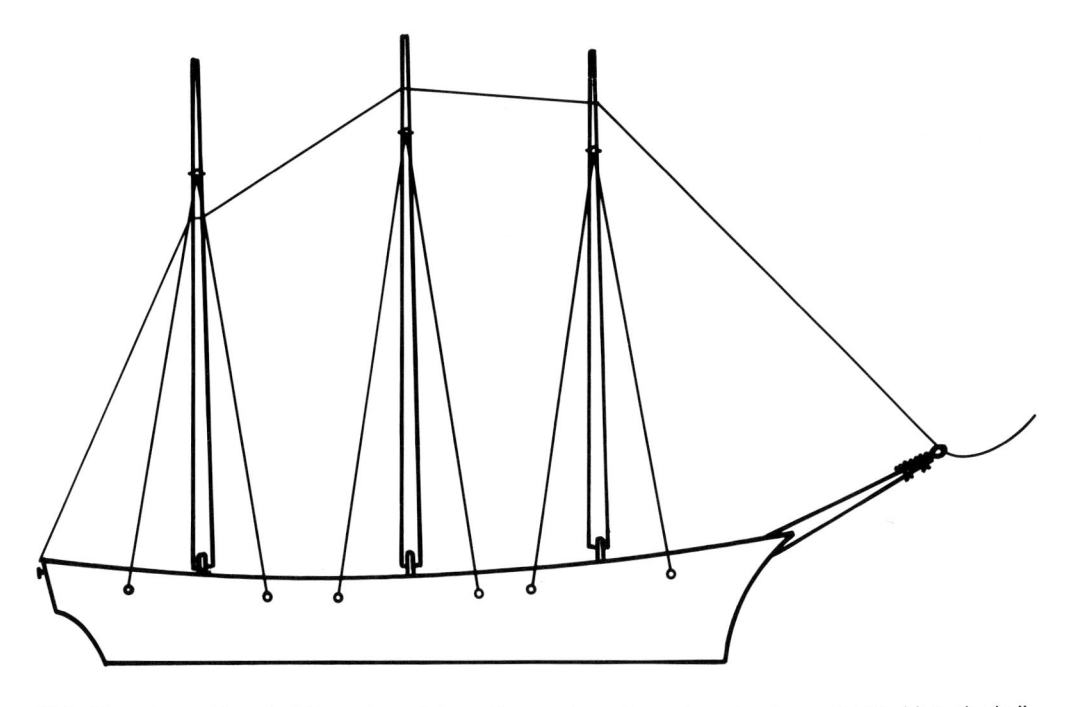

Fig. 15-9. Shrouds are threaded through eyelets on the masts and run down to pins embedded into the hull.

187

lower the masts down to test. Make adjustments which allow for the smooth raising and lowering of all masts and yards.

Now is the time for a dry run to check for proper clearance. Hold onto the bowsprit and insert the stern of the vessel through the opening in the neck. Insert the folded model only partway into the neck of the bottle; otherwise, it may be pushed beyond the point of no return and remain irretrievable. Note any hang-ups and think of ways to alter or eliminate such problems. Remove the model from the bottleneck and make any required adjustments.

Deck structures are constructed next. They may include, but are not limited to, deckhouses, cabins, hatch covers, ship's wheel, cannons or guns, hand pumps, capstans, and rigging equipment. Although such objects should be constructed and painted, they are not usually installed on or attached to the ship until after it is inserted into the bottle and the masts are raised. This delay in final assembly provides for a more compact folding of the vessel, resulting in smoother passage through the bottleneck.

Schooners

Some of the preceding instructions refer only to a square-rigged sailing vessel. Naturally, not every rigging configuration can be included without adding volumes to read. A few pointers in the construction of a schooner, however, will help you to become more inventive in discovering ways to adapt almost any type of rigging configuration to this method of bottling a ship. Careful planning and extensive experimentation will eventually result in solving even the most difficult of fold-up engineering problems. It is usually a matter of developing patience and determination.

A ship rigged as a schooner requires the use of a boom and gaff attached to each mast, as shown in Fig. 15-11. These important components must

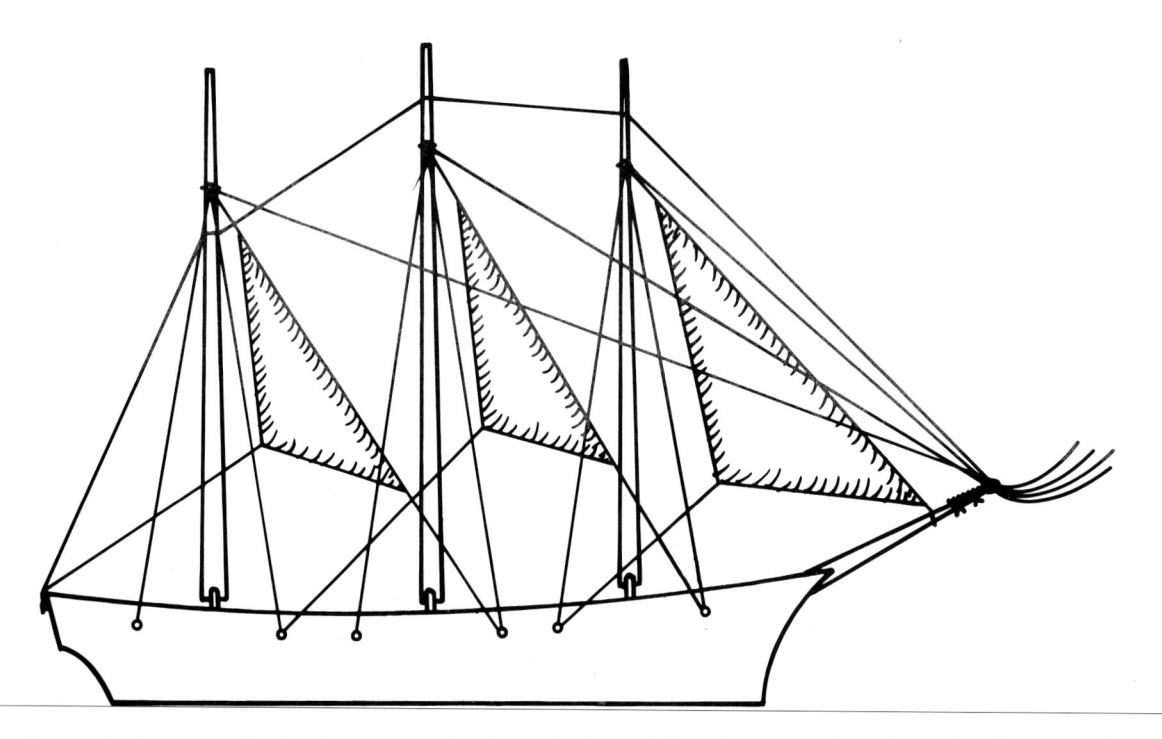

Fig. 15-10. Lines supporting the jib and staysail run from pins located along the upper edge of the hull, up through eyelets on the masts, and down through the bowsprit eyelet.

trol the positions of the boom and gaff. The boom and gaff may be set at an angle to the keel as if set in tack with the wind direction. A schooner rarely sails with the boom and gaff exactly parallel to the vessel's keel. For that matter, it is accurate to say the same for square-rigged vessels. One rule must always be followed: the boom and gaff together must create a vertical plane, unless, of course, the vessel represents a shipwreck. Therefore, the gaff cannot hang out over the starboard gunwale, while the boom remains parallel with the keel, nor can it hang out over the port side. Since a sail is stretched between them, that rule only makes good sense.

Although some builders may disagree, cloth sails may be preferable to paper ones on a schooner. Considering all the folding of masts, booms, and gaffs, paper sails will become permanently creased and mauled. Of course, paper sails could be installed after the ship is inserted into the bottle and the masts are raised permanently; however, such installation of curled paper is difficult. Cloth, on the other hand, is much more durable and crease-resistant. Beyond that, cloth is durable enough to endure being sewn to the masts and spars.

INSERTION

Finally the big day has arrived! All the construction has been completed, and all the parts have been assembled, as in Fig. 15-12. A dry run or two has determined that everything will operate properly once inside the bottle. The next big step is the actual insertion of the folded ship into the bottle. Prior to actual insertion, you must make some decisions. Some craftsmen prefer to cement the ship model directly to the glass bottle once the ship is inside. Others plunge the hull of the ship into the modeling clay or sash putty representing ocean water. Either method will work well; however, you must be very sure of all vertical measurements when securing the ship model with putty or modeling clay. If the hull of the ship model is unable to be embedded deep enough into the "ocean," the tops of the masts may strike the inside of the bottle glass when they

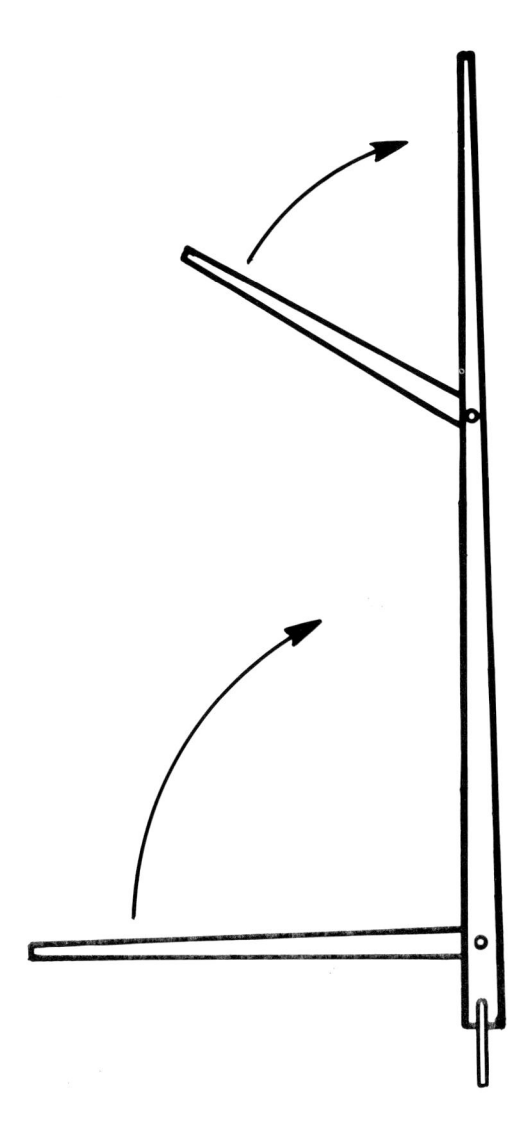

Fig. 15-11. The boom and gaff of a schooner-rigged mast must be able to be pivoted up out of the way during insertion into the bottleneck.

also fold with the action of the masts. The mast ends of the gaff and boom (the points at which they connect to the mast) may be hinged on a small pin or loosely lashed with thread or thin wire to allow for easy movement. The schooner-rigged mast is hinged and operated in the same way as the previously mentioned square-rigged mast. A retaining line is used to hold the mast in the proper upright angle, while additional lines are used to con-

Fig. 15-12. Construction of the model itself is complete and all the parts are ready to be inserted into the bottle.

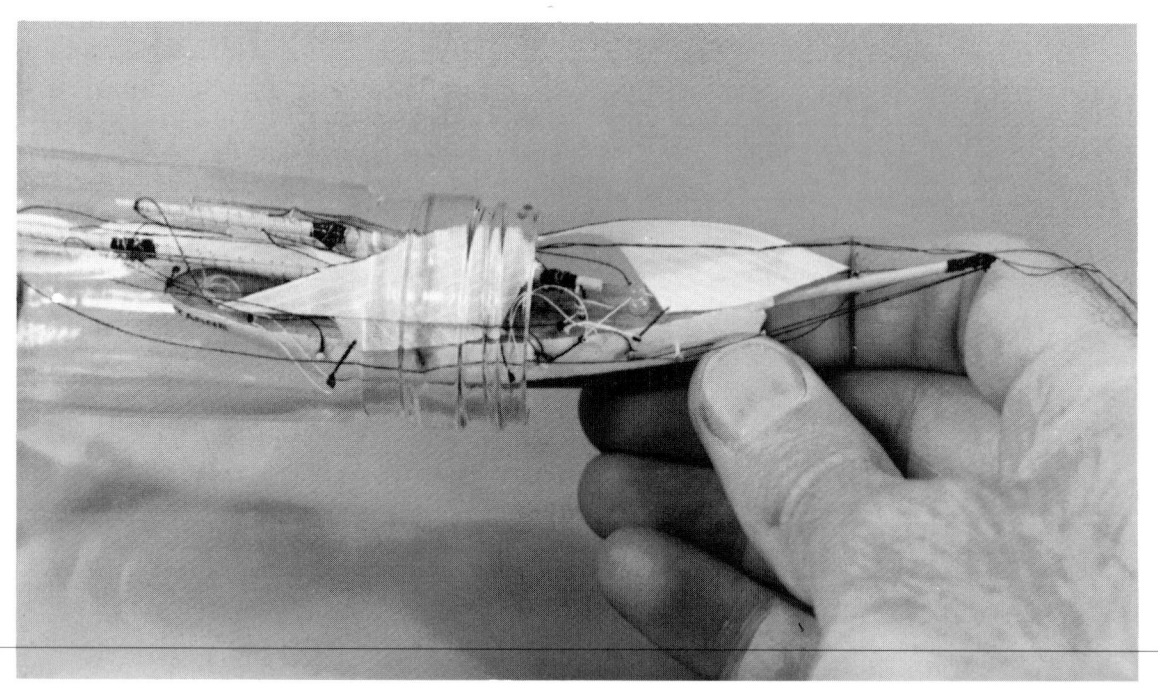

Fig. 15-13. The main portion of the snip model is inserted into the neck by hand. The remaining parts will be inserted later.

are raised. When the ship model is inserted into the bottle, it is positioned and then pressed vigorously into the putty or modeling clay using the boat-press tool (Fig. 14-1). Be aware that modeling clay has been known to release a model from its grip using this method. The sash putty, on the other hand, almost never fails.

The advantage of cementing the ship model to the glass prior to surrounding it with putty or modeling clay is that it provides you with the peace of mind that the ship is extremely secure. Epoxy cement is mixed and inserted into the bottle, using the wire tool, at the exact location where the ship will stand. Then, the ship is inserted through the bottleneck (Fig. 15-13) and maneuvered into position atop or into the cement, again using the wire tool. It also works well to lift the folded ship model over to the cement to avoid having the rigging or sails drag or fall into the cement. The ship is left undisturbed a full 24 hours (Fig. 15-14). Only after the masts are raised and secured is the "ocean" applied lump by lump around the base of the ship's hull. Later, shaping and painting of waves create the required realism. Remember to wait until the epoxy cement has dried before doing anything. You must resist all temptation which might result in a disaster.

Now, it is time for a fun and exciting task. Pulling the strings which raise the masts is perhaps the most gratifying task required to complete the bottled ship. The builder watches intently as the results of many hours of engineering and craftsmanship spring to life. Position the bottle in a location which allows the strings to dangle over the edge of a table or counter. Gently pull the strings, all together, or one at a time to avoid tangles. When the

Fig. 15-14. The vessel remains partially folded while the epoxy cement which secures the hull to the glass cures or dries completely.

Fig. 15-15. After you pull the strings which raise the masts to their fully upright position, apply weights to each string, and spread a small amount of white glue on and around the bowsprit eyelet.

masts have been raised to their full, upright position and all sails and lines are pulled taut, weights are applied to each string, as illustrated in Fig. 15-15. Clothespins will work especially well for this purpose.

After all the weights have been applied (hanging over the edge of the table or counter), smear a small amount of white glue over the bowsprit eyelet and the lines running through the eyelet. Make sure the glue is applied all around the strings, allowing it to penetrate between them. This is a major stress point which must be strong and secure. A small amount of glue should saturate the strings to a point 1/4 inch out beyond the eyelet to allow for a cleaner severing of the strings later.

The weights should remain undisturbed for several hours or even overnight. Later, use the line cutter (Fig. 4-15) to cut through the strings just outside the eyelet with a wiggling action.

The deck structures are installed next. Using the bent-wire tool, smear a small amount of white glue onto the deck at the location intended for each part. Then, attach a small wad of modeling clay to the end of a bent-wire tool and pick up a part and set it into the glue. Maneuver it into the exact position using another wire tool. The bottled ship should now be complete (Fig. 15-16).

Sealing the bottle is the next step. Allow any moisture which has accumulated during installation to evaporate. To do so, simply leave the bottle uncorked for several days. Any condensation appearing on the inside of the bottle during a sudden change in temperature will indicate excessive moisture remaining inside the bottle. It will eventually

Fig. 15-16. The completed bottled sailboat is ready for final sealing with a cork closure.

evaporate. After all the droplets of water have disappeared, the bottle can be sealed with a permanent closure. The bottle's original cap, a cork, or an elaborate device, described in previous chapters, may be employed to seal the bottle for eternity.

It should be abundantly clear that extensive experimentation, careful planning, and exhaustive testing are essential to achieve success of a seemingly impossible undertaking. By following the simple instructions in this chapter, you can manage to fold up, insert, and unfold most any rigging configuration. Using common sense, being inventive, and learning from your successes and mistakes will enable you to develop the skills required for tackling even more difficult challenges. Happily, there will always be those more difficult challenges waiting to be met.

16 The Sectioned Method Of Construction

Interest in bottling sailing ships continues to be strong despite the emergence of mechanically powered vessels. The need to accommodate the bottling of these modern ships, such as steamers, riverboats, military ships, and many other vessels without sails, however, became increasingly apparent as more types of them evolved. A new method of bottling modern vessels was developed. In theory, the ship model is simply constructed in a number of separate pieces, each of which is inserted into the bottle as an individual unit. In other words, the ship is bottled in sections. Since a bottled ship is composed of so many fewer pieces than a bottled house, you can build the entire ship on the outside of the bottle and then reassemble it on the inside. It is that simple! There are both advantages and disadvantages to using this method of construction. One major advantage is that since the mechanics of fold-up structures have been eliminated, there is usually more room for additional and more accurate details. There is also increased builder concentration on these improved details, since attention can be turned away from complex mechanical functions. Accuracy is especially enhanced with this construction method. Another advantage of this method is that a wider variety of ships, or other objects for that matter, can be constructed and bottled. You are no longer limited to sailing ships. On the other hand, one disadvantage is that the surface on which the sectioned vessel is to be mounted must be perfectly flat for proper section alignment. Rarely are the inside, glass walls of a bottle flat enough. You must take additional care to provide a flat surface. Consequently, you will find that flat-sided bottles are easier to work in than round ones. Round bottles must be partially filled with some additional material in order to level-off a suitable mounting spot, as illustrated in Fig. 16-1. A vessel should not be mounted directly onto a rounded or curved surface, because the sections of the model will not line up evenly. In contrast, flat-sided bottles require no extra materials for leveling off, but merely a flat spot on which to assemble and mount the model. Another disadvantage is that your craftsmanship must be of the very highest quality. Each section should fit together with its adjoining neighbor with only a tiny, visible crack. Greater success will be achieved if you can assemble the sections without noticeably conspicuous cracks or seams. The real disadvantage presents itself only if you are unable to achieve this level of craftsmanship. As with all learned skills, however, the early works of art provide practice to develop your improved craftsmanship for use on later, more advanced projects. **PRELIMINARY STEPS.** Completion of a few preliminary tasks will help lay a proper

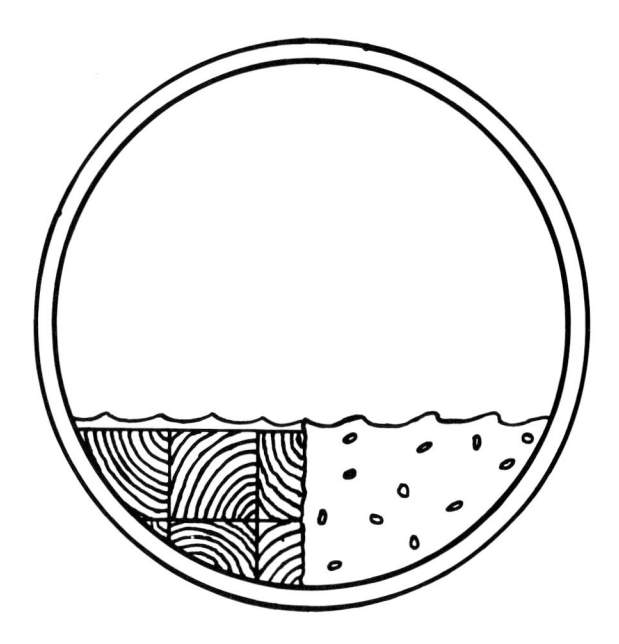

Fig. 16-1. This cross section of a round bottle shows how a level area must be formed to accommodate the ship model.

foundation in preparation for the actual construction processes occurring later. These preliminaries should not be abbreviated, but rather completed with all the care and attention to detail as in the actual construction of the model.

You must first select a suitable vessel and an appropriate bottle which relates well to that vessel. If you are a novice builder, you should select a vessel composed of simple shapes and modest details. A model which is overwhelming to complete, because of its excessive complexities, can discourage a beginner from ever attempting another bottled ship. Keep the first project simple. Next select a bottle of appropriate shape and size. Consider the overall shape of the vessel when choosing a bottle. The bottle's shape should relate closely with the ship's. Remember, too, that usually, but not always, the bottle will lie on its side. Therefore, a short, squatty bottle would be a poor choice for an aircraft carrier. On the other hand, if you are taking generous "artistic license" with the design of the aircraft carrier, a highly stylized version might just fit into such a bottle, creating a very interesting statement. It all depends upon your intent. Size is still another consideration. Select a bottle which will provide enough room to hold a model large enough to allow some details to show. The smaller the bottle, the less detail can be presented. Conversely, if it is your intent to construct on a tiny scale, a small bottle is the only possibility.

Clean the botttle if necessary. Remember that new beverage bottles which are freshly emptied usually require simple rinsing, while antiques may need extensive scrubbing. Allow the bottle to drain and dry thoroughly. Then, cork or seal the bottle to keep out dust. It is wise to select a suitable closure and have it ready for use.

Begin considering sizes. First, measure the bottle using the techniques outlined in the preceding chapter. Then, scale down the size of the watercraft to be bottled. Keep in mind that this process is extremely important and should be checked and double-checked for accuracy. There can be no room for errors with this craft. Once the proper scale has been selected, the actual construction may begin.

CONSTRUCTION

Begin by building a flat spot on which the hull of

the ship will attach. This may be a very flat piece of wood or plastic 1/8 inch thick and as wide as the bottleneck will allow for easy passage. The length will be determined by the scale of the vessel being bottled (length of the model's hull). This flat spot must not be visible after the hull is inserted and glued into place (except when looking through the glass wall serving as the bottom of the artwork). Accordingly, the size of the flat spot should be somewhat smaller than the bottom surface of the ship's hull to help keep it hidden from view. After cutting and shaping, cement the flat spot onto the inside wall of the bottle by mixing epoxy cement and inserting it through the neck with the wire tool. Smear a generous portion of the cement onto the glass. Then, insert the flat spot and plunge it into the pool of cement. Adjust its location to the middle of the bottle (suitable to the location of the vessel) and carefully level it off. Leave the bottle undisturbed for 24 hours.

Another method may be slightly more difficult to execute, but it results in a much more refined appearance upon completion. First, colored putty is applied to the bottle glass to represent the water surrounding the vessel. Remember to coat the glass surface with white glue prior to applying the putty, and allow it to dry completely. White glue dries clear. Smear the putty against and over the glue surface for a secure bond. After the putty is applied, cut a 3/32-inch-thick piece of plywood (or any rigidly flat material) just wide enough to fit through the bottleneck. This piece should be wide enough and long enough to provide a flat assembly area atop the putty. It is similar to the flat spot. Drill a hole through one end and attach a pull string, 12 to 18 inches long, tied securely through the hole. Insert the plywood into the bottle, allowing the string to dangle outside. Position the plywood in the middle of the putty area, but avoid putting any pressure on it. The plywood should not be allowed to stick to the putty. Assembly and gluing of the vessel's hull is accomplished atop this plywood assembly area. Do not glue the hull to the plywood. After the hull is assembled, glued, and dry, the string is gently pulled to remove the plywood from the bottle. Position the assembled hull over the exact spot intended for final sailing. Then, press the hull into the putty using the wire boat press (Fig. 14-1). Level or pitch the hull as desired, while making sure it is embedded securely enough to remain there for eternity.

The actual hull construction is the first task to be completed that involves the vessel itself. Surprisingly, there are two methods for building the vessel's hull in small enough sections. The best way is to cut and form wood strips, each of which will pass through the bottleneck. Assembled together they should equal the total size required for the completed hull. Then, wooden, metal, or plastic pins are planted along one connecting edge of all but one of the sections (Fig. 16-2). Assemble all the sections, and shape the hull as required. This technique ensures that all the sections will line up evenly and remain aligned. Remember, however, that the pins must also clear the bottleneck along with each wooden section; so make the pins short.

In the other construction method, the hull is formed as a single unit rather than in pieces. Later, after all the shaping has been completed, the hull is cut into carefully measured pieces using a very thin-bladed saw. Afterwards, some additional shaping (sanding) may be required to help make the resulting cracks disappear from between the sections. The only problem with this method is in keeping all the sections aligned at all times. This minor problem, however, is usually overcome by most builders with little difficulty. Rubberbands can be fantastic tools.

Testing remains important. Prior to painting the sections composing the hull, they should be inserted into the bottle to check for proper alignment and fit. This testing process also provides you with additional practice in maneuvering objects into position inside the bottle. Make sure the two middle sections are carefully balanced atop the flat spot. Check how neatly the two sections fit together. Next, remove all the pieces from the bottle and reassemble on a very flat surface. Again check the cracks between sections. Trim or add wood putty to improve the fit and minimize the size of the cracks.

Continue constructing the various parts com-

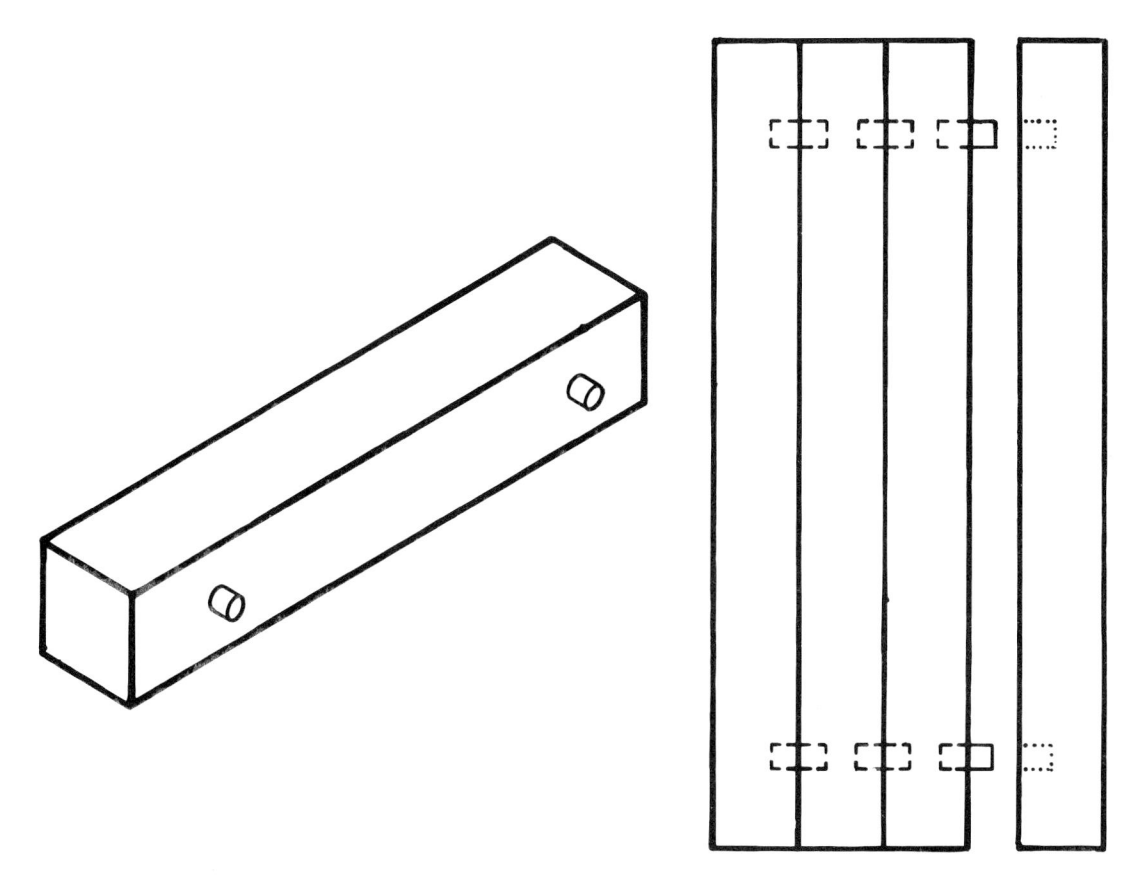

Fig. 16-2. Pins are used to hold the different sections together while their proper hull shape is being cut and refined.

Fig. 16-3. A wooden flat spot is inserted into the bottle and cemented directly to the glass.

posing the ship model. Deckhouses, hatch covers, smokestacks, radio and radar antennae, masts, and all other structures must be constructed, usually by carving them from solid wood, and sectioned depending on their final size. Remember to calculate their size according to the scale you selected. Many parts may remain in a single unit and still pass easily through the bottleneck. After all the pieces have been constructed, assemble them atop a flat, level surface. Note how well each piece fits along the surface of each deck. Everything must fit together neatly with only the smallest of cracks. Make sure pieces can be assembled using only a wire tool. Pieces should not be required to snap together, but rather to slide together easily.

Painting is the next major consideration. After all the sections and individual pieces have been sanded smooth, they must be painted. Glossy-finish enamel model paints look very appropriate on most parts of modern watercraft, while matte-finished paints seem to look best on much older steamers and sailing ships. Naturally, the decision on which type of paint to use is your option. If you are trying to reproduce a wreck of a fairly modern vessel, matte-finished paints would help portray the decaying and rusting remains of the ship. Luckily, the great variety of model paints provide you with a number of useful alternatives for almost every possibility.

If modeling clay is being used to represent water, some should be inserted into the bottle and applied around the flat spot just prior to the insertion of the first section (Fig. 16-4). Make sure to avoid mounding the clay up too high. This undesirable condition would allow the clay to interfere with the overhang of the hull sections, which extend out,

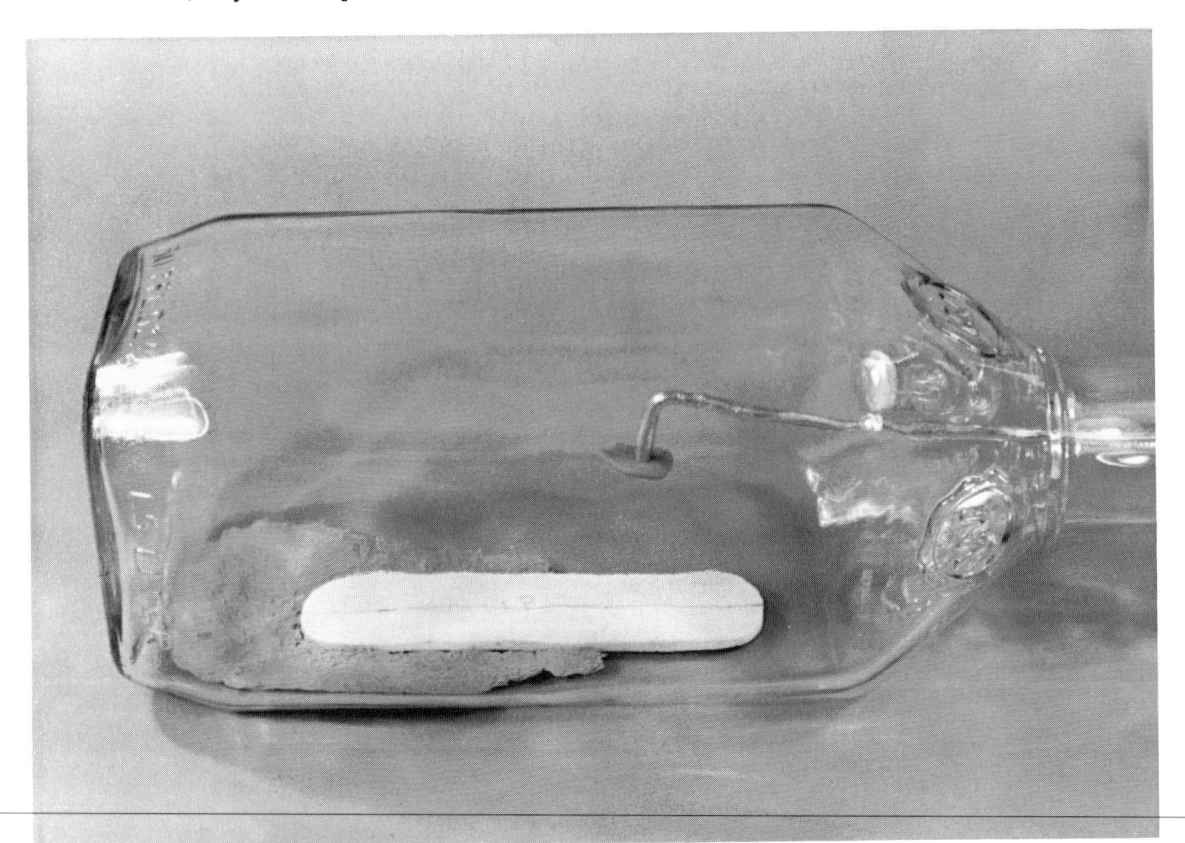

Fig. 16-4. A thin layer of modeling clay is applied to the glass around the flat spot in such a way as to avoid interference with the bottom area of the hull sections.

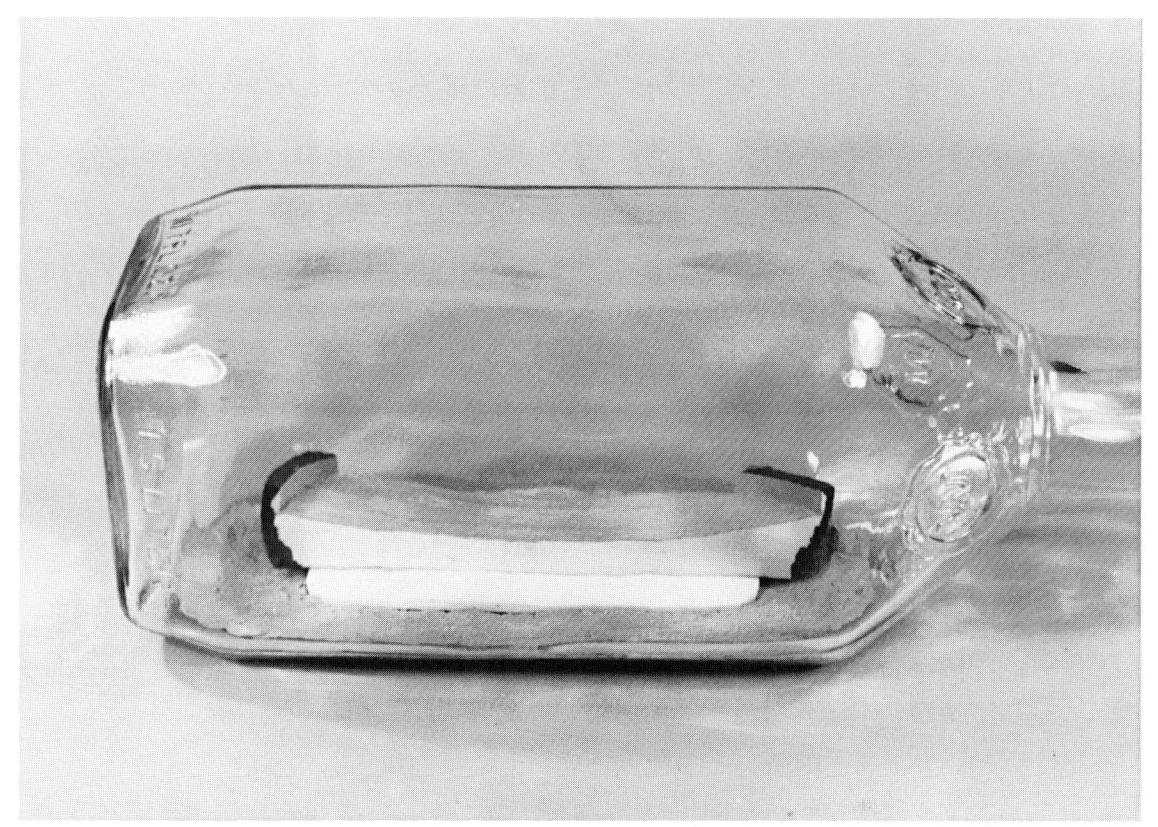

Fig. 16-5. The first of two center hull sections is inserted into the bottle, maneuvered into its intended location, and glued to that spot.

over the edges of the flat spot. Simply keep the level of the clay below that of the top surface of the flat spot. Additional clay can be smeared onto this thin layer after the hull has been fully assembled and permanently secured to the flat spot.

Begin inserting the sections of the hull into the bottle, assuming that all the shaping, refining, painting, and adjusting, for fit have been completed. One of the center sections is installed first. Insert the section through the bottleneck using your fingers. Once inside the bottle, the section is maneuvered onto the wrong, or opposite, side of the flat spot using the bent-wire tool. Next, glue is applied to the correct side of the flat spot using any wire tool. The bent-wire tool is used to maneuver the section onto the correct side of the flat spot atop the smears of glue. Figure 16-5 shows the first section of the hull secured in its permanent position.

Avoid leaving any glue smeared on the sides of the section, especially on surfaces to be joined with the sides of other parts. Make final adjustments and allow the glue to dry overnight.

The adjoining center section is inserted into the bottle next. Maneuver it off to the side away from the flat spot to allow the application of glue. Apply the glue to the top surface of the flat spot in the usual way, but also smear a small amount of glue onto the connecting surface of the first section you installed. Then move the second section into its final position using the bent-wire tool. Care should be taken to adjust the second section until its edges are flush with the edges of the first section. Allow the glue to set for an hour or two before continuing to assemble the remaining hull sections.

The outer sections are inserted into the bottle next. Since the flat spot is now fully covered by the two center sections, it is no longer a foundation for mounting additional sections. Therefore, glue must be applied carefully to the connecting surfaces of the two center sections. Try to apply the glue to the lower area of the connecting surface in order to avoid having glue squeeze out on top of the deck. Insert the first, outer section and maneuver it into its intended position. Allow the glue to set for an hour before you install the last section. On the following day, complete the installation of modeling clay around the finished hull. This is the best time to build up waves and paint their whitecaps.

The main deckhouse is installed next. Insert the first section and maneuver it away from its intended location on the deck. Apply glue using the bent-wire tool to the correct portion of the deck. Move the deckhouse section onto the glue (Fig. 16-6) and allow it to dry completely, overnight if necessary. Make sure no glue oozes out from cracks to interfere with the other section. If it should, wipe it away with the bent-wire tool. Next, install the other deckhouse section using the same technique. Allow complete drying before you install additional structures.

It should be abundantly clear at this point that the installation techniques used thus far will continue to be effective for installing most of the remaining sections and parts of the watercraft. It may be easier, however, to use the modeling-clay and wire tool (Fig. 4-14) to install small individual parts. Apply glue inside the bottle at the intended installation spot. Then, stick the part in the modeling clay at the end of the wire tool and insert the part into the bottle, delivering it to the glued spot. Touch the glue with the connecting surface of the part and it should release. Make final adjustments for proper location, and avoid disturbing until dry.

Some small parts require special handling.

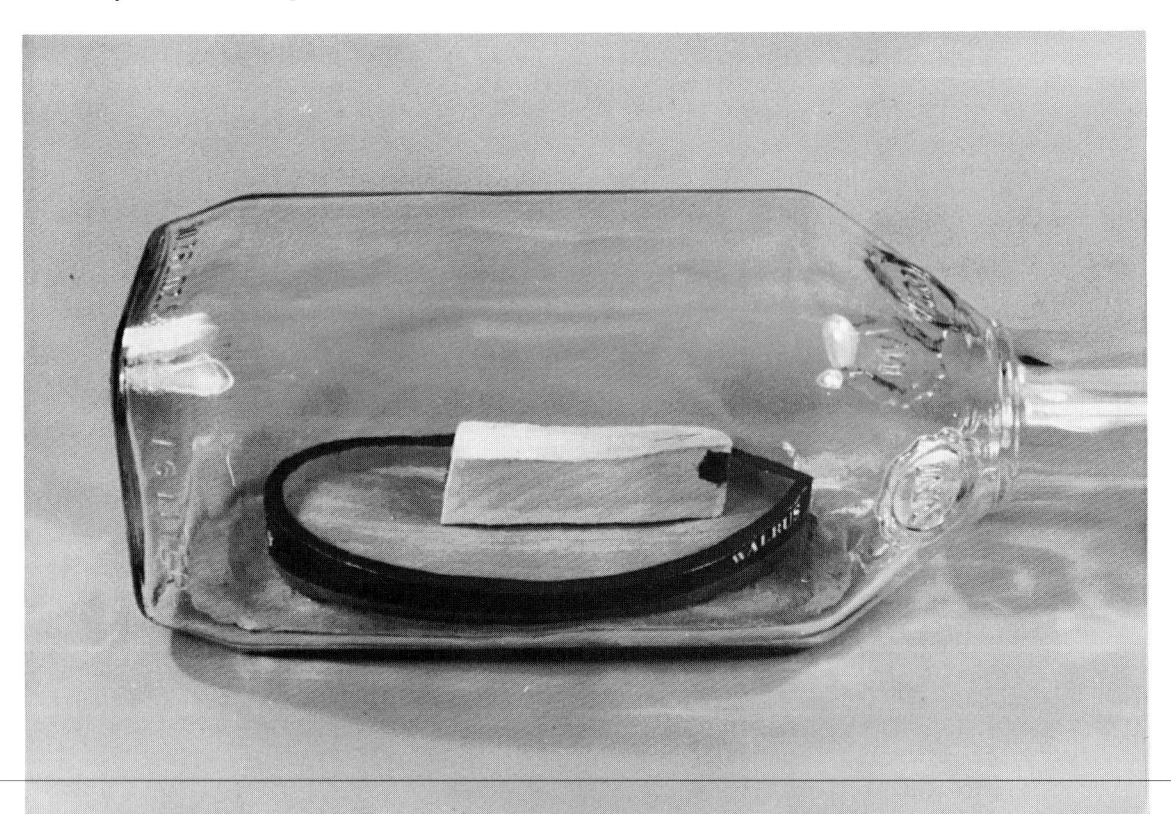

Fig. 16-6. The first section of the deckhouse is installed atop the completed hull structure.

Fig. 16-7. After all the sections and individual parts have been installed and the vessel is completed, the bottle is permanently sealed.

These are parts whose shape will not permit them to be inserted through the bottleneck without turning them on their sides. An example of such a part is a tall smokestack. These parts are light enough in weight to be picked up again once inside the bottle and moved around using the modeling-clay and wire tool.

Start by setting the bottle on its original bottom. Pick up the part with the tool and insert it through the neck. Deposit it on the inside bottom of the bottle. Just set it on the bare glass. Then, change its position or orientation relative to the bottled vessel by maneuvering it into a vertical position using the wire tool. Apply glue to the exact location to which the part will be attached. Next, pick up the part again with the modeling-clay and wire tool and set it in its correct location and reset the bottle on its side. Press the part into the glue, and the tool should release the part easily. Make final adjustments and clean up any glue drips using the bent needle-wire tool. Continue this process with each part until the vessel is complete (Fig. 16-7). Seal the bottle for the final time with an appropriate closure.

MAST INSTALLATION

Sailing vessels present special problems using the sectioned method. Masts are especially difficult to install. There are, however, at least two possible techniques for accomplishing the task. One method is to install each complete mast individually with the ratlines attached (measured and trimmed) along with the other shrouds and support lines. Install and glue the base of the mast into an appropriate hole in the hull and allow it to dry. Later, the shrouds and ratlines, hanging from the masts, are glued to

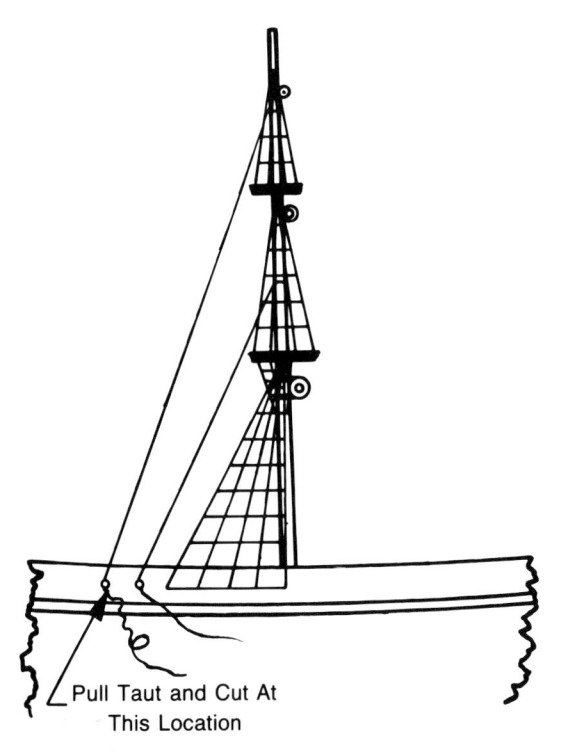

Fig. 16-8. The ratlines are unfurled and glued against the ship's hull. Shrouds are maneuvered around pins, pulled tight, glued at the pin, and weighted until dry. Later, the excess shroud line is cut away at the pin.

the sides of the hull. Paper sails are installed next and glued to the yards or booms and gaffs. Lines running from the yard ends and sail corners must be stretched down to tiny tacks or brads (any formation designed to receive and hold such lines) and glued while pulled taut with weights outside the bottle. Later, the excess line is cut in a similar manner as with the fold-up method. (See Fig. 16-8.) Use extreme care when cutting away excess line to avoid cutting or damaging other lines or wooden structures.

The other technique is a variation of the fold-up method. All the masts are hinged to a center hull section and raised after all the other hull sections have been installed. Shrouds, ratlines, and other lines are allowed to hang freely from the masts and are attached to the hull, glued, and cut, as outlined before. One major disadvantage with this method is the confusion of all the different lines, which tangle easily among masts. Nobody said it wasn't challenging, but then, no measure of difficulty can discourage the efforts of a truly determined craftsman.

POSTSCRIPT

Consideration of all the other hundreds of ship configurations you may wish to reproduce is a continuing concern of mine. Volumes of instructions would be required to explain the construction processes of every possible maritime structure. I hope you are now better prepared to use your own initiative in figuring out how some of the other unusual vessel shapes can be bottled. This kind of builder self-reliance increases self-confidence, as well as personal pride. These benefits do not offset the serious responsibilities of thinking, being inventive, experimenting, and practicing. Admittedly, it is hard work creating a workable step-by-step process for constructing a complex vessel in a bottle. Combining initiative with the common sense most of us have the fortune to possess, you can find success with whatever challenge you might encounter or create for yourself.

As with so many other things, creativity begins with dreaming and thinking, eventually evolving into organized ideas. Some complex ideas require extensive engineering and problem-solving. The testing of both materials and building techniques often demands copious experimentation. Practicing complex building processes helps develop essential hand-eye coordination, as well as skills in fine craftsmanship. Although all of that seems like an awful lot of hard work, the resulting success can bring terrific rewards. Who can shun self-satisfaction, pride, confidence, maybe even fame and fortune?

Appendix: Resources

BOOKS

Albion, Robert. *Five Centuries of Famous Ships*. New York: McGraw-Hill Book Co. 1978.

Baeder, John. *Gas, Food, and Lodging*. New York: Abbeville Press, Inc. 1982.

Bartley, Richard F.C. *Models In Bottles*. London: Percival Marshall Co., Ltd. 1951.

Blackburn, Graham. *The Illustrated Encyclopedia of Ships, Boats, Vessels, and Other Water-Borne Craft*. New York: Overlook Press. 1978.

Boeriche, Art, and Shapiro, Barry. *Handmade Houses: A Guide to the Woodbutcher's Art*. San Francisco: Scrimshaw Press. 1974.

Casson, Lionel. *Ships and Steamship in the Ancient World*. Princeton: Princeton University Press. 1971.

Chapelle, Howard I. *The National Watercraft Collection*. Washington: Smithsonian Institution Press. 1960.

Chapelle, Howard Irving. *The History of American Sailing Ships*. New York: W.W. Norton & Co., Inc. 1935.

Christensen, Per. *Ting Og Sager I Flasker* [*Things and Such In Bottles*]. Egaa, Denmark: Tommeliden. 1984.

Cichy, Bodo. *The Great Ages of Architecture*. New York: G.P. Putnam's Sons. 1964.

Diagram Group, The. *Handtools of Arts and Crafts*. New York: St. Martin's Press, Inc. 1981.

Foster, Michael. ed. *Architecture: Style, Structure, and Design*. New York: Excalibur Books, 1982.

Hamlin, Talbot. *Architecture Through the Ages*. New York: G.P. Putnam's Sons. 1953.

Heine, William. *Historic Ships of the World*. New York: G.P. Putnam's Sons. 1977.

Hoag, Edwin. *American Houses: Colonial, Classic, Contemporary*. Philadelphia and New York: J.B. Lippincott Co. 1964.

Kemp, Peter. *The History of Ships*. London: Orbis Books. 1978.

Landstrom, Bjorn. *Ship, an Illustrated History*. Garden City, N.Y.: Doubleday & Co., Inc. 1961.

Lobley, Dougleas. *Ships Through the Ages*. New York: Octopus Books, Ltd. 1972.

Pratt, Richard. *A Treasury of Early American Houses*. New York: Whittlesey House, a division of McGraw-Hill Book Co. 1949.

Robinson, Ethel Fay, and Robinson, Thomas P. *Houses In America*. New York: Viking Press, Inc. 1961.

Shipway, Vera Cook, and Shipway, Warren. *The Mexican House: Old and New*. New York: Architectural Book Publishing Co. 1960.

Van Schouten, Joop. *Sailing In Glass*. Boston: Sail Books, Inc. 1981.

Villiers, Alan John. *Men, Ships, and the Sea*. Washington: National Geographic Society. 1973.

Watson, Aldren A. *Hand Tools: Their Ways and Workings*. New York: W.W. Norton & Co., Inc. 1982.

OTHER SOURCES

Many Goode's
P.O. Box 5161
Torrance, CA 90510
small dowels

Midwest Products Co.
400 S. Indiana St.
Hobart, IN 46343
wood products

Ships-In-Bottles Association of America
P.O. Box 550
Coronado, CA 92118
$10 annual dues

Glossary

aesthetics—The philosophy that studies and promotes quality in the compositions of art.

aft—Towards the stern or rear of a ship, boat, or other vessel.

amidships—At or pertaining to the middle of a watercraft or aircraft.

artistic license—The right of an artist to rearrange or add and delete objects in a composition of art in the interest of aesthetics or personal preference.

battlements—A structural formation for the purpose of defensive maneuvers mounted atop a wall or other towering form.

bay window—A protrusion of windows extending beyond the flat plane of an outside wall.

beam—A long structural form made of metal, wood, or stone and whose cross-sectional shape may be either square or rectangular.

boom—A horizontal spar used to secure the bottom edge of a fore-and-aft sail.

bow—The front end of a ship or boat.

bowsprit—An important spar or mast extending beyond the bow of a sailing ship.

bridge—A raised observation and control platform from which a ship is steered and other systems are monitored.

bulkhead—Walls or any other vertical structure inside or on a ship or other watercraft.

buoy—A floating device used to mark navigational channels or hazards.

capstan—A piece of deck equipment aboard a ship or boat used as a horizontal winch for winding up and feeding out ropes, cables, and chains.

centimeter—A metric unit of measure equal to 1/100 meter (.3937 inch).

closure—A stopper, cap, lid, or any other device which can be used to seal the opening of a bottle.

connecting surface—The exact plane, face, or area of an object on which another part is attached using glue or cement.

craft—An activity or trade requiring manual skills.

craftsman—A man or woman who works at a craft or hobby, doing the designing, carving, gluing, and painting; a builder.
cross section—A theoretical view of an object in which its cut-away shape is revealed in order to help clarify its construction.

davit—A special crane used to secure, lower, and raise lifeboats.
deck—The floor of each level of a boat or ship.
dimensions—The measurements in metric or English units for every feature and direction (thickness, length, and width).
dowel—A round-shaped rod usually made of wood and often available at a length of 36 inches with diameters ranging from 1/8 inch to 1 inch.
drafting—A process by which pencil or ink lines are drawn on paper in order to represent objects or parts of objects which are yet to be constructed.
dry dock—A cradlelike dock used to lift a boat or ship out of the water or repair or modification.

earth—The earthen or ground base on which the house is constructed.

facade—The high and decorative front area of a building.
flight deck—A tremendously long and wide flat deck dominating an aircraft carrier and used as a field from which aircraft are launched and retrieved.
flush—A condition in which one surface is level or even with another surface forming a smooth surface plane.
footprint—The shape or mark of an object as it contacts a flat plane.
fore-and-aft rigging—A system of sails and lines which are set fore and aft (in a line or direction running from the bow to the stern of a watercraft) when not trimmed for actual sailing.
foremast—The vertical standing mast nearest the bow of the ship.
forward—Toward the bow or front of the ship.
fuselage—The main, central body of an aircraft.

gable—A roof configuration in which two angled roof planes form a pyramid, while the resulting vertical end is enclosed or ended with a flat wall (Fig. 7-2).
gaff—A diagonal spar which supports the top of any sail running along the length of the ship; a fore-and-aft sail.
galleon—A large, high-decked, square-rigged vessel used extensively during the fifteenth and sixteenth centuries.

hardwood—A classification of wood species which is deciduous in origin and whose wood is hard and dense.
helm—The steering wheel or tiller of a ship or boat.
hobby—A recreational activity of personal interest and relaxation; a craft.
hold—A large storage area in the hull of a ship.
hull—The massive portion of a boat or ship which is partially submerged in the water but is designed in most cases to keep the water from leaking into the vessel.

incise—To cut small openings or holes through a flat material.
insert—To pass a part or tool through the neck or opening of a bottle.
install—To measure, cut, insert into the bottle, and glue into its intended location any part used for the construction of an object in a bottle.

jib—A sail in the shape of a triangle supported only by lines and located forward of the foremast.

keel—The "backbone" of the skeletal frame of a watercraft, running along the bottom of the hull.
ketch—A sailing vessel rigged fore and aft on two masts—one taller, main mast and a smaller mast located forward of the steering tiller or wheel.

lash—To bind or attach together two or more linear parts using string, twine, rope, thread, or chain.

lintel—A heavy, horizontally placed member located above doors or windows supporting the wall materials above it.

macrame—The art of knotting rope or light cord into interesting designs and geometric patterns to form belts, fringes, spheres, and other shapes.

mast—The tall, vertical pole or spar used to hold the sails or spars and rigging high above the hull of a ship or boat.

meter—A metric unit of measure equal to 39.37 inches.

milling—A process by which a lumberyard or mill cuts most wood products to exact and specified sizes.

miter—To cut linear materials at an angle in such a way that two of these cut pieces may be joined at a predetermined angle.

mizzenmast—A mast which is shorter than and located behind the main mast.

molding—A long decorative strip of wood whose cross-sectional shape is artistically contoured.

needle-wire tool—A tool combining an aluminum wire with a sharp needle and whose function is to insert, place, and release individual parts used in bottle-house and -ship construction.

outboard motorboat—A small motorized vessel in which the motor and accompanying propeller are attached to the outside of the boat's hull at the stern.

parapet—A wall often with openings for the purpose of defence or for protecting the edge of a roof or balcony.

pitch—The angle at which a roof rises; the thick, viscous sap of trees used for sealing out water or moisture.

plank—A structural form usually of wood whose shape is flat and long.

plank on frame—A very accurate method of model ship construction in which wood planks are attached (sometimes with wooden pegs) to the individual framing members composing the skeleton of ship's hull.

port—A nautical term referring to the left or left side; a harbor or group of landings for watercraft.

ratlines—Rope ladders extending from the sides of a sailing ship upward to the first crosstree of the mast.

rig—To attach lines used to secure and control masts and sails on sailing boats and ships.

router—A portable, handheld, power tool used for shaping a decorative edge on a piece of wood.

scale—The size relationship or ratio between a plan and the actual object which the plan represents.

shim—A paper, cardboard, or wood form used to take up space or level-off angles in preparation for attaching another part.

schooner—A sailing ship whose masts and sails are arranged in a fore-and-aft formation supported by gaffs and booms.

shrouds—Support lines or ropes running from midmast down to the sides of the hull.

siding—Sheet material used for covering the outside walls of wood-framed houses.

softwood—A classification of several species of woods which are coniferous in origin.

spar—Any ridged pole used as a sailing ship's mast, boom, gaff, or bowsprit.

square-rigger—A sailing ship whose masts and sails are arranged in a square sail formation.

starboard—A nautical term referring to the right or right side.

staysail—A triangular sail much like a jib but located between masts.

story—A level or floor of a building whose rooms occupy the same continuous floor.

stucco—A plasterlike material usually made of cement and sand applied to a mesh structure of chicken wire covering the outside walls of a building.

superstructure—Any formation or building which rises out of or above the top, main deck of a vessel or watercraft.

surface—Pertaining to or at the water's top face, level, or surface.

tack—The general angle of the sails, and even the watercraft itself, in relationship to the direction of the wind.

tiller—A lever attached to a boat's rudder and used to steer the watercraft.

trim—to adjust a sail's position or angle in such a way as to take best advantage of the wind while sailing a boat or ship.

vise—A device with adjustable, clamping jaws used to securely grasp objects on which work is being performed.

veneer—A thin sheet of wood, often with paper-backing for strength, used to cover other wood of lesser quality.

weather decks—Housings and decks above the hull and its main deck.

wing—A section of a building which extends out, usually at right angles from the main body of the structure.

yard—A horizontal spar attached at its center to a vertical mast for the purpose of supporting or hanging the top of a sail of a square-rigged ship.

yawl—A sailing vessel, rigged fore and aft on two masts, one taller, main mast and a smaller mast located behind the steering tiller or wheel.

Index

A
adapting an existing house, 37
adapting your own design, 37
adhesives, 168
adobe style, 35
adobe wall, 106
aft, 205
air plant, 112
aircraft carrier, 154
Alki, 123
amidships, 205
Andrea Doria, 144
annealing, 7
asphalt shingles, 102
automobile carrier, 134

B
balconies, 93
band saw, 27
barges, 134
bark, 148
battle wagons, 156
battlements, 205
bay window
   hanging, 100
bay windows, 97
bent-wire tool, 58
Blenko Glass, 13
Bluenose, 124

boards
   sandpaper, 62
boat, 127
   tour, 145
boats
   fishing, 128
bottle, 5
bottle and its contents, 8
bottle characteristics, 8
bottle cleaning, 24
bottle closures, 26, 116, 164
bottle qualities, 8
bottle seams, 12
bottle shape, 161
bottled house
   care of, 117
bottled ships
   variations, 121
bottlemaking
   history of, 5
bottleneck, 5
bottles, 161
   finding old, 18
   types of, 163
bottling ships, 120
Bounty, 150
bow, 205
bowsprit, 205
box saw, 53

brick walls, 104
broadcloth, 170
brownstones, 34
Buccaneer Queen, 150
building materials, 65, 166
building mountains, 74
building nonwood walls, 104
building site
   flat, 75
building tools, 51
bulkheads, 166
buoy tender, 159

C
Camp Minnow Trap, 22
cap shingles, 91
Cape Cod style, 33
capstan, 205
care of bottled house, 117
carpenter's square, 57
carrier
   aircraft, 154
   automobile, 134
   container, 130
   helicopter assault, 154
   ore, 131
carriers, 130
carved posts, 82
castles, 34

209

catamaran, 142
cement, 72
chimneys, 94
clamps
   metal, 54
clapboard, 33
cleaning
   bottle, 24
closures
   bottle, 26, 116, 164
cloth, 169
clothespins, 54
   miniature, 54
coloring
   variegated, 111
Columbia, 163
compass, 57
conning tower, 125
Constellation, 123
Constitution, 152
construction
   plank-on-frame, 122
   roof, 89
   second floor, 89
   sectioned method, 194
construction fold-up method, 179
container carrier, 130
coping saw, 53
cotton batiste, 170
cotton thread, 170
covering
   wall, 85
cracking off, 6
Crosby
   Vic, 125
Cuajhtemoc, 149, 150
Cutty Sark, 181

D

da Vinci
   Leonardo, 2
David, 65
demijohns, 21
design
   adapting your own, 37
   house, 29
desk lamp, 56
destroyers, 156
doors, 84
drafting lamp, 56
drafting triangle, 57
dreadnoughts, 156
dry brushing, 71

E

eaves, 91
epoxy cement, 60

F

file, 56
finding old bottles, 18
fingers

   mechanical, 56
fireboats, 134
fishing boats, 128
flat building site, 75
floor joists, 106
flooring, 79
fold-up method of construction, 179
foliage materials, 111
framing
   wall, 80
freighters, 130
frigate, 159

G

gingerbread, 33
glass
   Mexican, 14
glass quality, 162
glue, 72
gouges, 52
Great Expectations, 122

H

hairs, 170
hanging bay window, 100
hat pins, 55
headers, 82
helicopter assault carrier, 154
historic vessels, 146
homemade tools, 58, 176
   other, 61
Hornblower's Flotilla, 123
house
   existing, adapting an, 37
house design, 29
house modification, 29
Hunchback of Notre Dame, 65

I

inserting ships into bottles, 189
installation of masts, 201
Intrepid, 124
Irish linen, 170

J

jar, 5
jeweler's saw, 53
joists
   floor, 106

K

ketch, 141, 142

L

La France, 144
lamp
   desk, 56
   drafting, 56
landscaping, 111
light
   work, 55

liners
   ocean, 144

M

main roof, 100
making trees, 112
Mary Celeste, 125
mast installation, 201
materials, 161
   building, 65, 166
   building, cement, 72
   building, cloth, 169
   building, glue, 72
   building, modeling clay, 69
   building, paint, 169
   building, paints, 69
   building, paper, 69
   building, pins, 172
   building, plastics, 72
   building, polystyrene foam, 71
   building, putty, 171
   building, stone, 65
   building, wire, 172
   building, wood, 65
   building, wood putty, 71
   foliage, 111
mechanical fingers, 56
Memory Lanes Antique Mall, 20
metal clamps, 54
Mexican glass, 14
miniature clothespins, 54
Mission Revival style, 34
mizzenmast, 142
modeling clay, 69, 171
modification
   house, 29
mold marks, 12
motorboats, 142
mountains
   building, 74
Mutiny on the Bounty, 150

N

Nautilus, 125
naval vessels, 152
New Jersey, 159
nonabsorbable surgical suture, 171
nonwood walls, 104
nylon fishing line, 171

O

ocean liners, 144
oil tanker, 131
Old Ironsides, 152, 181
ore carrier, 131

P

paint, 169
paintbrush, 55
paints, 69
panels, 85

210

paper, 57, 69, 166
pencil, 57
pins, 172
  hat, 55
pitch, 91
plant
  air, 112
planters, 113
plastics, 72
pointed tweezers, 54
polyester, 170
polystyrene foam, 71
pontil, 6
posts
  carved, 82
press
  shingle, 62
protractor, 57
Pueblo style, 35
putty, 171

Q

quality
  glass, 162
Queen Mary, 144, 150, 151

R

rafters, 91
recreational vessels, 138
ribs, 122
riverboat, 151
rock roof, 102
roof
  asphalt shingle, 102
  decorative rock, 102
  main, 100
  Spanish tile, 102
  tar paper, 102
  wood shingle, 102
roof construction, 89
Rose Bowl, 20

S

sail, 125
sailboats, 142
San Diego Maritime Museum, 148
sanding, 55
sandpaper, 55
sandpaper boards, 62
saw
  box, 53
  coping, 53
  jeweler's, 53
schooners, 188
seams, 12
second floor construction, 89
second-story walls, 100
sectioned method of construction, 194

shape
  bottle, 161
shingle press, 62
shingles
  cap, 91
ship, 127
ships
  bottled, variations, 121
  bottling, 120
  inserting into bottles, 189
Sina, 123
site
  flat, 75
Spanish style, 34
Spanish tile roof, 102
square
  carpenter's, 57
square-riggers, 182
Star of India, 148, 150
steamships, 144
stone, 65
stone walls, 104
store-bought tools, 51, 174
structural supports, 78
stucco wall, 106
studs, 80
style
  adobe, 35
  Cape Cod, 33
  Mission Revival, 34
  Pueblo, 35
  Spanish, 34
  Tudor, 33
  Tudor Revival, 33
  Victorian, 33
styles
  architectural, 29
submarine, 154
supports
  structural, 78
suture
  nonabsorbable surgical, 171

T

tanker
  oil, 131
tapping off, 7
tar paper roof, 102
tender
  buoy, 159
The Bottle Shipwright, 121
The Bounty, 150, 181
The Princess Louise, 151
thermoshock, 117
thread, 169
tie, 78
tiller, 142
Titanic, 122
tool
  bent-wire, 58
tools, 174
  building, 51

  homemade, 58, 176
  other homemade, 61
  store-bought, 51
tour boat, 145
tower
  conning, 125
tract home, 34
trees
  making, 112
triangle
  drafting, 57
trimaran, 142
Tropicale, 144
Tudor Revival style, 33
Tudor style, 33
tugboats, 128
tweezers
  pointed, 54
types of bottles, 163
types of watercraft, 127

U

United States, 124, 144

V

variegated coloring, 111
veneer, 166
vessel, 127
vessels
  historic, 146
  naval, 152
  recreational, 138
  recreational, motorboats, 142
  recreational, other, 144
  recreational, sailboats, 142
  water taxi, 134
  work, 128
  work, barges, 134
  work, carriers, 130
  work, fireboats, 134
  work, fishing boats, 128
  work, tugboats, 128
  work, other, 136
Victorian style, 33
Virginia, 122

W

Waddell, 157
wall
  adobe, 106
  stucco, 106
wall covering, 85
wall framing, 80
walls
  brick, 104
  building nonwood, 104
  second story, 100
  stone, 104
Walrus, 136
warships, 152
watercraft, 127
water taxis, 134

   types of, 127
Weldwood, 66
window
   hanging bay, 100
windows, 82

bay, 97
wire, 172
wood, 65, 166
wood putty, 71
wood shingles, 102

work light, 55
work vessels, 128

Y

yawl, 140

OTHER POPULAR TAB BOOKS OF INTEREST

44 Terrific Woodworking Plans & Projects (No. 1762—$12.50 paper; $21.95 hard)

How to Repair Briggs & Stratton Engines—2nd Edition (No. 1687—$8.95 paper; $15.95 hard)

Security for You and Your Home ... A Complete Handbook (No. 1680—$17.50 paper; $29.95 hard)

46 Step-by-Step Wooden Toy Projects (No. 1675—$9.95 paper; $17.95 hard)

The Kite Building & Kite Flying Handbook, with 42 Kite Plans (No. 1669—$15.50 paper)

Building Better Beds (No. 1664—$14.50 paper; $19.95 hard)

Organic Vegetable Gardening (No. 1660—$16.50 paper; $25.95 hard)

The Woodturning Handbook, with Projects (No. 1655—$14.50 paper; $21.95 hard)

Clock Making for the Woodworker (No. 1648—$11.50 paper; $16.95 hard)

Steel Homes (No. 1641—$15.50 paper; $21.95 hard)

The Homeowner's Illustrated Guide to Concrete (No. 1626—$15.50 paper; $24.95 hard)

Kerosene Heaters (No. 1598—$10.25 paper; $16.95 hard)

Clocks—Construction, Maintenance and Repair (No. 1569—$13.50 paper; $18.95 hard)

The Underground Home Answer Book (No. 1562—$11.50 paper; $16.95 hard)

Airbrushing (No. 1555—$20.50 paper)

Basic Blueprint Reading for Practical Applications (No. 1546—$13.50 paper; $18.95 hard)

Central Heating and Air Conditioning Repair Guide—2nd Edition (No. 1520—$13.50 paper; $18.95 hard)

The Complete Book of Fences (No. 1508—$12.95 paper; $19.95 hard)

How to Sharpen Anything (No. 1463—$12.95 paper; $19.95 hard)

Building a Log Home from Scratch or Kit (No. 1458—$12.50 paper; $17.95 hard)

Build t with Plywood: 88 Furniture Projects (No. 1430—$1 3.50 paper; $18.95 hard)

The G ANT Book of Metalworking Projects (No. 1357—$1 95 paper; $19.95 hard)

The W lder's Bible (No. 1244—$13.95 paper)

The GIANT Handbook of Food-Preserving Basics (No. 1727—$13.50 paper; $17.95 hard)

Ventilation: Your Secret Key to an Energy-Efficient Home (No. 1681—$8.95 paper; $15.95 hard)

Tuning and Repairing Your Own Piano (No. 1678—$12.50 paper)

Superinsulated, Truss-Frame House Construction (No. 1674—$15.50 paper; $21.95 hard)

Raising Animals for Fun and Profit (No. 1666—$13.50 paper; $18.95 hard)

Practical Herb Gardening ... with Recipes (No. 1661—$11.95 paper; $15.95 hard)

Effective Lighting for Home and Business (No. 1658—$13.50 paper; $18.95 hard)

Constructing and Maintaining Your Well and Septic System (No. 1654—$12.50 paper; $17.95 hard)

Maps and Compasses: A User's Handbook (No. 1644—$9.25 paper; $15.95 hard)

Woodcarving, with Projects (No. 1639—$11.50 paper; $16.95 hard)

Sign Carving (No. 1601—$13.50 paper; $19.95 hard)

Mastering Household Electrical Wiring (No. 1587—$13.50 paper; $19.95 hard)

Cave Exploring (No. 1566—$10.25 paper; $16.95 hard)

The Radio Control Hobbyist's Handbook (No. 1561—$19.50 paper)

Be Your Own Contractor: The Affordable Way to Home Ownership (No. 1554—$12.50 paper; $17.95 hard)

Beekeeping—An Illustrated Handbook (No. 1524—$10.95 paper; $15.95 hard)

101 Model Railroad Layouts (No. 1514—$11.50 paper; $17.95 hard)

53 Space-Saving, Built-In Furniture Projects (No. 1504—$17.50 paper)

The Home Brewer's Handbook (No. 1461—$10.25 paper; $16.95 hard)

Constructing Outdoor Furniture, with 99 Projects (No. 1454—$15.50 paper)

Draw Your Own House Plans (No. 1381—$14.50 paper; $19.95 hard)

The Fiberglass Repair & Construction Handbook (No. 1297—$11.50 paper; $17.95 hard)

TAB TAB BOOKS Inc.

Blue Ridge Summit, Pa. 17214

Send for FREE TAB Catalog describing over 750 current titles in print.

STACK